VEHICLES

VEHICLES

NIGEL HAWKES

Macmillan Publishing Company
New York

Maxwell Macmillan International
New York · Oxford · Singapore · Sydney

A Marshall Edition
This book was conceived, edited, and designed by
Marshall Editions, 170 Piccadilly, London W1V 9DD

Macmillan Publishing Company
866 Third Avenue
New York, NY 10022

Macmillan Publishing Company is part of the
Maxwell Communication Group of Companies.

Library of Congress Cataloging-in-Publication Data

Hawkes, Nigel.
    Vehicles/Nigel Hawkes. — 1st American ed.
      p.   cm.
    Includes bibliographical references and index.
    ISBN 0-02-549106-7
    1. Vehicles—Popular works.   I. Title
  TL146.5.H38 1991   91-17772 CIP
  629.04—dc20

Macmillan books are available at special discounts for bulk
purchases for sales promotions, premiums, fund-raising, or
educational use. For details, contact:

Special Sales Director
Macmillan Publishing Company
866 Third Avenue
New York, NY 10022

First American edition

Editor: Anthony Lambert
Art Editor: Peter Laws

Assistant Editor: Lindsay McTeague
Editorial and Picture Research: Elizabeth Loving
Editorial Research: Heather Magrill
Production: Janice Storr

Editorial Director: Ruth Binney
Art Director: John Bigg
Production Director: Barry Baker

Typeset by Servis Filmsetting Limited, Manchester, UK
Origination by Imago Publishing Ltd, Thame, UK
Printed and bound in Germany by Mohndruck Graphische
Betriebe GmbH

10 9 8 7 6 5 4 3 2 1

CONTENTS

INTRODUCTION

From earliest times, man has been an explorer. The more successful cultures have had a curiosity about the world around them and a belief that somewhere over the horizon is a place where life is easier, the Sun warmer and the Earth more fruitful. The great journeys of discovery that first established the shape of the oceans and continents were made not in pursuit of abstract knowledge but of wealth and power.

Those who succeeded were those who had provided themselves with the best means of transport. This book celebrates the continual quest to push back the frontiers of technology, design and human endurance in transportation. Every vehicle has been designed to improve on what went before, with a specific purpose in mind: to explore the Earth; to test the toughness of a machine and its design; to carry ever greater loads; to provide the most opulent surroundings in which to travel; to reach other planets.

The vehicles and journeys described in the book have been chosen because they are the first, the toughest, the fastest, the most singular or the most significant in the history of transportation. No book of normal length can pretend to be comprehensive, so a timetable charting the vital steps in transportation is provided at the end.

CHAPTER ONE

ACROSS THE OCEANS

F or most of humankind's history, the immensity of the oceans created a barrier that seemed impenetrable. Small boats might skirt along a coast to fish and trade, or explore a modest ocean like the Mediterranean, but the Atlantic appeared boundless and the Pacific was unknown. At the outer edge of the great oceans lay an emptiness where no one might venture with any certainty of a safe return.

Suddenly, in medieval Europe, the constraints of geography were broken by navigators who struck out boldly across the oceans. They had ships capable of great journeys of exploration, but, more important, they had an idea of how the Earth was made that convinced them and their patrons that such voyages would be possible and worthwhile. To overcome the dangers of the open sea they had first to subdue the doubts in their own minds. In the space of a few years Columbus had discovered the New World and Magellan had circumnavigated the Earth, feats of courage and seamanship that transformed human perceptions.

Since these pioneering voyages, the oceans have been travelled by a huge variety of ships. Some have been designed for speed, like the tea clipper *Cutty Sark* and the liner *Mauretania*, while others made a virtue of their ordinariness, like the humble Liberty ships that kept the supply lines open during World War II. Men like Joshua Slocum and Francis Chichester have challenged the oceans alone, responding to an adventurous instinct. They endured hardships of a quite different kind from the crew of the nuclear submarine *Nautilus*, who sat in air-conditioned comfort as they faced the unknown dangers of the first journey beneath the Arctic ice cap.

Yet, in spite of all the changes and the development of new technologies like satellite navigation, the oceans still retain something of the dread they had for ancient man. On land nature has been largely tamed, but at sea it retains its power to terrify and to subdue. In this section we examine some of the more remarkable craft that have set to sea and follow the voyages that made them famous.

Pioneer Voyage to the New World

The three small ships that first sailed to the New World in 1492 occupy one of the most puzzling gaps in the history of exploration. Everybody knows that they were commanded by Christopher Columbus and financed by King Ferdinand and Queen Isabella of Spain. Most would agree that the small fleet—the *Santa Maria*, the *Pinta* and the *Niña*—discovered America, although these days the more particular are inclined to say they merely "encountered" it, out of respect for the aboriginal Indian peoples who predated Columbus. However we describe it, the voyage was of huge and lasting importance to world history, yet the vessels that made the journey are ill-documented and poorly understood.

"Nobody knows what *Niña*, *Pinta* and *Santa Maria* really looked like," wrote Samuel Eliot Morison in his biography of Columbus, *Admiral of the Ocean Sea*. There have been plenty of attempts to draw the ships, or even to build copies of them, but each has inevitably involved a lot of guesswork. None of the reproductions sails as well as Columbus's ships did, suggesting that they had some secret now lost which accounted for their excellent performance.

No original plans exist for the caravels, the ships that made possible the great age of discovery in the fifteenth and sixteenth centuries. Contemporary drawings lack details, and no wreck of a caravel has ever been unambiguously identified. It has been said that more is known of the ships of ancient Greece and Rome than of the caravels that extended the European imagination across the oceans.

Santa Maria was the largest ship in Columbus's fleet and therefore his flagship, but she was not his favourite vessel. She was broader in the beam than the *Pinta* or the *Niña*, suggesting that she was probably not a caravel at all, but a cargo vessel of the type known in Spain and Portugal as a *nao*. For voyages of discovery, speed is worth more than cargo capacity and Columbus wrote in his journal that *Santa Maria* was unwieldy and not well-suited to the task. He put the blame on the people of Palos, the Spanish port that had been ordered by King Ferdinand and Queen Isabella to put the ships at his disposal as recompense for certain offences they had committed against the crown.

But in fact the royal decree demanded two caravels, not three, and these were duly provided: the *Pinta*, which belonged to Christobal Quintero of Palos, and the *Niña*, which belonged to Juan Nino of the nearby town of Moguer. Officially the *Niña*'s name was the *Santa Clara*, but in those days ships usually had nicknames given by the crew, often taken from the name of the owner.

Two ships were insufficient for Columbus's purposes, so a third had to be hired by the crown to make up the fleet. None of the shipowners in Palos who owned caravels was willing to let them be hired, so Columbus had to be content with a *nao* belonging to Juan de la Cosa of Santona, near Santander. She was called *Santa Maria* but because she had originally been built in Galicia was known by the crew as *La Gallega*.

Santa Maria was only slightly larger than the other two ships, perhaps a little over 80 feet long and 28 feet in the beam. She was rated at 90 to 100 tons, which meant that she could carry that many tuns, or barrels, of wine. Since a Spanish *tonelada* of wine contained 213 gallons, it weighed almost a ton in weight. The *Niña* and the *Pinta* were shorter than the *Santa Maria*, at around 70 to 80 feet long, but they were about 3 feet narrower in the beam and, at 60 tons, had less cargo capacity.

When the ships finally sailed on 3 August 1492, it marked the culmination of a long campaign by Columbus to be allowed to undertake a voyage of discovery. He believed that by sailing far enough westward he would eventually reach the shores of Asia, a conception of geography that left the entire American continent out of account. Nobody knew it was there, and Columbus had wrongly calculated that the circumference of the Earth was about 18,750 miles, some 6,300 miles too short. This led him to claim that it would be possible to sail to the coasts of Asia if he set off westward and kept on going for long enough.

After failing to persuade the Portuguese to support his expedition, Columbus sent his brother Fernando to England to try to solicit support from King Henry VII. Nothing came of this so Fernando next tried King Charles VIII of France. Columbus himself was about to travel to France to press his suit when Queen Isabella was persuaded by a priest to take the proposition seriously. She summoned Columbus, and

FACT FILE

Columbus's flagship on his first voyage to the New World

Date: 1492/93

Duration: 7 months 12 days

Christopher Columbus (1451–1506)
Born in Genoa, Columbus went to sea as an illiterate young lad. After many years on merchant ships, he developed a conviction that the Atlantic Ocean was quite narrow and that Asia could soon be reached by sailing west. Three further voyages of exploration followed Columbus's epic voyage; they met with only limited success and he was to die at Valladolid in Spain a frustrated and embittered man.

Pioneer Voyage to the New World

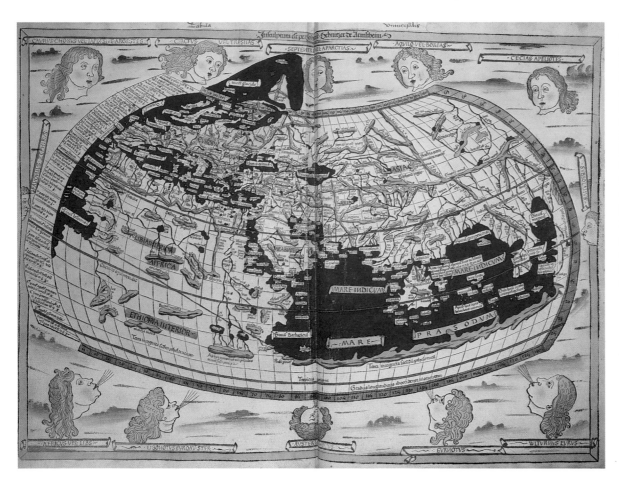

A map of the world published in 1482 at Ulm in Germany and based on Ptolemy's system of latitude and longitude. Ptolemy's work was lost with the fall of the Roman Empire, and it was only in 1400 that a manuscript copy of his Geographia, *with maps, was found in Constantinople. He gave winds both names and personalities, illustrated here in the border.*

eventually agreed to finance the expedition.

Some historians consider that Columbus's trump card was his recognition of the existence of the trade winds, which he believed would blow him all the way to the Indies if he stuck to the southerly part of the ocean, and all the way back if he took a more northerly course. Although his geography was hopelessly muddled, his instinct about the winds was right, and may have helped him convince the queen.

On 17 April he signed an agreement with Ferdinand and Isabella covering the terms under which the expedition would operate. Columbus was to be appointed admiral, and would become viceroy and governor-general of any "islands and mainlands which he may discover or acquire". He would be entitled to 10 percent of any valuable merchandise he might obtain. For their part, the king and queen would provide the ships and pay the crews four months' wages in advance. The people of Palos were ordered to provision these ships within ten days, a timetable which could never have been met. In fact, it was ten weeks before they were ready to sail.

Ninety men sailed in the three ships. On *Santa*

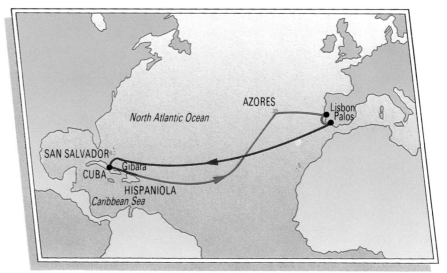

Columbus's first landfall in the Caribbean was the island called Guanahani by the natives and which he named San Salvador. He explored the islands of Cuba and Hispaniola before heading back to Spain 155 days after first setting out.

ANNIVERSARY RECONSTRUCTIONS

The reconstructions being built for the 500th anniversary celebrations include copies of all three ships, financed by the Spanish government at a cost of $4 million. These pictures illustrate the *Santa Maria* at Barcelona. A copy of *Santa Maria* is being built for the Japanese government. Geo-Arts of Bath, Maine, plans to reproduce the whole squadron, while the city of Columbus, Ohio, and the Mexican government are content with copies of *Santa Maria*. A citizen in Florida is building a copy of *Nina*.

Maria, Columbus was assisted by the captain and owner of the ship, Juan de la Cosa. The flagship also carried a pilot, a royal inspector, a surgeon, a secretary, a man who could interpret from Hebrew, Aramaic and Arabic, and about 30 artisans, including a carpenter, a caulker, a cooper and a master gunner. The *Pinta* was commanded by Martin Alonso Pinzón, while his brother Vicente Yanez Pinzón commanded the *Niña*. The owners of both ships also sailed with the fleet.

The voyage started with problems. Columbus had to put in to Lanzarote, the closest of the Canary Islands, to repair the *Pinta*'s rudder and to replace the *Niña*'s lateen (triangular) sail with square sails which would be better suited to the following winds which Columbus expected from here onward. All this took time, and it was 8 September before the fleet finally set sail again.

The fleet sailed swiftly. According to Dr Morison, during one five-day stretch it averaged 8 knots running before the favourable winds, an excellent performance. The maximum speed of the two caravels appears to have been about 11 knots, which compares quite well with the speed of any sailing ship except fast clippers or racing yachts. On 10 October, the fleet covered 59 leagues, equivalent to more than 215 miles, and the crew began to grow restless, so far had they now strayed from familiar waters. Columbus

Pioneer Voyage to the New World

reassured them, and two days later the crew of the *Niña* found a twig floating in the water, encouraging evidence that land might be near. On 12 October, a lookout on the *Pinta* sighted land, and two hours after midnight the fleet hove to about 7 miles from the shore to await daylight.

The land Columbus had found was a small island in the Caribbean, which he named San Salvador. Subsequently he sailed to Cuba, landing at a point thought to be near Gibara, and to an island he called Hispaniola (now shared between Haiti and the Dominican Republic). He found such friendly natives there that he determined to found a settlement. But on Christmas Eve disaster struck when control of the flagship was left overnight in the hands of a boy who allowed it to drift ashore on to the reef. Realizing that the *Santa Maria* was lost, Columbus abandoned ship and transferred the crew to the *Niña*. He set up the first Spanish settlement in the New World and left some 40 settlers to establish it. On 4 January 1493, he set sail back to Spain.

Both Columbus and Pinzón, the captain of the *Pinta* who had meanwhile engaged in some freelance exploring, had collected quantities of gold from the natives they met. On the way home they met a terrible storm and Columbus feared that all his discoveries would be lost before he could report them to the Spanish crown. Finally they made landfall at the Portuguese island of Santa Maria, the easternmost of the Azores. From there they sailed home, surviving another terrible storm, in which waves swept continuously over the decks of the two small ships. They reached Lisbon, where they were welcomed by the Portuguese king, and then sailed on to Palos, arriving on 15 March 1593.

The completion of the voyage was testimony to the excellent qualities of the ships, particularly the two caravels, and to Columbus's abilities as a navigator. Yet frustratingly little is known of the details of the ships' construction: historians believe that any such details were deliberately kept secret by the Portuguese and Spanish for reasons of strategy. As a result, no drawings were allowed to be published.

Most caravels had a tall deck at the stern, raised well above the level of the main deck. This was called the tolda, and later evolved into a fully developed sterncastle, a platform from which the ship would be navigated and from which attacks on other ships could be launched. To begin with, caravels did not have a similar raised portion at the front because this would

EARLY NAVIGATION METHODS

When Columbus set sail in 1492, navigational methods were rudimentary. The Phoenicians in the first millennium BC undertook preplanned ocean voyages, reaching the Azores and the Scilly Islands by their knowledge of the stars. The Scandinavians developed navigational skills during the first millennium AD, sailing regularly to Iceland and Greenland by AD 900.

The first navigational aids were the astrolabe, magnetic compass and chart. The first two may have been in use by *c.* 1300, but it was not until the early fifteenth century that the first attempt at scale maps was made. The accuracy of early compasses was reduced by ignorance over the angle between magnetic North Pole and the true North Pole.

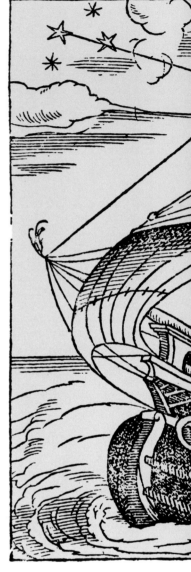

have got in the way of the lateen sails. But on the later square-rigged caravels, the bow was raised to form a tilda, which developed into a forecastle. It is assumed that the *Santa Maria* had both a forecastle and a sterncastle, but the details remain obscure.

Unless the wreck of a caravel is discovered, these questions are unlikely to be answered. In 1976, treasure hunters in the Turks and Caicos Islands found a wreck that appears to have been a caravel or small warship of the sixteenth century, but little was left for the nautical archaeologists to pore over. Their best hope remains that of finding what is left of two caravels beached by Columbus on his last voyage

The astrolabe (far left) was a simple device used to measure the altitude of the Sun or a star. A thick graduated ring of brass is suspended by a cord to hang vertically. Pivoted at the centre of the ring is an alidade, or sighting rule, which was turned on its axis to align with the star and the altitude reading was then taken from the ring. The difficulty of using it on a pitching deck is obvious, so navigators were provided with a platform mounted on gimbals (left). This picture is taken from Le Cosmolabe . . . *by Jacques Besson, published in 1567.*

The precise function of the vertical timbers attached to the outside of the hull remains a mystery. They may have been fenders or designed to reinforce the attachment of the shrouds to the hull. It is not known whether the caravel's stern was rounded or square or whether it had a crow's nest for lookouts.

in 1503. With timbers penetrated by worms and leaking heavily, the *Capitana* and the *Santiago de Palio* were deliberately driven ashore by Columbus in St Ann's Bay, off the northern coast of Jamaica, on 23 June 1503.

It is assumed that the two caravels were gradually covered by sand and silt and may still be in a reasonable state of preservation. In recent years a series of attempts has been made to discover what may be left of them, using increasingly sophisticated scientific instruments to probe beneath the mud. Nautical archaeologists from Texas A. & M. University are leading the search, using sonar devices to try to detect the presence of timbers. If they succeed,

the 500th anniversary of Columbus's voyage may be marked by fresh understanding of the remarkable vessels he used.

The absence of knowledge is not, however, preventing the building of a series of replicas to mark the 500th anniversary celebrations. At least ten reproductions of the various ships used by Columbus are either built or planned. It seems plain that 1992 will see more caravels sailing the seas than have been afloat since the sixteenth century, although whether any of them will bear close resemblance to the originals is open to doubt. Nevertheless, it should make for an enjoyable celebration of a crucial anniversary in European and American history.

Circumnavigating the Globe

FACT FILE

The first ship to sail around the world

Date: 1519–22

Duration: 3 years

On 6 September 1522, seventeen weary men sailed into the harbour of Sanlucar de Barrameda in southern Spain aboard a small vessel, the *Vittoria*. They were the only survivors of the greatest journey ever undertaken, 42,000 miles around the world, more than half of it through waters no Christian had ever entered. As a feat of seamanship and navigation it had no equal, yet the man responsible was not on deck as *Vittoria* crept to her berth. Ferdinand Magellan had not survived to see his voyage through, and those who did had reason to disparage his achievement and cast doubt on his leadership. As a result, Magellan has never enjoyed the fame that he undoubtedly deserves.

He had set out three years before in order to find a new route to the Spice Islands of the Far East. These were what are now known as Indonesia, a group of islands centred on the Moluccas. They produced coconuts, palm oil, hemp, various dyes, sandalwood, spices and pepper. Today it seems strange that such products could excite the greed of kings, but without pepper medieval society would have been hard-pressed to survive. In central and northern Europe there was such a shortage of winter fodder that more than three-quarters of all cattle and sheep had to be slaughtered each autumn and their carcasses cured.

For that, both salt and pepper were needed; and while salt was easily to be had, pepper had to be imported from the Indies. It was a hugely profitable trade, making middlemen rich at every stage, all the way from the point of production. Small wonder that an alternative direct route to the Indies was desperately sought, and that the Spanish crown should have agreed to finance an expedition by the Portuguese navigator Magellan to try to find it.

The potential gains of the voyage help to explain the tensions on board the five ships that set sail under Magellan's command: the *San Antonio* (120 tons), the *Trinidad* (110 tons), the *Vittoria* (90 tons), the *Concepcion* (90 tons) and the *Santiago* (75 tons). These ships were caravels, stout cargo ships about which we know pathetically little. They had three masts, square sails and a simple deck. Below deck was an open bilge and a lower deck that effectively ran like a shelf around the inside of the hull. Life on board these ships was insanitary, uncomfortable and often short.

Magellan had not won the command without inspiring jealousy, and the ships were provisioned in an atmosphere poisoned by political intrigue. Connections at court had won a number of people positions in the fleet which they did not merit by experience or personal qualities, while ordinary seamen were reluctant to sign on. They had not been told the object of the voyage, but knew they had to enlist for at least two years.

Magellan ordered sufficient food to be loaded aboard the ships—including 213,800 lb of biscuit, 72,000 lb of salt beef and 57,000 lb of salt pork—but much of it was pilfered. And, as we now know, the rations lacked the very thing that the crew would need to fend off the dreaded scurvy. Without vitamin C in the form of fruit or green vegetables, more sailors died from scurvy than from wind, wave or shipwreck. Magellan did not know this, or he could have saved himself and his men much grief. Instead, he ordered cheeses and enough wine to give each of his men almost a pint a day.

The fleet also carried huge quantities of spares for making repairs along the way, a shallow draught boat for exploring inshore, and an adequate armoury for fighting their way out of trouble. The cargo consisted of quantities of copper and mercury, bracelets, bells, cheap knives, mirrors, scissors and combs, fishhooks, cloth and crystals cut into the shape of jewels, enough to exchange for a full cargo of pepper for the return journey. There were 277 men at the farewell mass in the dockyard church; only 1 in 15 was to see his homeland again.

Already mutiny was in the minds of some who resented Magellan's command and resolved to murder him at the first opportunity. But he refused to rise to their taunts and provide an excuse. Setting a course southward, his intention was to cross to the mainland of South America, and then travel down the Brazilian coast until he reached the southern cape and could turn west.

He then expected to cross a narrow ocean and reach the Moluccas swiftly. There were at least two serious errors of geography here: first, the southerly extent of South America and second, the width of the Pacific Ocean. Magellan can hardly be blamed for these mistakes, however, for no man had sailed this way before.

As the fleet crossed the equator, Magellan's chance came to deal with his rebellious subordinates. The boatswain of the *Vittoria* had been caught in the act of sodomy, and Magellan ordered a trial. The three Spanish captains of the other ships attended and took the opportunity of

Ferdinand Magellan (c.1480–1521)
*Born at Villa de Sabrosa in Trasos-Montes, Magellan spent his early years as
an attendant at the Portuguese court of John II. He first went to sea on a
voyage to India in 1505, followed by visits to the Spice Islands. Falling from
favour for alleged trading with the enemy in Morocco, Magellan went to
Spain, where he won the support of Charles V for his epic journey. This
portrait hangs in the Uffizi Gallery in Florence.*

Circumnavigating the Globe

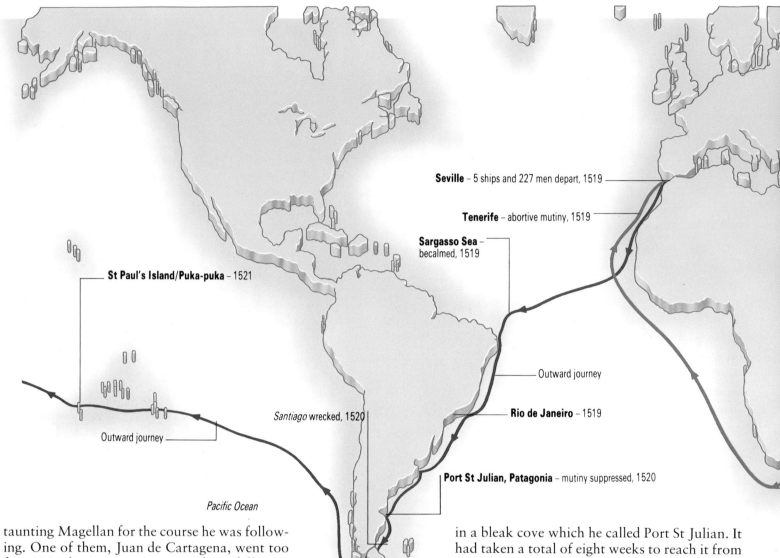

Seville – 5 ships and 227 men depart, 1519

Tenerife – abortive mutiny, 1519

Sargasso Sea – becalmed, 1519

St Paul's Island/Puka-puka – 1521

Outward journey

Santiago wrecked, 1520

Rio de Janeiro – 1519

Outward journey

Port St Julian, Patagonia – mutiny suppressed, 1520

Pacific Ocean

Tierra del Fuego – desertion of *San Antonio*, 1520

taunting Magellan for the course he was following. One of them, Juan de Cartagena, went too far. "No longer am I prepared to follow a hazardous course set by a fool!" he shouted out. Magellan accused him of mutiny, stripped him of his command and threw him in irons.

Led by the flagship *Trinidad*, the fleet ploughed south. Delayed by the doldrums in the Sargasso Sea, they finally found a wind and made the coast of Brazil early in December. After two weeks' resting in the bay of Rio de Janeiro, where to the joy of the crew the Guarani Indians willingly sold their daughters for a shiny bell or a cheap German knife, they sailed on down the coast. When the wide estuary of the River Plate was reached, they confidently sailed into it, believing that it must be the southern cape that would lead them toward the Indies. They realized to their disappointment that it was a river, and sailed on.

By the end of March, with the winter fast approaching, Magellan was forced to anchor

in a bleak cove which he called Port St Julian. It had taken a total of eight weeks to reach it from Rio through terrible seas, including six days during which the *naos*, trapped in a bay on a lee shore, had been forced to tack hopelessly to and fro to avoid being driven aground. As they struggled on, they sighted penguins, the first Europeans ever to see them, but no sight of human beings. It was a tired and disaffected crew who finally dropped anchor in the cheerless bay of St Julian.

Here the Spanish captains attempted another mutiny, which Magellan with an element of luck was able to crush. The ringleader, the released Cartagena, was banished with a priest on to the mainland of Patagonia—a miserable prospect, but Magellan would have been within his rights to execute him. Another Spaniard, Gaspar de Quesada, was beheaded, the executioner his own secretary who took on the task in exchange for a pardon. Quesada's body, together with that of another Spaniard, Captain Luis de Mendoza,

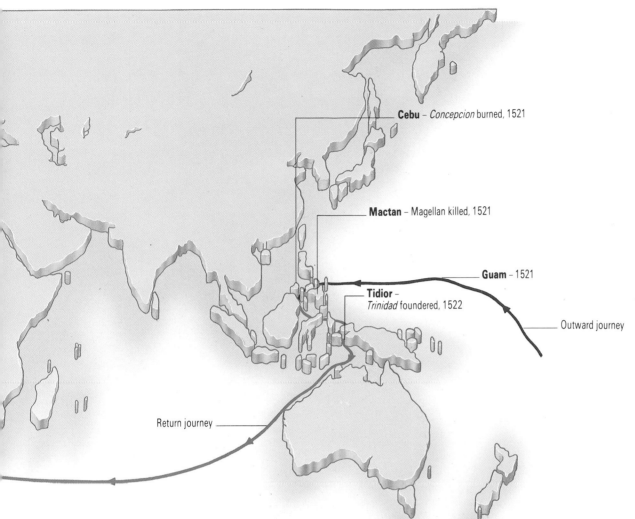

Cebu – *Concepcion* burned, 1521

Mactan – Magellan killed, 1521

Guam – 1521

Tidior –
Trinidad foundered, 1522

Outward journey

Return journey

The principal human discovery of Magellan's voyage was the race of giants standing about 7 feet 6 inches tall, found in Patagonia. They are described by Pigatta in the only chronicle of the voyage to survive. Later travellers, like Sir Francis Drake, concur in reports of the existence of the now extinct race; all that remains is the name Patagonia—land of the big feet. Magellan took two of the friendly giants aboard, but neither survived.

The trading caravels forming Magellan's fleet remain a mystery to maritime archaeologists. There are no accurate illustrations of them, but these Portuguese carracks were a development of the caravels, with high fore and stern castles.

Circumnavigating the Globe

who had been killed in the mutiny, were drawn, quartered and strung up on gibbets.

In this freezing and gruesome place the fleet spent its winter with Magellan's authority now unquestioned. Stout huts were built, the provisions shifted to them, and the ships drawn up on shore and repaired. Here Magellan discovered to his consternation that only half the provisions he had ordered had in fact been loaded. He set the crew to hunting, fishing and trapping to make good the deficiencies.

By the time Magellan was ready to sail, the *Santiago* had been lost in a storm. Just 300 miles farther south, Magellan finally found a strait which he began to explore. It was the *San Antonio* and the *Concepcion*, advancing alone, which discovered that the strait indeed led into a wide expanse of ocean which stretched as far as the eye could see toward the setting sun. Magellan was overjoyed and determined to sail on, but the *San Antonio* mysteriously disappeared. Her crew had had enough and were sailing back to Spain with defamatory accounts of Magellan's leadership in an attempt to justify their desertion.

On the large island that lay to the south, Magellan's men saw the campfires of the Indians, and named the place Tierra de los Fuegos (land of the fires). As they emerged into the ocean, which Magellan optimistically named the Pacific, he thought they would have only a few days' sailing to reach the Spice Islands. In fact, it was two miserable months before they sighted land, by which time the crew were reduced to eating ox-hides, sawdust and rats. Even rats eventually became so scarce that they had to be auctioned off to the highest bidder.

Magellan was unfortunate in the course he chose, which passed north of the Society Islands and led him into the empty reaches of the Pacific. Scurvy took its toll, and men began to die. By mid-January, a third of the crew were so ill they could hardly walk and only a handful could manage the sails or the helm. When they finally did sight an island, on 24 January 1521, it was uninhabited, and they were forced to sail on. (We now believe that this island, named St Paul's by Magellan, was Puka-puka, the most northerly of the Society group.)

Finally, after another agonizing month, they made landfall on some inhabited islands near Guam, about 1,700 miles northeast of their destination in the Moluccas. Here there was a row with the native people, many of whom were

The channel now called the Magellan Strait did not look promising as a passage to the Pacific when Magellan entered it in 1520. It seemed too narrow and overpowered by mountains to be the right channel, but it wound its way between the peaks and led into the huge expanse of the eastern Pacific. Varying in width from $2\frac{1}{4}$ to 70 miles, the strait is 365 miles long. Although not thoroughly explored until 1826–36, it was charted in the sixteenth-century Vaz Dourado map, from the collection of the Duke of Alba.

slaughtered and their food stolen to feed the starving European crew. After a rest, they went on, reaching the Philippine island of Cebu early in April.

Here at last was a known land, with a recognizable language and the unmistakable artefacts of the East. Magellan realized that after 555 days he had reached the Indies and if he continued he would complete a circumnavigation of the Earth. It was a moment of triumph he did not have long to enjoy, for instead of making immediately for the Moluccas he lingered in the Philippines and found a taste for preaching the gospel of Christ. He erected a cross on a hill and took possession for Spain of the group of islands.

Today the Philippines remain the only Christian nation in Asia. Having converted the local ruler, Magellan rashly promised to help him deal with his enemies. The Rajah replied that he did, indeed, have a dispute with the neighbouring island of Mactan, and Magellan sailed to visit the might of the Spanish armouries on these poor innocents. The result was disaster: not only did he fail to conquer the people of Mactan, but he was himself killed in the battle. Deserted by his

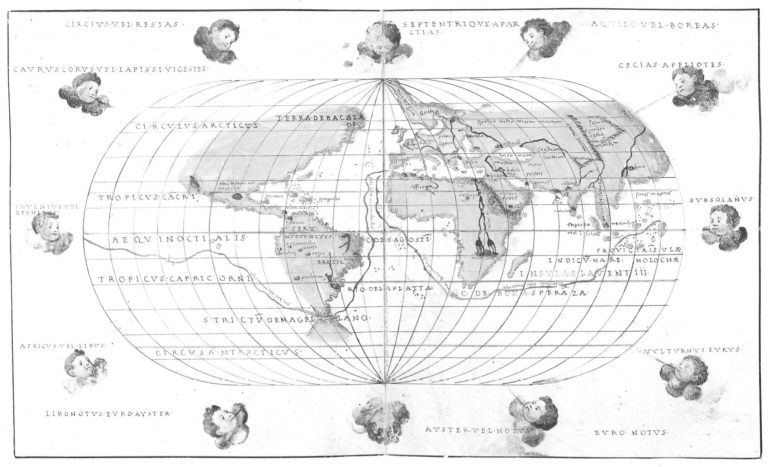

Spanish officers, Magellan was speared to death in shallow water by the enraged natives. "And so they slew our mirror, our light, our comfort and our true and only guide" wrote Antonia Pigafetta, the chronicler of the voyage, whose loyalty to Magellan was unquestionable.

What followed was muddle and chaos. The Rajah owed no loyalty to those who had betrayed Magellan, and took the first opportunity to slaughter as many as he could. The rest escaped and roamed the seas as pirates, stealing cargoes from any ship they met. Early in November 1521, the *Trinidad* and the *Vittoria* reached the Spice Islands, *Concepcion* having been burned—together with most of Magellan's papers—because she was unseaworthy.

In January 1522, *Vittoria* set sail alone, for by this time *Trinidad* too was unfit for sea. As *Vittoria* struggled home, men died of hunger, disease and scurvy. The 17 men who finally staggered ashore were all that was left of the 277 who had sailed. Among them was the captain, Juan Sebastian del Cano, to whom went the honour of being the first circumnavigator of the Earth. But the real honour was Magellan's.

The discoveries of men like Vasco da Gama and Columbus gave a great impetus to chartmaking in Spain and Portugal. Few charts that predate 1500 still exist, but many fine sixteenth-century charts survive, including this 1554 map by the Genoese Battista Agnesi showing Magellan's route (above). The tradition of placing representations of winds around a map goes back to Ptolemy's maps. Evidence survives that globes were used in navigation during the sixteenth century. On the right is a facsimile of the globe made by Georg Hartmann (1489–1564), a German maker of navigational instruments.

Convoy of Floating Prisons

At five o'clock on the morning of Sunday 13 May 1787, a fleet of 11 ships weighed anchor at the Mother Bank outside Portsmouth. It was barely dawn as the ships dropped out of sight of land, on a spring morning which offered little comfort to 759 wretches huddled below, chained and in pitch darkness. Never before had so large a fleet attempted so ambitious a voyage.

Their destination was Botany Bay on the southeastern coast of Australia, discovered 17 years before by Captain James Cook and now designated a penal colony for those unfortunates who had offended against the law of England. It was a destination as remote to the eighteenth-century imagination as the Moon is to ours, an oubliette for the petty criminals who now lay below decks. Ahead was a journey of eight months to a continent occupied by strange, wild men and even stranger creatures.

The First Fleet was led by the frigate *Sirius*, the flagship of the expedition's commodore, Captain Arthur Phillip. It was accompanied by another armed ship, *Supply*, and three store ships, *Golden Grove*, *Fishburn* and *Borrowdale*, which carried sufficient food and stores to last two years. The convicts were carried in six ships—*Scarborough*, *Lady Penrhyn*, *Friendship*, *Charlotte*, *Prince of Wales* and *Alexander*—each accompanied by a detachment of marines. Below, the convicts cowered in the darkness, for they had no portholes, and candles or lamps were not permitted for fear of fire. The air was fetid with the stink of vomit and worse; the stench from the bilges rose and overpowered them. Many must have felt they would have preferred a public execution at Tyburn.

Transportation of criminals was nothing new in English law. Banishment had first been ordered as a punishment for rogues and vagrants in the reign of Queen Elizabeth I and transportation to the American colonies had begun in the seventeenth century. But the American War of Independence had closed off that option, leaving Britain with a growing number of criminals and no clear idea what to do with them. To the educated and cultured minority in the eighteenth century, the cities seemed every bit as threatening as do parts of New York to smart Manhattanites today. With no police force, a rising population, the easy availability of gin, and the moral authority of the Church in decline, there was a justified fear of crime. The penalties for breaches of the law were extraordinarily harsh.

Among those aboard the First Fleet (as Australians call it) was a 70-year-old woman, Elizabeth Beckford, sentenced to seven years' transportation for stealing 12 lb of Gloucester cheese. A West Indian man, Thomas Chaddick, was aboard for the crime of entering somebody's kitchen garden and picking 12 cucumbers. A nine-year-old chimney sweep, John Hudson, the youngest on board, was being transported for seven years for stealing some clothes and a pistol. The oldest convict was 82-year-old Dorothy Handland, who had got seven years for perjury.

The transports that carried the convicts were not purpose-built. They were ordinary sailing ships of the day, in reasonable condition. The oldest, *Scarborough*, had been launched in 1781. They ranged in size from the *Alexander*, at 452 tons, to the *Friendship*, at 278 tons. Even the *Alexander* was only 114 feet long and 31 feet in beam, and it had to carry 213 male convicts, together with 2 lieutenants and 35 marines, not counting officers and crew.

The convicts had been put aboard the ships several months before they sailed, causing Phillip considerable anxiety. "It will be very difficult to prevent the most fatal sickness among men so closely confined," he warned the Admiralty. Sure enough, in March typhus broke out and 11 of the prisoners on board *Alexander* died. The convicts were taken off the ship, which was scrubbed with creosote and quicklime to purify it. Another five convicts died, but the outbreak was brought under control and even served a useful purpose, for it enabled Phillip to insist on proper food which was being denied him by a dishonest contractor.

The man entrusted with command of the First Fleet was a solid, reliable sort. Arthur Phillip was half-German, the son of a language teacher from Frankfurt who emigrated to London and married an English girl. Phillip's career in the Royal Navy had not been especially distinguished, and his own marriage had failed. Twice he had retired from the Navy to his farm at Lyndhurst in the New Forest, but had been drawn back by the sea. For several years during the 1770s he had served in the Portuguese Navy, once delivering 400 convicts from Portugal to Brazil without

FACT FILE

The long journey by ordinary British merchantmen taking the first convicts to Australia

Scarborough

Built: 1782

Overall length: 111 feet 6 inches

Width: 30 feet 2 inches

Height between decks: 4 feet 5 inches

The founding of Australia by Captain Arthur Phillip, RN, is depicted in this painting by Algernon Talmage, RA (1781–1839), *which hangs in the Royal Commonwealth Society, London. Convicts were chained at the neck and hands (left) for the walk from prison to barges at Blackfriars, which took them to transports down the River Thames.*

Convoy of Floating Prisons

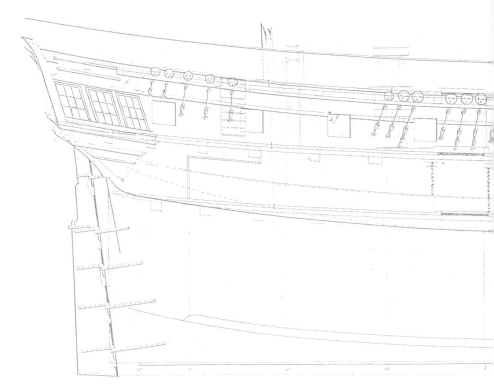

losing a single man, a remarkable achievement.

By 1782 he was at last master of a ship of the line, the 64-gun *Europe*, but in 1784 he retired again on half pay to his farm. In 1786 he must have been surprised to be entrusted with a long and difficult voyage in command of unwilling convicts, to a land where he would be responsible for setting up a penal colony in the wilderness. But he turned out to be an excellent choice, an honest man who would not be fobbed off with half measures and who supervised every detail of the preparations. More than once he wrote furiously to the Admiralty about the conditions of the prisoners and the inadequate provisioning of the fleet.

As far as he could, Phillip insisted on a decent diet for both crew and convicts. The bane of long sea voyages was scurvy, caused by vitamin C deficiency and first conquered by Captain Cook who, during his voyages between 1768 and 1771, issued sauerkraut, a liquor made of malt, and a meat broth reduced until it became a kind of cake. The juice of citrus fruits would have been more effective, but Cook was unaware of that, even though it had been discovered nearly 20 years earlier by Dr James Lind.

For short journeys to the Americas, scurvy was less of a problem, but Phillip realized that if his fleet lacked the right provisions on their long voyage, many would die. "The garrison and the convicts are sent to the extremity of the globe as they would be sent to America—a six-week's passage," he complained.

Once at sea, things went more smoothly. The official history of the voyage records one attempt at mutiny aboard *Scarborough*, detected and frustrated by the officers. The leaders were brought to the *Sirius* and punished, presumably by flogging. The fleet reached Tenerife on 3 June, where one prisoner escaped but was quickly recaptured. The next port of call was Rio de Janeiro, far south enough to pick up the westerlies across the South Atlantic for the Cape of Good Hope. As they slipped south and the weather became hotter, conditions aboard deteriorated.

Rats, cockroaches, lice, bedbugs and fleas proliferated, crawling up from the bilges and tormenting convicts and crew alike. In the doldrums, water was rationed to three pints a day, but then the wind freshened and the fleet reached Rio on 4 August. A month was spent provisioning before Phillip set sail for Cape Town, where another month was spent buying plants, seeds and livestock for the new colony.

HMS Sirius *began her existence as an East India Company merchantship named* Berwick *in 1780. Within a year,* Berwick *was gutted by fire and bought by the Royal Navy. She was put into dry dock and rebuilt as a storeship (above) in 1782, to carry anything from water casks to powder and shot. In October 1786 she was renamed* Sirius *and classified as sixth rate— a ship of no fewer than 26 guns and no more than 28. Apparently a slow sailor,* Sirius *was 110 feet long, 32 feet wide and weighed 540 tons. Although Captain Phillip travelled on her,* Sirius *was under the command of Captain John Hunter. She was wrecked off Norfolk Island in the South Pacific in 1790.*

Out of Cape Town, the weather turned dark and gloomy, with the occasional violent storm. On 19 January 1788 Botany Bay was sighted, and the next morning they were anchored. Of roughly 1,000 people aboard the 11 ships, 48 had died—40 convicts, 5 convicts' children, one marine, the wife of another, and the child of a third. This may sound terrible, but in the circumstances of the time it was a remarkable achievement, one of the greatest feats in the annals of navigation. Later transports, under less efficient leadership, did far worse. The Second Fleet, which sailed between July 1789 and January 1790, lost 267 prisoners out of roughly 1,200 at sea, and at least another 90 after landing. On the *Scarborough*, which completed the first voyage without losing a life, 73 out of 253 died.

Captain Phillip quickly found that Botany Bay was unsuitable for a penal colony. It had a shallow harbour, a shortage of fresh water, and a bare and open soil. Leaving the convicts ashore, he sailed north to investigate another harbour noted favourably by Cook from a glimpse as he sailed past its narrow entrance. It had everything that Botany Bay lacked: deep anchorages, "where a thousand sail of the line may ride with the most perfect security", good landings, fresh water and eucalyptus trees. It was, Phillip told Lord Sydney of the Admiralty, "the finest harbour in the world". He named it Sydney Cove. Today it is better known just as Sydney, one of the world's greatest cities.

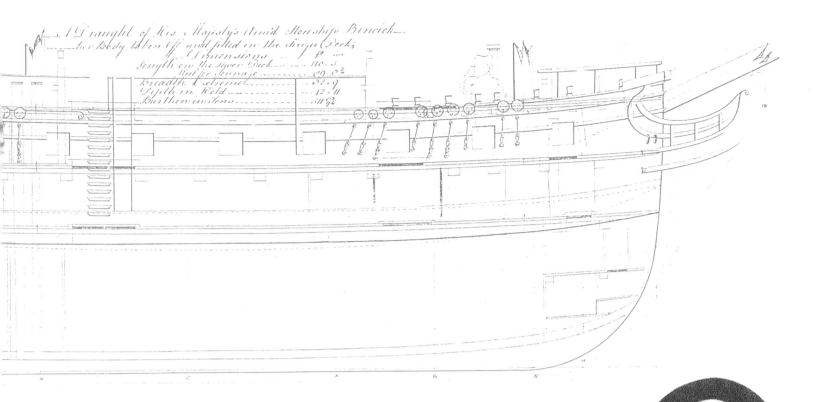

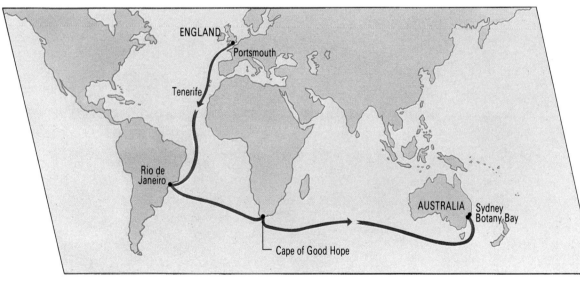

Captain Arthur Phillip (1738–1814) *was born in London and trained at Greenwich before joining the navy in 1755. After serving with Admiral Byng in the Mediterranean, he was at the taking of Havana in 1762. He became the first governor of New South Wales, guiding the colony for four years until ill-health forced him to return to England. He was made a vice admiral in 1810.*

Captain Phillip's concern with diet on the eight-month voyage was reflected in the time spent provisioning. The fleet stocked up in Rio, and in Cape Town, the Friendship's *female convicts were transferred to other ships and it was filled with 500 animals— bulls, cows, sheep, pigs and poultry.*

For the bicentennial celebrations of the founding of Australia in 1988, the voyage of the First Fleet was re-enacted by reconstructions of vessels that either took part in the voyage themselves or were thought to resemble ships associated with the early history of the country. These included HMS Bounty *(right)*.

Alone Around the World

Joshua Slocum *was born in Nova Scotia in 1844. His family included several seafarers, but his father was a farmer. He left home at the age of 12 when his father beat him for making a model ship when he should have been grading potatoes. He signed on as a sailor and by the age of 26 had command of a barque. In the course of a full life, he acquired enormous knowledge, not only learning the skills of sailing and navigation, but boat-building too. Surprisingly few photographs have survived of* Spray *to help artists depict the boat's epic journey (opposite).*

FACT FILE

First boat to carry a lone sailor around the world

Built: 1892–94

Length: 36 feet 9 inches

Width: 14 feet 2 inches

Weight: 9 tons net

At the age of 51, Captain Joshua Slocum set out to sail around the world, alone. No man, he asserted, had done it before, which seemed reason enough to try. Slocum was a tough sea captain from the age of sail, adaptable and not easily cast down by circumstance. He had little formal learning, but he could write with a wry, simple-hearted charm; his *Sailing Alone around the World* remains one of the great classics of the sea. The only thing he could not do was swim.

The boat in which Slocum was to undertake his journey was an ancient sloop called *Spray*. She was a virtual wreck when Slocum found her, but in 13 months he had rebuilt the sloop as strong as he could make her.

When finished *Spray* "sat on the water like a swan," Slocum wrote, and sailed so securely that he found he could set course, lash the tiller and go below to sleep in the certain knowledge that she would not wander.

He spent a season fishing in *Spray*, but by this time had resolved to sail her around the world, serving as captain, mate and crew. On 24 April 1895 he left Boston, and after fitting out in Gloucester, Massachusetts, he set sail on 7 May. He called at a few ports up the coast and at one of them bought an old tin clock with a broken face and no minute hand for the sum of $1. This was the timepiece he used to navigate during the entire voyage.

Spray made good time, covering 1,200 miles in the first eight days, her sails drawing steadily all night as Slocum dozed in between going aloft from time to time to make sure all was well. He passed several ships, shouting messages to them as he went; one Spanish captain, who was 23 days out from Philadelphia, sent him a bottle of wine across, slung by the neck. The loneliness, once conquered, never returned.

Slocum stopped briefly in the Azores, then sailed for Gibraltar. Here the Royal Navy made a great fuss of him, giving him a berth alongside several great battleships. The governor came to visit and signed his name in Slocum's log. Vegetables and milk were supplied by the Admiralty, and a tug was provided to tow *Spray* out of harbour when Slocum sailed. He left Gibraltar westward, crossing the Atlantic once more, bound for Brazil. Once in the swing of the trades, the sailing was easy and Slocum spent his time reading and writing, or making small repairs to rigging and sails. Flying fish that landed on the deck provided most of his meals, together with biscuits and potatoes.

He made landfall at Pernambuco, then sailed on to Rio. Leaving Rio for Cape Horn, Slocum encountered a northerly current which made it necessary to hug the shore, but in doing so he ran aground. With great difficulty he managed to lay out the anchor to hold the sloop firm, carrying anchor and cable in his little dory which was swamped by the weight and the waves breaking over it. "I grasped her gunwale and held on as she turned bottom up, for I suddenly remembered I could not swim," Slocum wrote. After repeated efforts he managed to right the boat and clamber aboard, and with one of the oars which he had recovered he was able to paddle to the shore to rest.

Soon *Spray*, high and dry on the beach, was surrounded by curious and acquisitive locals, but Slocum bought them off with a few biscuits, and with the help of two other men was able to refloat his ship on the next high tide. She had been damaged, but not mortally, and was easily put right at Montevideo, where the local agents of the Royal Mail Steamship Co. docked and repaired her for nothing, as well as giving Slocum £20. He was happy to have it, for he had set off with very little money and was dependent during his voyage on gifts or what he could earn. Ahead lay the greatest challenge of the whole trip, Cape Horn.

Slocum planned to squeeze through the Magellan Strait rather than sailing around the very tip of Cape Horn. He was warned that foul weather was not the only danger he might face. The Fuegians who inhabited those remote regions were neither friendly nor law-abiding, and Slocum was advised to wait for a gunboat to accompany him, or at least to carry a crew to help fight off attacks. He could find nobody.

As Slocum sailed between the remote islands of the Magellan Strait, he soon met the Fuegians. When the weather permitted, they came out in canoes to beg and threaten. Slocum, anxious not to show them he was alone, rigged an old piece of bowsprit forward as a lookout, dressing it as a seaman and attaching a line to it so that he could create the impression it was alive. Several times he was forced to fire over the heads of boarding

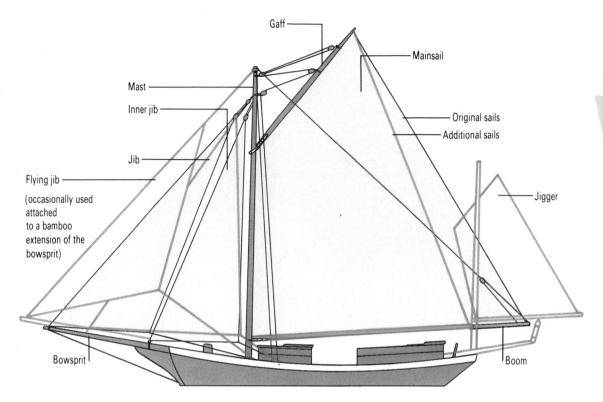

Gaff

Mainsail

Mast

Inner jib

Original sails

Additional sails

Jib

Flying jib

(occasionally used
attached
to a bamboo
extension of the
bowsprit)

Jigger

Bowsprit

Boom

THE REBUILDING OF SPRAY

Slocum found *Spray* propped up in a field at Fairhaven, Massachusetts. To rebuild her, he used local timber which he steamed, bent and caulked himself. The planks were of Georgia pine $1\frac{1}{2}$ inches thick, the keel was a stout oak, the deck $1\frac{1}{2}$-inch pine pinned to beams 6 inches square. He created a cooking galley and a cabin 10 feet by 12. Between

cabin and galley was a midship hold sufficient to store water and salt beef for many months.

Her rig began as a sloop but was altered to a yawl during the journey. For a ship's boat, Slocum found an old dory and cut it in half, boarding up the end where it was cut. It also served as a tub to wash clothes in and as a bath.

parties, and when he finally escaped from the strait he was caught by a tremendous storm.

Stripped of her sails, *Spray* bore south under bare poles, two long ropes paid out astern to steady the ship and stop her broaching. Under these conditions, Slocum cooked an Irish stew, for his taste for proper food seldom deserted him. As he was swept south around Cape Horn he began to make plans to head for Port Stanley in the Falkland Islands, so hopeless was it to contemplate beating north. But suddenly he saw land and made for it. It was Cockburn Channel, leading him back into the strait from which he had so recently escaped.

He broke away from the treacherous waters of the Horn on 13 April 1896, next making landfall at Juan Fernandez, the island where Alexander Selkirk, prototype for Robinson Crusoe, lived alone for almost five years. Slocum visited Selkirk's cave and a local woman made him a new flying jib in exchange for some of his tallow.

Then he was away across the Pacific to Samoa, where he met the widow of Robert Louis

Stevenson and passed some idyllic days. Reluctantly he left, and "crowded on sail for lovely Australia", a nation which he knew well.

Slocum lingered in Australia for nine months, visiting Sydney and Melbourne and cruising around Tasmania. The Australians showed an enormous interest in his voyage, and he gave many public lectures, as well as charging people sixpence to visit *Spray*. Eventually he left, sailing north of Australia to the Keeling Cocos Islands, Rodriguez and then Mauritius.

In South Africa Slocum had a memorable encounter with Paul Kruger, the president of the Transvaal. Kruger believed the world was flat, and retorted sharply when told that Slocum was sailing around the world that it could not be.

Finally all there remained of the great journey was yet another crossing of the Atlantic, for the third time. Slocum reached his native shore by way of the Caribbean, then up the eastern seaboard of the US to drop anchor in Boston on 27 June 1898, "after a cruise of more than 46,000 miles round the world, during an absence of

After crossing the Atlantic, Slocum had intended to travel through the Mediterranean and down the Suez Canal, but the danger of attack by pirates along the North African coast changed his mind. Slocum's accurate navigation was remarkable because he measured his longitude by calculating with a sextant the distance between stars. He was then able to work out the time at the Greenwich meridian using tabular data first produced in the late 1750s. Comparing that with local time enabled him to calculate his longitude.

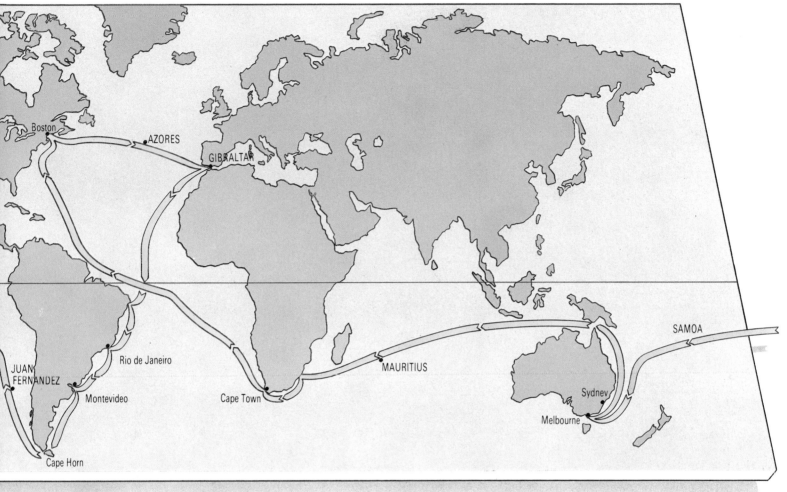

T. FOGARTY.

Slocum read avidly *during his voyage. He had been warned that the Fuegians of southern Patagonia would probably try to board his boat. To deter such interruptions to his sleep or reading, Slocum used a bag of carpet tacks that an Austrian sea captain had given him en route. He spread them over the deck while he anchored near the Cockburn Channel; he was woken about midnight by howls that were "like a pack of hounds . . . They jumped pell-mell, some into their canoes and some into the sea."*

three years and two months." He was well and weighed a pound more than when he had sailed. As for *Spray*, "she was still as sound as a nut, and as tight as the best ship afloat. She did not leak a drop—not one drop!" A few days later Slocum took her right home, tying her up at Fairhaven, Massachusetts, to the same cedar pile driven into the bank to hold her when she had been launched. "I could bring her no nearer home," he noted.

Slocum's appetite for sailing never diminished. Almost every winter he sailed *Spray* down to Grand Cayman in the West Indies, and in November 1909, at the age of 65, he set out once more, outward bound from Bristol, Rhode Island, for the River Orinoco. He was never seen again. Most likely *Spray* was run down in the night by a steamer while Slocum was below. For years afterward there were rumours that Slocum had been seen on some South American river or another, for he appeared indestructible. But he was finally declared legally dead. His book, and his reputation, remain imperishable.

The Wooden Fortress Against the Ice

Seldom has a ship been given a more appropriate name than the SS *Discovery*, which carried Captain Robert Scott on his first voyage to Antarctica in 1901. *Discovery* was a robust ship, built in Dundee, Scotland, strong enough to spend two winters locked in the Antarctic ice and emerge undamaged. Later, after spending many years as an ordinary trading ship, *Discovery* was re-equipped and sent on a pioneering scientific cruise in the southern oceans, establishing many of the basic data upon which the science of oceanography is founded.

Scott's voyage of 1901 was the most ambitious scientific expedition that had ever sailed from England. The questions he sought to answer were fundamental ones: how large was Antarctica, how deep the ocean surrounding it, how impenetrable the ice cap that surmounted it? His crew were to make meteorological observations every two hours and a painstaking magnetic survey of the regions south of the 40th parallel. They were to explore the greatest unknown landmass in the world, striking farther south than anyone had gone before.

The expedition was sponsored by the Royal Society and the Royal Geographical Society, funded to the extent of £45,000 by the government, and supported by the Admiralty. To carry this expedition the first ship ever built in Britain for scientific exploration was commissioned.

Immense care went into deciding what form *Discovery* should take. Should she follow the saucerlike lines of *Fram*, the Norwegian polar ship, which survived pack ice by riding upward under its pressure? Or should she be based on the shape of the old whalers, tough, seaworthy craft whose record spoke for itself? The expedition's sponsors opted for the latter, specifying a ship 172 feet long by 33 feet broad, and made of wood, for no other material could provide the combination of elasticity and strength needed to survive the pack ice. By October 1899, when the lengthy specification was issued, few shipyards in Britain still had the skills to build in wood, and only one firm with sufficient experience responded. So it was in Stevens' Yard, on the River Tay, that the keel was laid in March 1900.

The ship was built spectacularly strong, with huge beams and a double thickness of hull. The bow was even tougher, made of huge pieces of oak fitted together and fastened by strengthening bolts. At the bow a layer of steel was laid on top of the timber, to produce greater strength when *Discovery* crashed into the ice, riding upward on it before crashing down under her own weight to break it.

Discovery was undoubtedly strong, but she was not a graceful sailor. She was slow and rolled horribly and, despite the many-layered hull, she leaked mysteriously and persistently. The only time the leaks stopped was when she was trapped in the pack ice. For the rest of the time, the pumps were at work, since even the most careful examination in dry dock in New Zealand failed to find the source of the leak.

After sailing to New Zealand and unsuccessfully seeking to stem the leak, *Discovery* set off south on Christmas Eve 1901. There were 44 men on board, mostly very young. Scott himself was only 33, and the average age was 25. The ship passed without too much trouble through the belt of sea ice that lies around Antarctica, and reached land. On 21 January they passed Mount Erebus and were in sight of the great ice sheet which extends outward from the land for 500 miles. Then Scott retraced his steps and, having found a sheltered anchorage in McMurdo Sound, decided to spend the winter there.

It was an unwise decision, for it was to be two winters before the ice shifted enough to allow *Discovery* to escape. Soon the winter set in, and the expedition was left alone in an isolation now impossible to imagine. There was no radio, nor any hope of messages reaching them until the following summer. It was dark, for in the winter the Sun never rose above the horizon.

The following summer was spent in observations and expeditions, Scott making an epic but mismanaged journey inland. He had too few dogs, and those he did have were grossly overloaded, so could hardly pull the sledges. The group of three who set off—Scott, Ernest Shackleton and the expedition's surgeon, Dr Edward Wilson—were provided with wholly inadequate amounts of food, of the wrong sort, and tents which could not easily survive the kinds of winds that are common in Antarctica.

They had just $7\frac{1}{2}$ ounces of pemmican, a cake of dried meat, to eat a day; today it is known that at least a pound a day is necessary to keep going in such conditions. The men worked heroically, none more so than Scott, but emerged exhausted

FACT FILE

One of the last ships built in wood and iron of titanic strength

Date built: 1900/01

Overall length: 220 feet

Power output: 500 horsepower

Weight: 485 tons

Discovery *was trapped by ice,* near Observation Hill (above), for two winters. The crew (left) did not have to endure the privations of some marooned expeditions. Breakfast consisted of porridge, bread and marmalade, the main meal of seal or tinned meat and a fruit tart. On the mess deck, "shove ha'penny" was the favourite entertainment, while the wardroom held debates on issues such as women's rights and enjoyed lantern slide talks.

The Wooden Fortress Against the Ice

and near to death. There was evidence here of the same kind of blind heroism that was later to lead Scott to disaster on his final bid to reach the Pole in 1910–12.

As summer arrived, so did a relief ship, the *Morning*, bringing mail and fresh supplies, to find *Discovery* still firmly anchored by the ice and with little chance of escaping. The expedition settled down for another winter. When summer finally came around again, fruitless efforts were made to escape by cutting through the ice with saws. The ice was 7 feet thick and froze up again almost as soon as it had been cut.

That summer not one relief ship but two had arrived, *Morning* and *Terra Nova*, sent by the Admiralty which had panicked unnecessarily. They brought orders that if *Discovery* could not be freed by the end of February, Captain Scott was to abandon ship and return home in the relief ships. This proved unnecessary because a swell arrived to break up the pack ice and quite suddenly *Discovery* was free. What followed, however, was even more alarming and might have broken a weaker ship into fragments.

Leaving her harbour, *Discovery* almost immediately ran ashore. The wind got up and the heavy sea pounded the ship on the shore, breaking off the false keel. She was aground for eight hours, grinding relentlessly to and fro, but by good fortune drifted off again and set sail for New Zealand. Next her pumps failed, and the leak, grown worse after two years in the ice, threatened to sink her. At last steam was raised in an auxiliary engine on deck and the pumps were made to work. *Discovery* was saved. There remained only a broken rudder to replace and she was able to make New Zealand.

When the expedition returned in triumph to London, having achieved much, *Discovery* was soon forgotten. She was sold to the Hudson's Bay Company in 1905 and for six years sailed to and fro carrying supplies from West India Dock, London, to Hudson Bay. From 1912 to 1914 she lay idle in dock until World War I provided new opportunities. She sailed to Russia, and then worked briefly for the French Ministry of Commerce. In August 1916, she sailed to rescue members of Ernest Shackleton's expedition, stranded after their ship was crushed by ice, but arrived after Shackleton had contrived his own escape in an open boat. *Discovery* went back to routine trading until in 1923 she was bought by the Crown Agents for the Colonies to undertake scientific research in the South Seas.

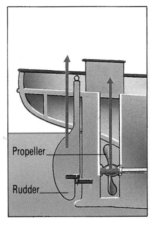

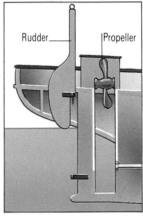

She spent two years carrying out a variety of work, including studies of the population of whales, until in 1925 she was commissioned again to visit the Antarctic as part of a joint British-Australian-New Zealand scientific expedition. On two expeditions *Discovery* surveyed another 1,500 miles of Antarctic coastline to add to the 1,000 miles surveyed under Scott.

She passed after this into the hands of the government of the Falkland Islands, and then, in 1937, to the Boy Scouts. Moored along the Embankment she was a familiar sight to Londoners for 50 years, until finally she was taken back to Dundee for restoration and to become part of a museum in the town where she was built. Few ships have been responsible for more distant or more dangerous voyages, or can claim to have located more territory than *Discovery*. Few have been more soundly built or have survived more perils.

The frame of Discovery *(above) was of English oak 11 inches thick, covered by planking 4 inches thick. Outside that were two layers of planking, one 6 inches thick and the other 5. The frames were placed close together so that for much of her length* Discovery's *hull was a full 26 inches thick. Three tiers of beams ran from side to side, 11 inches square and in the lower levels no more than 3 feet apart.*

The rudder was protected by an overhanging stern, since the rudder and propeller were always the weakest points of an Antarctic ship. In case of damage, the propeller and rudder could be detached and raised through the upper deck for repair (left).

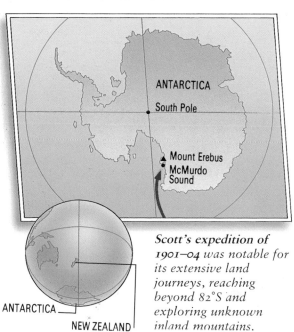

Scott's expedition of 1901–04 was notable for its extensive land journeys, reaching beyond 82°S and exploring unknown inland mountains.

Discovery's accommodation *had been well planned for her crew to come through two icebound winters (above) in good spirits. Individual cabins for officers were provided off a wardroom 30 feet by 20, but as a result of their position over the freezing coal bunkers they were rather cold. The crew's quarters were larger and warmer. Discovery's propensity to roll (left), even in modest seas, contributed to the loss of sheep from the decks on the way south.*

Exploring the Antarctic

The search for a great south land, or Terra Australis Incognita, preoccupied explorers of the sixteenth and seventeenth centuries. Credit for confirming its existence goes to Captain James Cook who undertook three voyages between 1772 and 1779. A series of modest discoveries preceded the "heroic" age of Antarctic exploration, which produced some of the most remarkable stories of human courage and endurance: Scott, Oates, Shackleton and Amundsen have become household names.

Since World War II, scientific discovery has replaced geographical discovery and the area has been uniquely protected from commercial exploitation and pollution by the Antarctic Treaty. Pressure from some countries to allow the mining of minerals places the world's last unspoiled wilderness in jeopardy.

The Terra Nova *(above) was the three-masted barque which took Captain Robert Scott (left) on his fatal Antarctic expedition of 1910–13. Scott and four companions perished on the return journey from the South Pole to base camp. They had reached the pole only to find that the Norwegian Amundsen had beaten them to it. Built in 1884 and weighing 749 tons, the Terra Nova had been the "biggest whaling ship afloat".*

The Endurance *(left), a* **Norwegian sealer** *of 350 tons, carried Sir Ernest Shackleton's Imperial Trans-Antarctic Expedition of 1914–16 to the Weddell Sea. In January 1915 the ship was trapped by ice floes off the Caird Coast. After nine months of tremendous pressure, beams began breaking and Shackleton gave orders to abandon ship. When they left the ship the next day, decks had buckled, masts had snapped and spears of ice had penetrated the bulkheads. In mid-November the party watched her sink. The 800-mile journey by Shackleton and 5 others in a 22-foot boat to South Georgia to organize the rescue of the expedition has been called the most remarkable boat voyage in history.*

The first mechanical vehicle *to be used on Antarctica was the Arrol-Johnson motor car (below), taken by Shackleton on his British Antarctic Expedition of 1907–09. Driven by a 15-hp air-cooled engine, the car was fitted with special steel-ribbed tyres. It proved of little use on soft snow, however.*

The Longest Journey into Battle

FACT FILE

The arduous voyage of the Russian Baltic fleet to a disastrous defeat by the Japanese at Tsushima

Date: October 1904– May 1905

Distance: 18,670 miles

Duration: 222 days

Admiral Heihachiro Togo (top) was trained in England and commanded the Japanese fleet at Tsushima. The Russian leader was Admiral Sinovi Petrovich Rozhestvensky (above).

Few more hopeless journeys have ever been undertaken than the voyage of the Russian Baltic fleet during the winter and spring of 1904/05. A poorly equipped and badly led navy set out on mission impossible: to sail 18,000 miles around the world, without benefit of friendly ports or coaling stations, in order to engage a Japanese fleet which had already proved its effectiveness. In the heat of war, many ill-considered decisions are made, but seldom one as fateful as that of Tsar Nicholas II to send 45 ships and 10,000 sailors to disaster.

The war between Russia and Japan, two nations which both had imperial designs on Manchuria and Korea, had gone badly for the Russians. On 5 February 1904 the Japanese commander-in-chief, Admiral Heihachiro Togo, launched an attack on the Russian Pacific fleet as it lay at anchor at Port Arthur, the most northerly ice-free port in the Pacific. Serious damage was done, but it was not mortal; the Russian fleet in the East still outnumbered the Japanese and for the next year engaged in a series of skirmishes as the war raged on land and the Japanese closed in on Port Arthur. An attempt by the Russians to break out and link up with their cruiser squadron at Vladivostok failed, and in desperation the tsar readied the Baltic fleet to steam around the world to relieve the blockade.

A curious selection of vessels old and new was assembled under the command of Admiral Sinovi Petrovich Rozhestvensky. His flagship was the *Suvorov*, a modern battleship designed for a displacement of 13,500 tons and a speed of 18 knots. But so much additional weight had been added, much of it in unnecessary fittings in the officers' quarters, that she weighed 15,000 tons, was top heavy and could reach only 16 knots at the most.

Some of the other battleships were worse: the *Alexander III* was good for only 15 knots, while the brand-new *Borodino* had had no time for trials to sort out her troublesome engines, which overheated at any speed greater than 12 knots. The *Orel*, another battleship, was plagued with troubles from the start: a fire, a near-sinking, and then the discovery that her propeller shaft had been coated with emery and brass filings in an attempt to sabotage her. The *Svetlana* was a modern ship capable of 20 knots, but was only a lightly armed cruiser.

The rest of the major warships were a poor lot in the opinion of Captain Vladimir Semenov, who had served in the Pacific fleet but had made his way back to Russia and was now aboard the *Suvorov*. Some were a joke. The cruiser *Dmitri Donskoi* was so old she had originally been rigged for sail as well as steam, while the *Almaz* was the commander-in-chief's yacht to which some armour and a few light guns had been added. The fleet could move only at the speed of its slowest member, which was 11 knots.

The sailors included a smattering of criminals who had been called up in order to get them out of the way. Small wonder that there was an air of alarm verging on panic in the fleet when it finally left Russian waters on 16 October 1904.

Men and officers were prey to a series of absurd rumours, of which the least probable but most widely believed was that the North Sea was full of Japanese torpedo boats. Nobody tried to explain how such tiny boats could have made their way around the world without detection, although the Russians suspected British connivance. The fact that Britain, though neutral, had supported Japan's side in the war deepened Russian doubts about British motives.

On 18 October the fleet fired on an innocent Danish trawler, and two days later on the Dogger Bank opened fire again on a fishing fleet out of Hull, believing it to be the fabled Japanese torpedo boats. One trawler, the *Crane*, was sunk and five more hit; two sailors were killed and six injured. In the pandemonium the Russians began firing at themselves; the cruisers *Aurora* and *Dmitri Donskoi* were hit and the chaplain of the *Aurora* was killed.

Thomas Carr, senior skipper of the Gamecock fleet of fishing vessels, kept a very stiff upper lip. In his report to the fleet's owners, he wrote laconically: "I don't know whether they mistook us for Japanese, or whether they were practising on us to get their hand in. There must be a mistake somewhere: they ought to have known that we were only innocent fishermen." He signed the letter Thomas Carr, "Admiral".

On the *Suvorov*, the fleet's engineer-in-chief, Eugene Politovsky, wrote in a letter to his wife: "Imagine the feelings of the people in these ships! They were, no doubt, fishermen. Now there will be a universal scandal." He was right. The British government mobilized the Home fleet

A popular classic woodblock by Hampo, issued by the Japanese in 1905.

The Longest Journey into Battle

and called the Channel fleet, then at Gibraltar, to a state of alert. By the night of 26 October the Royal Navy had 28 battleships either at sea or ready to go to sea, and for a while the prospect of war seemed quite possible.

Rozhestvensky, shadowed by four British cruisers, made his way through the Channel and south to Vigo Bay, in Spain. His explanation of the incident was unconvincing, but the Russian government offered reparations and agreed to cooperate in an inquiry. They detached a few officers from the squadron to give evidence. One of them, a Captain Klado, was no great loss to Rozhestvensky, for he was a troublemaker who spent as much time writing critical articles for the newspapers as serving as a naval officer. On his return to St Petersburg, Klado immediately began arguing that the fleet needed further reinforcements, with the result that some even older ships were sent to support Rozhestvensky.

His squadron had meanwhile split in two, the smaller vessels being sent through the Mediterranean and the Suez Canal, while the battleships with deeper draught took the long route around the Cape of Good Hope. Their greatest problem was coal. Before setting off they had been loaded to the gunwales with the stuff, *Suvarov* carrying more than 2,200 tons although she had bunkers for only half as much. There was coal everywhere, Semenov remembered, "not only up to the neck but over the ears". Coal was stored in bags on deck, in the lifeboats, in the heads, even in the food lockers.

Even so, it was nothing like enough, and with most of the world's coaling stations controlled by the British, the Russians had devised an extraordinary scheme to keep their ships steaming. A deal had been struck with the German Hamburg-Amerika Line to provide 62 colliers along the route, carrying 340,000 tons of coal to be transferred in neutral ports if possible but failing that outside the 3-mile territorial limit.

Loading the coal at sea was a horrible job, especially in the tropics. At Dakar in Senegal, where temperatures inside the bunkers reached 115°F, a young lieutenant, son of the Russian ambassador in Paris, dropped dead of heat-stroke. Coal dust was everywhere, in the cabins, in the cupboards, in everybody's clothes. Rozhestvensky's temper, never calm, was by this time close to boiling point. His main interest seemed to be to keep the fleet in perfect lines, exploding with rage when any of the ships deviated. After a volley of oaths, the order would

Damage to a Hull trawler from the incident at Dogger Bank. The sense of paranoia that led to Russian ships firing on British trawlers was fuelled by fanciful reports sent by Hekkelman, the head of the Russian intelligence agency. Based in Copenhagen, he had a hundred observers and nine boats to gather information, and sent warnings of Japanese torpedo boats. The incident produced demands from the British press and some members of Parliament for retribution, but an offer of compensation was accepted.

come: "Signal that idiot a reprimand!"

The fleet at last arrived at Madagascar to hear the news that Port Arthur had fallen to the Japanese, with the complete elimination of the Russian Pacific fleet. Rozhestvensky also heard the equally unwelcome news that reinforcements he had not sought and did not want were on their way. Overcome by exhaustion and despair—or perhaps even suffering a stroke—he retired to his cabin for several days, emerging pale and dragging one of his feet as he walked. He now had to sail the rest of the way to Vladivostok while the whole of the Japanese fleet lay in home waters waiting for him.

For weeks after its departure from Madagascar the fleet simply disappeared. Without radio communication, nobody knew where it was as it struck out across the Indian Ocean, making regular rendezvous with the colliers. This was the first time that a modern battle fleet had ever made such a long journey across open sea, relying on no friendly port for assistance. On 8 April it was sighted off Singapore, steaming at a steady 8 knots, all the ships trailing great masses of vegetation just below the water line.

By 12 April they were at Cam Ranh Bay in

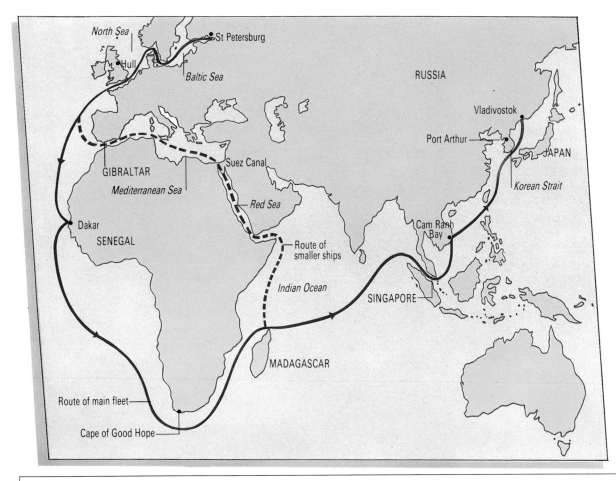

The route after the Dogger Bank debacle took in Vigo, where the Daily Mail correspondent Edgar Wallace elicited good copy from drunken Russian seamen. The smaller ships left to sail through the Suez Canal; the bigger ships sailed to Dakar and then around the Cape of Good Hope to Madagascar, stopping in isolated bays in French, German and Portuguese colonies to coal on the way. During two months of gunnery practice off the island few targets were hit, but one shell hit a Russian cruiser, and in manoeuvres two battleships had a gentle side-on collision.

COALING AT SEA

The most difficult part of taking 40-odd ships halfway around the world was the provision of coal for the voracious steam boilers. Most battleships had 20 boilers, one had 24. The desire of the German government to curry favour with Russia enabled Rozhestvensky's fleet to rely on German colliers. Agreement was reached with the Hamburg-Amerika Line to provide 340,000 tons of coal.

Rozhestvensky's fear of running short of coal led to frequent coaling at points between Denmark and Korea, and a stipulation that all ships should carry 50 percent more than their bunker capacity. The exertion of coaling in the tropics, and the dirt created by having coal stored in every possible place, did nothing for the crew's health or morale.

Generally, coaling was done using wicker baskets or sacks that the men carried on their backs or their shoulders—a long and laborious method. The delay to ships through the time taken to replenish a ship's bunkers encouraged the Royal Navy to begin in 1912 a programme to build British ships with oil-firing.

The Longest Journey into Battle

French Indochina (now Vietnam) where they halted for a full month to let the reinforcements catch them up. Given their deficiencies, the second squadron had made good time and reached Cam Ranh Bay on 8 May. But they added little punch; there was an elderly battleship, *Nikolai I*, an old cruiser and three coastal defence ships, together with seven auxiliary vessels. Rozhestvensky now had 45 fighting ships and numerous auxiliaries, some of which he sent to Shanghai but others he was obliged to keep with the fleet. Since they could make only 9 knots and had to be protected in a convoy, the whole fleet was slow and unwieldy.

Finally, though, it was ready for battle. The sensible course was to try to reach Vladivostok without encountering the Japanese, for then Rozhestvensky could rest, refit and prepare the fleet for battle without the encumbrance of the supply ships. But his best chance of doing so would be to go up the east coast of Japan, a longer route which would mean coaling off the coast. Up the Korean Strait was a shorter route, but it made direct contact with the Japanese more likely. For reasons we do not know— pride, fatalism or a desire for battle—he chose the Korean Strait. Admiral Togo guessed correctly that is what he would do and lay in wait.

On 27 May, on a moonlit morning, the Japanese sighted the Russian fleet. By 7 a.m. Japanese cruisers were shadowing it as it sailed northeast at 8 knots in misty weather and a heavily rolling sea. By 1.40 p.m. both battle fleets were in sight of one another, and the biggest naval battle since Trafalgar began. They were proceeding on parallel courses, in opposite directions, when Togo gave the order to turn about. He wanted to put his best ships in the right position to cause the maximum damage for the longest time, but he ran the risk that as his ships turned and masked each other's guns they would be vulnerable to the Russians.

The manoeuvre came off, and soon the Russian battleships were under withering fire. The Japanese concentrated on the *Suvarov* and the *Oslyabya*, the flagship of the second-in-command, Rear-Admiral Felkerzam. In fact, as Rozhestvensky knew but the rest of his fleet did not, Felkerzam already lay dead in his cabin. Ill since leaving Madagascar, he had died on the night of 23 May but the commander-in-chief had kept the fact secret for fear of spreading despondency.

Oslyabya, burning from end to end, turned

over and sank. The *Suvarov* was hit repeatedly, shells felling all but one funnel and one mast, and injuring many on the bridge, including Rozhestvensky. When *Suvarov*'s steering gear was disabled, the stricken ship left the line. By 3 p.m., the Russians were in disarray as the Japanese pounded them continuously. By the end of the day, *Suvarov*, *Borodino* and *Alexander III* had joined *Oslyabya* on the bottom and the rest of the fleet was scattered. Only one cruiser and two destroyers reached Vladivostok intact.

In all, on this and succeeding days, the Russians lost 34 warships and 4,830 lives, against 3 Japanese torpedo boats and 110 lives. There can hardly ever have been such a one-sided battle, or such a final and numbing defeat. After its epic journey around the world, the Russian Baltic fleet had stumbled naively to destruction.

The lesson was not wasted on other naval strategists. The Japanese victory had come from speed, better gunnery and superior leadership. The future of naval combat lay with swift ships, carrying big guns, as the British Admiralty had realized. The keel of a new class of battleship, HMS *Dreadnought*, had already been laid.

The cruiser Dmitri Donskoi *was the older of the two armoured cruisers in Rozhestvensky's fleet, built in 1883 with a full ship rig. She was damaged during the battle of Tsushima on 27 May 1905, and was scuttled the following morning off the island of Matsushima.*

The battleship Orel (left) was built in a yard on Galeray Island, St Petersburg, and launched in 1902. She was 397 feet long, and fully laden, she displaced 15,275 tons. Crewed by 29 officers and 796 men, the Orel was, like other Russian ships, painted black except for the canary yellow funnels, which helped the Japanese gunners. The upper deck of the Orel after the battle (below) indicated the severity of the damage sustained. The ship was amongst the remnants of the fleet which Rear-Admiral Nebogatoff surrendered the day after the battle.

The Aleksander II class battleship Imperator Nikolai I, flagship of Rear-Admiral Nebogatoff who commanded the reinforcements sent to catch up with Rozhestvensky. Launched in 1889, the Nikolai I was old and slow, but still the best of the "old flatirons and galoshes" as Captain Vladimir Semenov called them in his account of Tsushima. Nikolai I was surrendered to the Japanese.

The Indian summer of the clippers witnessed some memorable races between clippers and steamships. This painting by David Cobb commemorates the occasion in 1888 when Cutty Sark *overtook the P&O's crack new mailboat* Britannia *on the final run up the coast of Australia from Gabo Island to Sydney. Unloading the tea at East India Docks (right) was done as quickly as possible: the first of the new crop commanded the highest prices.*

Survivor of the Great Tea Race

The clippers that carried valuable cargoes of tea back from the Chinese ports in the middle years of the nineteenth century were some of the fastest sailing vessels ever built. The best of them could handle the shifting winds of the South China Sea as readily as the roaring forties or a brisk blow in the English Channel. Built for speed, they also possessed endurance and the power to fly before the fiercest storms, outpacing the mountains of green water that threatened to overwhelm them from astern. They were quite small ships, of 800 tons or so, with limited cargo capacity but able to navigate the poorly charted rivers and waters along the Chinese coast. The most famous of them, now preserved at Greenwich in London, was the *Cutty Sark*.

The tea clippers were racers, their job to be first back to London with the new crop of tea from the ports of China. Large bets were placed on these races by indulgent owners who treated their ships like thoroughbred racehorses. To be first back was both a commercial advantage and a source of pride. Ordinary trading ships would reduce sail and "snug down" each night, but for the clippers the rule was to cram on more sail in the hurry to be home. With favourable weather, they could complete the voyage from Shanghai in 90 days or less, and great prestige attached to the first ship home. On its maiden voyage to Australia in 1869 the great *Thermopylae* made Melbourne in 61 days, port to port.

In 1872 *Thermopylae* and *Cutty Sark* had a famous race home from China. They loaded together at Shanghai and sailed the same day, 18 June, but the first few days of fog and a dead calm produced little progress. At last, on 23 June, the wind picked up. By 26 June, both ships were off Hong Kong and in sight of each other. In light winds, *Thermopylae* showed at her best, but *Cutty Sark* regained at night much of what she had lost during the day. By 1 July, the ships had lost sight of each other. Through the South China Sea *Cutty Sark* met quirky weather, violent squalls, which carried away four sails, being followed by calms.

On 15 July, *Thermopylae* was again sighted in the Java Sea, and the two clippers beat through the strait between Java and Sumatra only a few miles apart. Captain George Moodie of *Cutty Sark* was well pleased to have held *Thermopylae*

over this tricky section of the voyage, for ahead lay the trades where he was confident *Cutty Sark*'s power would tell. He was right: with three consecutive daily runs of 340, 327 and 320 miles, *Cutty Sark* romped ahead, and the two clippers were never in sight of each other for the rest of the voyage.

In the middle of August, when *Cutty Sark* lay 400 miles ahead in the Indian Ocean, a tremendous storm struck her. The wind howled from the west, blowing a strong gale with heavy squalls. At 6.30 a.m. on the morning of 15 August, in the storm's last gasp, a heavy sea under the stern of the ship tore the rudder from its eyebolts, leaving *Cutty Sark* without a means of steering. The brother of the ship's owner, Robert Willis, recommended making for a South African port, but Moodie would have none of it and set about fitting a jury rudder at sea.

As luck would have it, two stowaways were aboard *Cutty Sark*, a carpenter and a blacksmith. They were set to work, together with the rest of the ship's company, to create a jury rudder out of a spare spar 70 feet long which the clipper carried in case of breakages. A forge was set up on deck for the blacksmith to make bolts and bars from the ship's stanchions. More than once the whole fire was swept away, and the smith himself was washed half overboard. Fixing the rudder in place was another awkward task, completed by 21 August when to everyone's delight it was found that it worked well. By this time, it is reckoned, *Thermopylae* was some 500 miles ahead, having caught and overtaken *Cutty Sark* while she lay stationary.

Ahead lay heavy weather, through which *Cutty Sark* had to be nursed, for her makeshift rudder could not be risked. She ran into a head gale which kept her down to only 465 miles in eight days, and the eyebolts holding the rudder came away. Once more the rudder was hauled on deck, repaired and refitted.

Finally, the last lap of the voyage from the Azores to the Channel was accomplished against strong gales, and *Cutty Sark* passed Dungeness in Kent on 17 October. *Thermopylae* had finished a week ahead, but *Cutty Sark*'s performance in making the Channel from the Cape with a jury rudder in 54 days was considered a marvellous achievement. *Thermopylae* had taken 115 days, *Cutty Sark* 122. The fastest

FACT FILE

The most famous of the celebrated tea clippers

Date built: 1869

Length: 212 feet 6 inches

Width: 36 feet

Registered gross weight: 963 tons

Sail area: 32,000 square feet

Survivor of the Great Tea Race

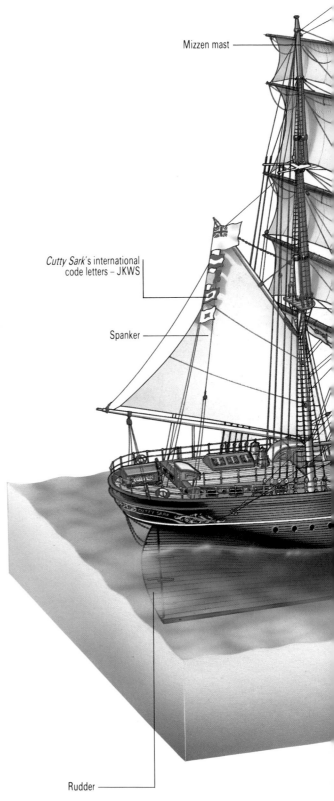

Mizzen mast

Cutty Sark's international code letters – JKWS

Spanker

Rudder

passage that year was by *Normancourt*, which left Macao on 14 September and made it home for Christmas after a passage of 96 days.

The clippers owed their inspiration to the eighteenth-century Yankee schooners, ships that had the ability to skim over the surface of the water. By the 1850s these had developed into fast passenger vessels, weighing more than 2,000 tons and carrying a huge area of sail. The tea clippers were smaller but with a similar racing profile: a sharp pointed bow, three masts raked astern and a set of sails that looked too powerful for what were really quite small vessels. To design such a ship successfully called for the nicest of judgement, for it had to be tough as well as fast.

Cutty Sark was commissioned by the ship-owner Captain John Willis, determined to produce a clipper to beat *Thermopylae*. Willis picked a young designer, Hercules Linton, who had recently started building ships on the Clyde at Dumbarton near Glasgow with a partner named Scott. The ship was built in 1869, a time when wooden construction had not yet given way entirely to iron. *Cutty Sark* used both, in what was known as composite construction.

Although designed for the tea trade, *Cutty Sark* carried every sort of cargo during her long career. Before loading the tea she would be cleaned out and fumigated, then lined with

Cutty Sark in dry dock at Greenwich (above). Her composite construction produced a tremendously rigid ship. The keel, frames and other main structural parts were of iron, with the outer skin in wood. The lower part of the masts was also of iron, and the deck of teak. Below, her cabins were panelled in teak and bird's-eye maple, and the captain was provided with a four-poster bed instead of the usual bunk. The cabin doors had yellow cut-glass handles, and the saloon a fireplace to keep the crew warm. She seldom leaked, and her pumps had little use. Even when 25 years old, she arrived in Hull with a cargo of wool after a voyage from Australia on which her pumps were not used.

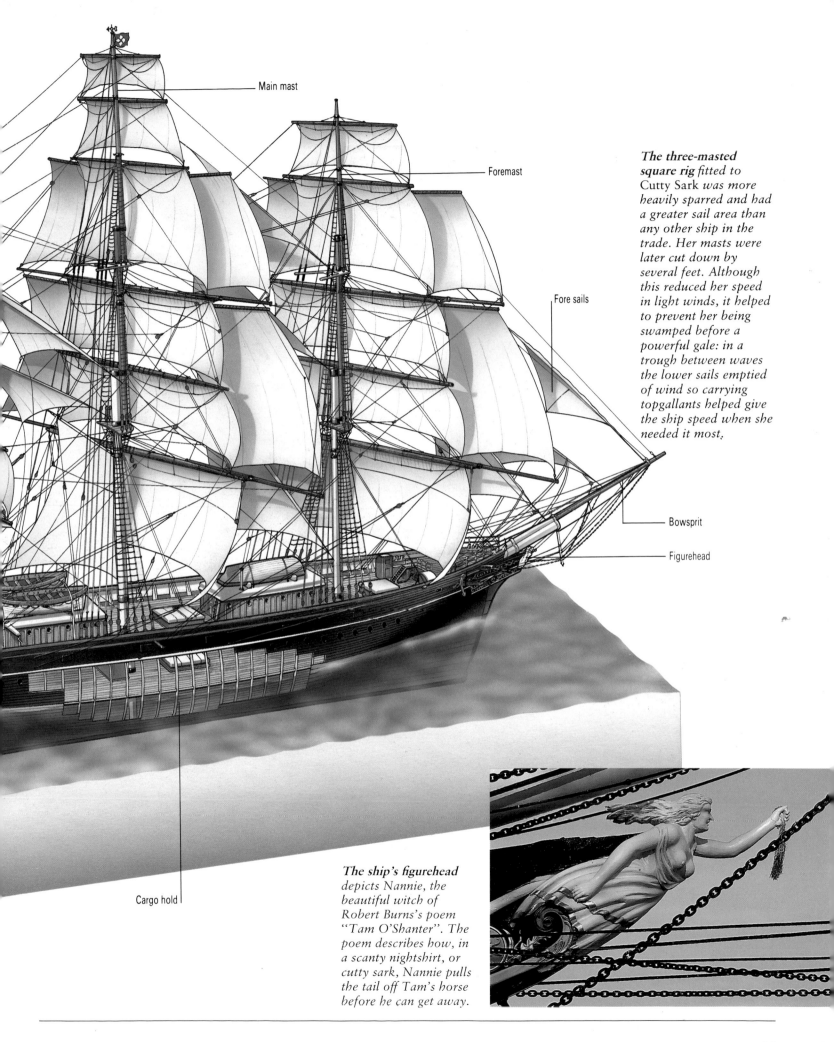

Main mast

Foremast

Fore sails

Bowsprit

Figurehead

Cargo hold

The three-masted square rig *fitted to* Cutty Sark *was more heavily sparred and had a greater sail area than any other ship in the trade. Her masts were later cut down by several feet. Although this reduced her speed in light winds, it helped to prevent her being swamped before a powerful gale: in a trough between waves the lower sails emptied of wind so carrying topgallants helped give the ship speed when she needed it most.*

The ship's figurehead *depicts Nannie, the beautiful witch of Robert Burns's poem "Tam O'Shanter". The poem describes how, in a scanty nightshirt, or cutty sark, Nannie pulls the tail off Tam's horse before he can get away.*

Survivor of the Great Tea Race

bamboo matting before the chests of tea were brought aboard and stowed. There was considerable skill in filling her awkwardly shaped holds, and in guessing how much ballast, in the form of washed stones, should be loaded below the cargo. Too much and the ship was down to her gunwales before the cargo was half-loaded; too little and she would spend the voyage home rolling on to her beam ends.

On the outward voyages *Cutty Sark*, like other clippers, would carry general cargoes to Australia, then load up with coal for Shanghai, before returning with the tea. It was a pattern that did not last very long; the Suez Canal had opened the tea trade to steamers, and by the end of the 1870s the clippers were forced to earn their livings elsewhere. Several turned to the Australian wool trade. *Cutty Sark* could cram as many as 4,500 bales of wool, worth almost £100,000, into her holds.

In 1885 *Cutty Sark* made a memorable passage from Australia, reaching Ushant in the mouth of the English Channel in 67 days and beating the rest of the fleet, including *Thermopylae*, by more than a week. But by 1895 the slow rise of the steamship had finally made sail uneconomical, and John Willis sold his most famous ship to a Portuguese company, Ferreira, which gave her its own name. Now she traded between Lisbon, Rio and the Portuguese colonies in Africa, with regular visits to New Orleans. In 1905 she turned up in Cardiff, with images of saints stuck up around her decks, then disappeared again.

In 1914 she appeared in the River Mersey at Liverpool with a cargo of whalebone and oil, and was visited by hundreds of sightseers. She loaded up with coal and bricks and sailed again for Africa just as World War I was breaking out. In 1916 she was dismasted in a storm off South Africa, narrowly escaping complete destruction. Her owners could not afford to replace the masts as they had originally been, so she was re-rigged as a brigantine until she was finally put up for sale in 1920.

Her new owner, also Portuguese, had some repairs carried out, and sailed for London, where the old ship was once more the centre of attention. As she left, a gale blew up and *Cutty Sark* was forced to take refuge in Falmouth, where an old seafarer, Captain Dowman, saw her and bought her for £3,750. So finally *Cutty Sark*'s career of more than 50 years came to an end, and she eventually went into retirement in dry dock at Greenwich.

TALL SHIPS

The graceful clippers and full-rigged, three-masted ships were gradually superseded during the last two decades of the nineteenth century by the four-masted barque. Until the mid-nineteenth century, barques had been relatively small sailing ships, but gradually larger vessels were built, particularly for the grain and nitrate trade between South American ports and Europe. Some were as heavy as 5,000 tons. Technological advances helped to make possible the increase: the replacement of rope by wire enabled much larger sails to be set; winches and capstans took over the control of yards and sails from block and tackle.

World War I took a heavy toll of sailing ships, which were mostly broken up rather than lost to naval action. Within a few years of the war most had gone from the main ports of the world. Some sail training ships remained and many decaying vessels could be found in far corners of the world, like the Falkland Islands. The rescue of a few is testimony to the affection felt for the age of sail.

The **Falls of Clyde** *(below) was built at Glasgow by Russell & Company in 1878. With a wrought-iron hull, she was 1,748 tons net and 266 feet long. She sailed to ports in India, Australia, the Far East and the United States before being sold to the Matson Line in 1898. It used her on a San Francisco to Hawaii service until 1921. Her sailing days over, she was taken to Alaska for use as a fuel store. She was subsequently rescued and eventually found a home at Honolulu in Hawaii.*

The Mersey *was one of the last ships* *built for Captain James Nourse who specialized in trade to India and remained loyal to sail while rivals were changing to steamships. Built by Charles Connell of Glasgow and launched in 1894, Mersey was 270 feet long and weighed 1,713 tons. She was designed as a general purpose cargo vessel, and it is thought that Nourse used her as a coolie ship, taking indentured labour from Mauritius to the West Indies and returning with a cargo of sugar. By 1908 Mersey was used as a training ship by White Star Lines; although cadets would serve on steamships, it was policy to train them in the principles of navigation on sailing vessels. In 1911 she became part of the Transatlantic Motor Ship Co. of Christiana (now Oslo), Norway, and was given the name of the company. She changed hands several times in Norway before returning to Britain in 1923 to be broken up.*

Racing Elegance

No more beautiful racing yachts have ever been built than the magnificent J-class which competed for the America's Cup in 1930, 1934 and 1937. Sleek, fast and carrying tall Bermudan rigs, the big yachts were racing machines *par excellence*, designed and built for nothing else. They needed wealthy enthusiasts to commission and sail them, for no expense could be spared if they were to prove competitive. For the first time, high technology became an integral part of yacht racing. The J-class yachts were also the closest Britain has ever come to lifting the America's Cup, in a thrilling series of races in 1934.

Earlier contests for the cup had been between yachts that often differed markedly in size and sail plan, with time handicaps being given in an attempt to ensure they competed on level terms. Some of these yachts were even bigger than the J-class; *Reliance*, the American defender of the cup in 1903, carried 16,159 square feet of sail, ten times that of a modern 40-foot yacht. She was the biggest yacht ever to sail in the America's Cup and easily defeated the challenger, *Shamrock III*.

One difficulty faced by any challenger from Britain was that it had to be solid enough to cross the Atlantic. In 1929 it was agreed that in future both defender and challenger should be built to the same minimum standards established by Lloyd's, and should sail against each other on equal terms, with no handicaps. The yachts were to conform to the New York Yacht Club's J-class, which permitted a waterline length of between 75 and 87 feet. The rules also specified the Bermuda rig, with its tall, narrow sails which drove the yachts more efficiently than the old gaff rigs.

For the 1930 series Sir Thomas Lipton, a millionaire and perennial challenger for the cup, went to Britain's top yacht designer, Charles Nicholson. The result was *Shamrock V*, a graceful but fairly conventional design with steel frames and deck beams and a hollow spruce mast. In spite of the 1929 Wall Street crash, no fewer than four defenders were built—*Enterprise*, *Yankee*, *Weetamoe* and *Whirlwind*. Their differences were not very obvious to the naked eye, their sail area being identical within 1 percent. Although *Enterprise* was the shortest, at 80 feet, she won the trials.

The truth was that *Enterprise* represented a leap forward in yacht design, stripped of all normal fittings and using a light, strong duralumin mast, 12-sided and held together with 80,000 rivets. It was stepped in a watertight steel tube filled with a dense liquid which gave it more flexibility. This incredible mast weighed 4,000 lb, 50 percent less than the conventional hollow wooden mast, and was so delicate that it had its own crew member, a "mast nurse", to look after it. It cost as much as the whole of *Shamrock V*.

The boom was equally extraordinary. It was triangular, with a broad flat top wide enough for two men to stand abreast, giving it its name, the Park Avenue boom. All along its length were transverse tracks into which the slides attached to the foot of the mainsail were fixed. This enabled the curve at the foot of the mainsail to be trimmed to the optimum for wind conditions.

John Nicholson, son of *Shamrock V*'s designer, admits that he felt rather despondent when he heard of these innovations after arriving in the US. His premonitions proved only too accurate. *Enterprise*, chosen to defend the cup after a close-fought series of eliminators, easily beat *Shamrock V* in four straight races at Newport, Rhode Island. As well as a considerable technological edge, *Enterprise* was brilliantly helmed by Harold S. Vanderbilt, who

FACT FILE

The most graceful racing design for the America's Cup

Endeavour I

Built: 1933

Length (at waterline): 83 feet 4 inches

Weight: 143 tons displacement

Sail area: 7,560 square feet

Endeavour I was considered the best J-class yacht of her day, though she failed in the challenge against the American defender Rainbow in 1934.

The Rhode Island course (right) *has been used for the America's Cup races in most years since 1852. However, San Diego has hosted the race and in 1986/87 it was held in waters off Fremantle, Western Australia. The America's Cup was originally presented in 1851 by the Royal Yacht Squadron at Cowes, the premier yacht club of Britain, to the winner of a race around the Isle of Wight. It was won by a 170-ton schooner* America, *entered on behalf of the New York Yacht Club against 15 British yachts.*

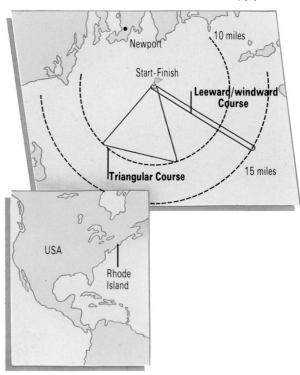

Racing Elegance

Sir Thomas Sopwith (b.1888) *made three challenges for the America's Cup; he is pictured (left) at the helm of the boat in which he made the challenge,* Shamrock V. *Sir Thomas was president of the Hawker Siddeley group that made its name building aircraft, many of which he designed. Besides owning three J-class yachts for his challenges, he later built a 1,620-ton motor yacht,* Philante, *which became the royal yacht of King Haakon of Norway, who renamed her* Norge.

Harold Stirling Vanderbilt (1884–1970), *businessman, author and yachtsman, successfully defended the America's Cup on three occasions. He helped William Vanderbilt establish the Vanderbilt Marine Museum on Long Island. His defender for 1930 was* Enterprise, *a J-class bare of all but essential fittings (right).*

organized his crew into a flawlessly efficient unit.

For the next challenge, in 1934, Nicholson responded by building for Sir Thomas Sopwith a much more technically sophisticated boat, *Endeavour*. By this time, the rules had changed to ban masts weighing less than 5,500 lb, which eliminated the possibility of another defence by *Enterprise*. The depression was at its gloomiest, but Vanderbilt put together a syndicate of yachtsmen to build a defender, *Rainbow*, designed by Starling Burgess.

Using as much equipment as possible from *Enterprise*, *Rainbow* was built for $400,000, a rock-bottom price, and sailed off against *Yankee*, one of those eliminated in the 1930 trials. To begin with, *Yankee* showed *Rainbow* a clean pair of heels, beating her ten times in succession in preliminary races. Vanderbilt then added 5 tons of ballast to *Rainbow* and his yacht began to improve. In the trials proper, *Rainbow* narrowly won and was chosen to defend the cup.

Endeavour was a worthy challenger, probably faster than *Rainbow*. She was 83 feet 4 inches long at the waterline and was made of steel throughout, except for her decks, joinery and rudder. Her mast was of welded steel, her boom of hollow spruce and constructed so that by the use of struts and tension wires it could be bent to give the sail the right aerodynamic profile. However, during trials in the English Channel the boom broke, and a hastily made Park Avenue boom replaced it.

Just before *Endeavour* was due to leave England, Sopwith's professional crew went on strike. Disdaining to negotiate, he sacked them all and put together a crew of amateur sailors from the Royal Corinthian Yacht Club; they had virtually no time to train together and many had never sailed J-class yachts before. This was a fateful error which almost certainly cost Sopwith the cup, for in every respect except the crew, *Endeavour* was a match for *Rainbow*.

The first race was called off for lack of wind with *Rainbow* well ahead, but when it was repeated two days later *Endeavour* won handily by 2 minutes 27 seconds. The second race also resulted in victory for the challenger, by 51 seconds. The third race was a different matter. After two legs of the triangular course, *Endeavour* was 6½ minutes ahead and the defender apparently beaten.

Vanderbilt handed over the wheel to Sherman Hoyt, a clever tactician who knew that Sopwith would always attempt to cover an opponent and

steal his wind, however far ahead he might be. Hoyt therefore set a course well wide of the finishing line and tempted Sopwith to cover him. When *Endeavour* came about in failing winds she lost headway and was forced to tack again. Coming up behind with better winds *Rainbow* was through, forcing Sopwith to go about again. *Rainbow* passed the finishing line 3¼ minutes ahead having made up 10 minutes on a single leg. Instead of being 3-0 down, Vanderbilt was losing only 2-1, with another four races to go.

The fourth race was marred by one of those rows without which no America's Cup series would be complete. When Vanderbilt refused to yield to a legitimate Sopwith manoeuvre as the two boats closed on each other, Sopwith issued a protest. But because he did not raise the protest flag until he neared the finishing line more than a minute behind, the committee refused to hear it. The decision caused fury. The result, however, was to put the two yachts level, 2-2. The fifth race went to *Rainbow*, though not without a

Shamrock V was designed by Charles Nicholson for Sir Thomas Lipton. It was to be Sir Thomas's fifth and last challenge. He was in his eightieth year, and felt confident of victory. Shamrock crossed the Atlantic with her designer, her manager and sailing master on board, while Sir Thomas made the passage in his luxurious steam yacht Erin. *The race was an easy victory for the defender,* Enterprise. *Shamrock was bought by Thomas Sopwith after Lipton's death in 1934.*

Racing Elegance

Endeavour I came as close to depriving the United States of the America's Cup as any other British challenger, winning the first two races in 1934. The final result, a 4–2 win for the American defender Rainbow, *might have been different had Sopwith's crew not gone on strike just before leaving England.* Endeavour's *possible advantage over her rival, a novel jib with double sheets, was copied by Vanderbilt in time for the race after a sharp-eyed American observer saw the sail on trial in the Solent.*

slice of luck. After a spinnaker split, Vanderbilt gybed in order to pull it in, and a man went overboard. He fortunately held on to a sheet and was quickly hauled aboard, and a race that was nearly lost was won by *Rainbow*.

The final race was desperately close. The two yachts were never far apart around the course, but *Rainbow* finally won by a bare 55 seconds, and the cup was retained. Never was Britain to come closer to winning, for the 1937 series was lopsided, the brilliant defender *Ranger* proving the fastest J-type ever built and easily defeating Sopwith's *Endeavour II*. Both defender and challenger were at the limit of the class, 87 feet along the waterline, and were equipped with bunks, panelling and other accommodation which the racers of 1930 had lacked. This was the result of a change of rules, which since 1934 had insisted the yachts be fully equipped.

Ranger was designed by Starling Burgess and Olin Stephens and was perfectly designed for the conditions of Newport. With a bulbous stem and

flattened stern she was not beautiful, but her speed was unquestionable. She easily defeated rival defenders and then won the actual races by a straight 4-0 victory. In the final race she covered the 10-mile leg dead to windward in 1 hour 14 minutes, an average speed of 8.01 knots, which still stands as the highest authenticated speed ever made good to windward by a sailing ship. *Endeavour II* finished 4 minutes behind.

This was virtually the last time the great J-class yachts raced. They were expensive to build and to race, for in anything over a stiff breeze there was always a serious danger of a mast being lost. Sailing in English regattas in 1935, both *Endeavour* and *Yankee* lost their masts, and *Ranger's* expensive duralumin mast was swept overboard near Cape Cod.

The unsuitability of the J-class for ordinary sailing may help explain why so few have survived into modern times. *Ranger* was broken up for scrap during World War II, the same fate that befell many of these great yachts.

ENDEAVOUR RESTORED

World War II put a temporary stop to the America's Cup, but the real tragedy of the war for the sailing fraternity was the loss of several J-class yachts for scrap. The huge cost of restoring the few survivors has deterred all but a few. *Endeavour* has been rebuilt by Elizabeth Meyer, and *Shamrock* was restored by Camper & Nicholson at Gosport in Hampshire during the 1970s. *Shamrock* was renovated again, at the Museum of Yachting in Newport, Rhode Island, also under Elizabeth Meyer. *Velsheda* has been restored and is now based at Southampton.

The restoration of Endeavour *ranks as one of the most thorough and expensive rescues of a yacht. Work began in Calshot (top right) before the boat was* *sold to the American Elizabeth Meyer, who completed her rebuilding, first at Calshot and then in Holland (left and above).*

Queen of the Atlantic

"If ever there was a ship which possessed the thing called soul, the *Mauretania* did," declared Franklin D. Roosevelt in August 1936, as the old liner was being broken up in Rosyth. The most famous ship ever to sail the Atlantic, she deserved in his view a more fitting end. "Why couldn't the British have remembered the *Mauretania*'s faithfulness—taken her out to sea and sunk her whole—given her a Viking's funeral, this ship with a fighting heart?"

Sentiment, however, comes pretty low on the shipowner's order of priorities, and by 1935 *Mauretania* had reached the end of her natural life. From her maiden voyage in November 1907 to her final trip in September 1934, she had been the flower of the North Atlantic, holder for 18 years of the Blue Riband for the fastest crossing and capable even in her final years of an astonishing turn of speed.

At her launch she was the biggest ship afloat, just a few feet larger than her sister ship the *Lusitania*, torpedoed by a German U-boat off the coast of Ireland in May 1915. With her four funnels and crisp lines, *Mauretania* looked more like a huge yacht than an ocean liner: "a ship which was a ship and not a damned freighthouse" as Roosevelt put it.

Mauretania was the product of a battle for supremacy in the Atlantic trade, and British worries that they were losing control of their merchant fleet to J.P. Morgan's International Mercantile Marine Company. In 1897 the *Kaiser Wilhelm der Grosse*, owned by Norddeutscher Lloyd, had captured the Blue Riband, and its successor in holding this important speed record was another German ship, the Hamburg-Amerika Line's *Deutschland*. The Cunard Steamship Company recognized that these fast German ships were winning the majority of the traffic at a time when immigration from Europe to the US provided a buoyant market. The takeover of White Star Lines by IMM in 1902 alarmed the Admiralty, for it appeared that Britain's Merchant Navy was falling into the hands of foreigners and would soon be unavailable for military service in time of war.

To meet these twin challenges, Cunard and the British government did a deal to build two high-speed express liners. In return for a loan, an operating subsidy and a guarantee of mail contracts, Cunard undertook to design the ships

to suit the Admiralty, staff them with British officers and a crew at least three-quarters British, and make them available for war service at prescribed rates. The results of this contract were two of the finest ships ever seen.

Much of the success of the *Mauretania* and the *Lusitania* arose from the choice of motive power—steam turbines rather than the reciprocating engines which drove the German ships. Steam turbines were then in their infancy, but Cunard convinced itself of the virtues of the turbine by comparing two identical ships, the *Caronia* and the *Carmania*, the first having reciprocating engines, the second turbines. *Carmania* was quicker and used less fuel. For the same amount of coal, she could produce an extra knot. She was also smoother and the engine room could be much smaller, leaving more room for passengers. The huge weight of reciprocating engines in the stern could be avoided, giving better weight distribution. The case for the turbine was proved.

The contract for building *Mauretania* went to Swan Hunter and Wigham Richardson at Wallsend on the River Tyne. Many changes were made as the design proceeded, but it was finally fixed on a ship 790 feet long and 88 feet broad which was to have a gross weight of 31,938 tons.

The *Mauretania* was launched on 20 September 1906, just 25 months after her keel was laid. The Dowager Duchess of Roxburgh named her, in the Cunard custom, after one of the ancient Roman provinces: in this case, a barren stretch of Sahara desert then called Spanish West Africa but now an independent nation, once more rejoicing in its original name. A ton of soft soap, $14\frac{1}{2}$ tons of tallow and 113 gallons of train oil did their work, and *Mauretania* slid slowly into the Tyne.

Mauretania was then fitted out in considerable splendour. The country-house architect Harold Peto designed the interior in an eclectic Edwardian style. Huge amounts of timber were used: French walnut veneer in the staircases, mahogany in the lounge, maple in the drawing room, weathered oak in the triple-decked dining room. The carving was spectacular: 300 craftsmen were brought from Palestine to the Tyne to spend two years creating high-relief mouldings, columns, capitals and bulkhead walls.

The first-class dining room was entirely

FACT FILE

The largest and one of the most sumptuous ships afloat in the 1920s

Date built: 1905–07

Length: 790 feet

Power output: 78,000 horsepower

Maximum speed: 29.7 knots

Registered gross weight: 31,938 tons

covered in straw-coloured oak, carved in a sixteenth-century style attributed to François I of France. The first-class lounge, or music room, 79 feet 6 inches long by 55 feet wide, was decorated in late eighteenth-century French style, with Aubusson tapestries and 16 lilac-coloured fleur-de-pêche marble pilasters. There was a high glass dome and crystal chandeliers, which appeared to hang free but were in fact locked in position so they did not swing when the Atlantic turned unfriendly. Cunard insisted on old-fashioned, bolted-down chairs, a nineteenth-century notion soon replaced by heavy but moveable furniture.

On 17 September 1907, *Mauretania* slipped out of the Tyne on some preliminary trials. Carrier pigeons took the results back daily to the builders. Her speed was fine, but there was a

Mauretania *leaving the* **Tyne** *for preliminary trials by T. Henry. The vibration that soon became apparent was caused by alternating stresses in the propellers that reacted with the hull in an unpredictable way. The vibration was reduced by fitting one-piece cast propellers. A silver match case embossed with the date 1907 (left) was given to first-class passengers. The brooches were for sale on board the ship.*

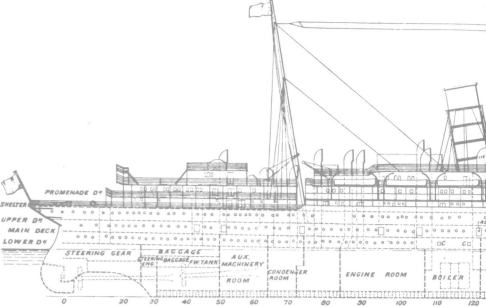

distressing vibration, just what they had hoped to avoid.

On her official trials, *Mauretania* satisfied the Admiralty by steaming 1,216 miles in two days at an average of 26.04 knots, and running the measured mile at 26.75 knots. Her first transatlantic crossing, in November 1907, was made into the teeth of a 50 mph gale, so no records were set. But on the return journey, despite a delay for fog, *Mauretania* got home in 4 days, 22 hours and 29 minutes, an average of 23.69 knots, and captured the Blue Riband from her sister ship *Lusitania*.

She held it until the maiden voyage of Norddeutscher Lloyd's *Bremen* in July 1929. Even then, *Mauretania* was not finished. Returning from New York in August 1929, she averaged 27.22 knots, completing the crossing in 4 days, 17 hours and 50 minutes. Between Eddystone Light and Cherbourg, 106 miles, she averaged 29.7 knots, an astonishing achievement for a ship 22 years old and designed for 25 knots. On 26 September 1934, the day after the *Queen Mary* was launched, she left New York for the last time. She was sold for scrap, her fittings removed and auctioned, her steel recycled into weapons for the war that was approaching. One man got a bargain, paying $20 a letter for the brass bow letters of her name.

Mauretania made a total of 318 return trips across the Atlantic during her career, as well as 54 cruises in the Mediterranean and Caribbean, particularly popular with Americans in the days of prohibition. Painted white, she looked, said a crew member, "like a bloomin' wedding cake", but no amount of white paint could conceal the fact that she was not really designed for cruising. With no air conditioning, few private bathrooms and no swimming pools, cruising in southern seas was a sweaty business. But still *Mauretania* maintained her record of speed and exceptional reliability. On one of her runs to Havana from New York in the early 1930s, she managed to beat the previous record by 13 hours and 28 minutes.

Few ships are as well remembered as *Mauretania*, for she symbolized a whole era in travel. Although more graceful in recollection than in reality—the majority of her passengers travelled third class—it is not mere nostalgia that has given her an affectionate place in the history of ships. Swift, elegant, reliable and safe, she served Cunard magnificently and for a generation made them kings of the North Atlantic.

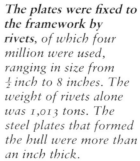

The quadruple screws, *each 17 feet in diameter, were driven by six Parsons turbines—four for going ahead and two for going astern. Steam was raised by 25 boilers in four boiler rooms which required a complement of 250 stokers to feed them 1,000 tons of coal a day. They were converted to oil after World War I.*

The plates were fixed to the framework by rivets, *of which four million were used, ranging in size from ½ inch to 8 inches. The weight of rivets alone was 1,013 tons. The steel plates that formed the hull were more than an inch thick.*

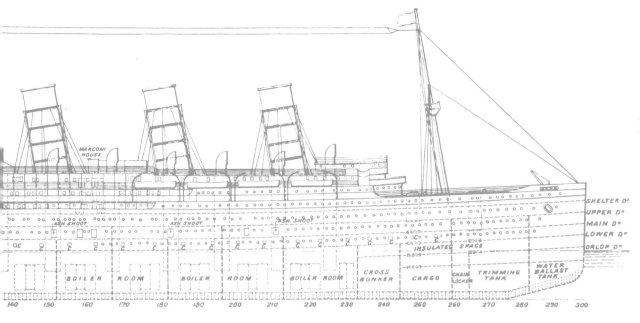

Labels on diagram: MARCONI HOUSE · ASH SHOOT · ASH SHOOT · ASH SHOOT · INSULATED SPACE · SHELTER Dᵏ · UPPER Dᵏ · MAIN Dᵏ · LOWER Dᵏ · ORLOP Dᵏ · BOILER ROOM · BOILER ROOM · BOILER ROOM · CROSS BUNKER · CARGO · CHAIN LOCKER · TRIMMING TANK · WATER BALLAST TANK · 140 150 160 170 180 190 200 210 220 230 240 250 260 270 280 290 300

Mauretania *carried* **2,145 passengers** *in greater safety than most ships. Her bottom was double plated and divided into separate cells like a warship. Some 175 compartments with watertight doors through the bulkheads, many of which could be closed from the bridge, made the ship less liable to sink.*

Golden Years of Transatlantic Luxury

The development of transatlantic steamship services began in 1838 with the 700-ton *Sirius*. Two years later the Liverpool-based Cunard Line won the British government contract to carry mail across the Atlantic; steamship sailings began between Liverpool and Boston.

The facilities of the early transatlantic ships were fairly basic, but they became gradually more opulent. Cunard's supremacy was eclipsed during the 1890s but construction of the *Lusitania* and *Mauretania*, launched in 1907, restored Cunard's fortunes. After World War I, the *Ile de France* set higher standards of luxury. Soon most new transatlantic liners were equipped with such facilities as swimming pools, squash courts, theatre, concert hall and vast apartments—the first-class dining room of the *Normandie* was 300 feet long.

Construction of grand liners continued during the 1930s and after World War II. The number of passengers grew to 1.2 million in 1958, but the start of jet airliner services in that year heralded the end of transatlantic liners.

Dancing on the promenade deck of the Aquitania *in 1922. With* Mauretania *and* Berengaria, Aquitania *was one of the "Big Three" of the Cunard fleet in the 1920s. Regarded as having the most sober character of the three, she drew passengers "of social consequence, people of title . . .". She lived to become the last four-funnelled liner, being withdrawn in 1939.*

The lounge on the Duchess of Bedford, *a Canadian Pacific Railway liner built by John Brown in Glasgow. Launched in 1928, she spent most of her life on the route between Liverpool and Montreal. She was renamed* Empress of India *and then* Empress of France *before being broken up in 1960.*

MENU

P&O

Competition between shipping lines *extended to food, with tempting dishes listed in ornate menus (above). The quantities of food and drink required for a transatlantic voyage were prodigious: 425 lb smoked salmon, 1,150 lb beef fillet, 70,250 eggs, 2,400 bottles of champagne, 48,000 bottles of mineral water and 15,000 cigars. To be one of the seven guests to dine at the captain's table was the ultimate recognition of a person's status: the fifteen guests invited to pre-prandial cocktails changed each evening, but the composition of the captain's table was the same throughout the voyage.*

The Pompeian Bath *on the P & O liner* Viceroy of India, *built by Stevens of Glasgow and launched in 1928. She sailed on the London to Bombay route until World War II, during which she was torpedoed off Algiers.*

Wartime Heroes Built by the Mile

FACT FILE

The largest class of ships ever built

First launched:
1941

Overall length: 441 feet 6 inches

Power output:
2,500 horsepower

Maximum speed:
11 knots

Registered gross weight: 7,176 tons

As efficiency in yards grew, Liberty ships were *built increasingly quickly. The SS* Pierre Dupont *was launched at Portland, Oregon, on 31 August 1942 (opposite). The only preserved Liberty ship, launched in June 1943, may be seen near Fisherman's Wharf, San Francisco (below).* Jeremiah O'Brien *has occasionally been steamed up and taken out to sea laden with fare-paying passengers.*

During World War II—or so the story goes—a lady was invited to the California shipyard of Henry Kaiser to launch a ship. Arriving at the launching platform, she found the bottle of champagne ready, but no sign of a ship. Had she come to the wrong yard, or on the wrong day? "No, ma'am," came the reply. "You just start swinging the champagne and the ship will be along soon enough!"

At the time, this must have appeared a pardonable exaggeration, for US shipyards were performing miracles of ship production never achieved before or since. In the month of September 1942 three new ships were delivered every day, a total of 93 in a single month. One of these ships had been launched just ten days after its keel was laid, and completed in another five days. Over the year as a whole, 8 million tons of shipping were launched in US yards in a desperate effort to keep up with the appalling losses inflicted by the Axis powers.

Mass production had been made possible by the adoption in January 1941 of a standard design of cargo ship. The Liberty ships, as they were called, were accepted with some reluctance by the US Maritime Commission, for they appeared ugly, sluggish and out of date, and their basic design was British. In practice they became the commonest ships afloat, and instead of the five-year life they had been given, many were still providing good service in the 1970s as

tramp steamers flying many different flags. Others were converted into troopships, oil tankers, army tank transports, a hospital ship and even a mobile nuclear power station.

In 1937, the US Maritime Commission had begun a peacetime programme of equipping its merchant navy with modern high-speed tankers and cargo vessels, at a rate of 50 ships a year. These were excellent ships, with turbine engines that gave them speeds of up to 17 knots. In November 1940, the Commission produced its first all-welded ship and showed that this method of production could save 600 tons of steel. The intention was to re-equip with up-to-date ships a merchant navy that had stagnated since World War I; there had therefore been little enthusiasm for a visit in September of a delegation from Britain intent on ordering 60 ships, to be built in American yards.

The design the group brought with them was unambitious, based on a ship called *Dorington Court* which had been designed and built by the Sunderland shipyard of J.L. Thompson & Sons in 1939. Using modest engines of 2,500 hp, the *Dorington Court* could carry 10,000 tons of cargo at 11 knots; slow but economical. Admiral Emory Land, Chairman of the US Maritime Commission, found little to praise in these "simple, slow" ships, suspected that Britain was going to lose the war anyway, and felt the Commission should dissociate itself from the whole idea by allowing the British to purchase the ships outright. The British agreed, but found there were insufficient slipways available in the US to build them; new yards would have to be laid out and new techniques, such as welding, used if the contracts were to be fulfilled.

By January 1941, it was clear that the American shipbuilding programme had been overtaken by events. The tonnage being sunk by German U-boats underlined the need for lots of cheap ships, which could be "built by the mile and chopped off by the yard". There was no time to create a new design, and Admiral Land was forced to accept that the British might, after all, have been right.

The plans of the 60 Ocean-class ships already ordered by Britain were modified and adopted for the new programme, announced by President Franklin Roosevelt in February. The president seemed no more impressed with the design than

85 DAYS
36 DAYS
35 DAYS
26 DAYS

30
29
28
27
26
25
24
23
22
21
20
19
18
17
16

Wartime Heroes Built by the Mile

The Oregon Ship Building Corporation at Portland built 322 Liberty ships on 13 slipways designed specially for their construction. Of the 18 yards building Liberty ships, the Oregon Corporation produced the highest number of ships per slipway, and launched one vessel ten days after keel laying. This record was exceeded by the No. 2 yard at Richmond, California, which established an unbeaten figure, assembly taking just over four days and outfitting another three.

Land, calling the ships "dreadful-looking objects". But Land, having reluctantly embraced the idea of mass-producing tramp steamers, realized that they needed a better image if the programme was to succeed. In a brilliant stroke he named the ships a "Liberty fleet", and soon they were known as Liberty ships.

The ships which the American yards set to building were not quite the same as the British original. Oil was used instead of coal to fire the boilers. The shape of the hull was simplified to reduce the number of plates which had to be shaped by heating and pressing, eliminating many double curves at bow and stern. The superstructure was reorganized so that all crew accommodation was midships, considered safer for Atlantic convoys and also cutting the expense of piping, heating and outfitting.

Steel decks were specified instead of wooden ones, and items such as radio direction finders, fire detection equipment, emergency generators and life-raft radios were omitted. The ships were not fitted with gyro compasses and many went to

sea with inadequate anchor chains. As steel ran short, the original specification of 300 fathoms of chain was reduced to 240 and later to 210. The only improvements on the British original were the provision of searchlights, domestic refrigerators and running water in the cabins, which doubtless reflected the different expectations of American merchant seamen.

Nine shipyards were established early in 1941 to make the ships. Many of them were completely new yards manned by workers with no experience of shipbuilding, but this did not matter much. Liberty ship production was an assembly process in which the component parts of the ship, produced in factories in 32 states, were welded together as rapidly as possible. Engines and boilers were interchangeable, while whole bow and stern sections were prefabricated ready for dropping into place.

The names of the ships were taken from famous Americans. The first, named *Patrick Henry* in honour of the American patriot who cried "Give me liberty or give me death!", was

Prefabrication of components was vital to achieve the rate of ship production required. The yards were assembly points for some 30,000 parts, all produced off site. Many of the yards had none of the usual shipyard machine tools and equipment. Here a deckhouse section is swung over a slipway in 1943.

Moored Liberty ships lined up at Withington, North Carolina, one of eight sites where ships were mothballed after World War II. Some vessels re-entered service during the Korean and Vietnam wars, but as their condition deteriorated and they became technically obsolete, they were sold for scrap en bloc.

Women worked on construction in increasing numbers as the war progressed. After June 1944, shipbuilding had an "urgency" rating for workers and many more women were taken on. By September 1944, 31 percent of the work force at the Oregon Corporation were women. Riveting was a hard and noisy job. Although some yards welded all joints, the older yards used rivets in the frames, seams and deckhouses. Later, after a series of Liberty ships had broken in half, strengthening sections were riveted in.

launched on 27 September 1941, ten weeks before the attack on Pearl Harbor brought the US into the war. It was the first of 2,710 ships which stretched the *Dictionary of American Biography* to its limits.

Some 200 Liberty ships, almost $7\frac{1}{2}$ percent of production, were supplied to Britain under the lend-lease provisions and were all given names beginning with Sam—*Samadang, Samaritan, Samgara*. Americans believe the Sam prefix indicates the beneficence of Uncle Sam, but the real explanation is more mundane. Sam, it turns out, stands for "Superstructure Aft of Midships" in British Ministry of War Transport jargon.

In 1947, when the British economy was at full stretch and the ships were desperately needed, the US demanded them back. Eventually, about 100 of them were bought by British shipping companies, for £135,000 each.

Many of the Liberty ships were lost to enemy action during the war, no fewer than 50 going down on their maiden voyages. Seven took part in the ill-fated convoy PQ17 from Iceland to

north Russia in June 1942, and four were sunk. Armed with their single 4-inch gun, a few took part in heroic naval actions. The *Stephen Hopkins* gained fame for sinking the much better-armed German raider *Steir* after a battle which left them both immobilized and sinking.

The many Liberty ships that emerged intact in 1945 did not all enjoy a quiet retirement. The *Benjamin R. Curtis*, renamed the *Grandcamp*, caught fire when loading ammonium nitrate fertilizer in Texas City on 16 April 1947. When firemen were unable to put the blaze out, the ship was towed into the stream but exploded before she could reach a place of safety. The blast set off a series of other explosions which destroyed most of the dockyard, a chemical plant and many other buildings. Fires burned fiercely for several days, setting light to another ship which also exploded, destroying a second Liberty ship, *Wilson B. Keene*, which was moored alongside, and forcing the evacuation of the town. Over 500 people died, and the *Grandcamp* vanished without trace, such was the force of the blast.

Record-Breaking Hydroplane

FACT FILE

Donald Campbell's ill-fated hydroplane that won him the world speed record on water

Bluebird K7 in final form

Built: 1954

Length: 26 feet

Width: 10 feet 6 inches

Engine: Bristol-Siddeley Orpheus

Power output: 5,000 lb of thrust

Maximum speed: 320 mph

Father and son in 1926. The elder Campbell, Sir Malcolm, was dynamic and a success in all he touched. He made a lot of money by insuring newspapers against libels, but also had a career as a journalist, author, car sales agent and director of many companies. Donald was not to have such a prosperous base for his costly ventures.

Donald Campbell was a man fated by his parentage to live and die by speed. His father, Sir Malcolm Campbell, was a successful racing driver who turned his attention in the 1930s to setting world speed records on land and water, always in vehicles called *Bluebird*. In 1935, at Bonneville Salt Flats in Utah, he set a land speed record of 301 mph in the most famous of the *Bluebird* cars. On 1 September 1937, his boat *Bluebird* K3 took the world water speed record at Lake Maggiore in Italy, at 126.33 mph.

Just a fortnight before the outbreak of World War II he increased it again in a new *Bluebird*, K4, to 141.74 mph. Record-breaking was forgotten for the duration of the war but in 1945 Campbell, by then 62, was anxious to have another try. He acquired a de Havilland Goblin II jet engine, developing 5,000 lb of thrust, and fitted it to K4. The boat was undergoing modifications when Campbell suffered a stroke and died peacefully in his bed.

His son Donald was in business making machine tools, but by 1948 had been seized by the record-breaking bug. He approached his father's mechanic, Leo Villa, and said he had heard that an American, Henry Kaiser, was going after his father's record. The younger Campbell told Villa that he wanted to try for the record himself: "I just want to keep the old flag flying, get the record, and call it a day."

Donald hardly had the pull, or the financial resources, of his father. The old man's money had been left in trust for his grandchildren and the jet engine of K4 had only been loaned to Sir Malcolm. For his first attempt at the record, Donald Campbell went back to propeller power, refitting the Rolls-Royce R Type engine into the boat again. With no experience, he got into the boat at Lake Coniston, England, and came within 2 mph of breaking his father's record. While the boat was being modified for a fresh attempt, news came that Stanley Sayres and Ted Jones, in their propeller-driven *Slo-Mo-Shun IV*, had beaten Sir Malcolm's record by 20 mph.

Sayres was friendly and helpful to Campbell, offering him advice and providing details of the design. Campbell then converted K4 into a prop-rider and made another bid at the record. At 170 mph on Lake Coniston, Campbell and Villa hit a submerged railway sleeper, destroying the propeller and ripping out the stern of *Bluebird*. As they struggled ashore she went down.

Before Campbell could raise the money for a new attempt, the world water speed record claimed the life of another Briton, John Cobb. His jet-propelled *Crusader* broke up on Loch Ness in September 1952.

Cobb's death did not deter Campbell, who set about replacing the wrecked K4 with a new boat. Calculations showed that a jet boat was needed, and Campbell was able to lay hands on three old Metropolitan-Vickers Beryl engines, capable of 4,000 lb of thrust. The engines were delivered to Campbell's home near Leigh, Surrey, and Campbell and Villa, who knew nothing of jets, scratched their heads and wondered how they worked. Using the instruction manual they rigged one up and ran it in rural Surrey, singeing two large oak trees.

At last, after three years' work, K7 was ready to try for the record. On 23 July 1955 Campbell made two runs along the measured kilometre (0.6 miles) at Ullswater, waiting between the runs for the wash to subside. The average of the runs was a new record—202.32 mph. When Villa went aboard *Bluebird*, he says that the two of them started howling like a couple of children, hugging each other as tears streamed down their faces. Donald Campbell had finally exorcized the influence of his glamorous father with a record of his own.

Although he had told Villa that he would give up as soon as he had beaten the record, by this

A triumphant Donald Campbell and his wife on Lake Dumbleyung (above). Practice for the attempt on the world water speed record had been dogged by wild duck, the stumps of gum trees in the water and having to fly timekeepers up from Perth at short notice when the easterly winds abated. On New Year's Eve in 1964, with only minutes to go before the descent of darkness, he took the record with a run of 276 mph (left).

Record-Breaking Hydroplane

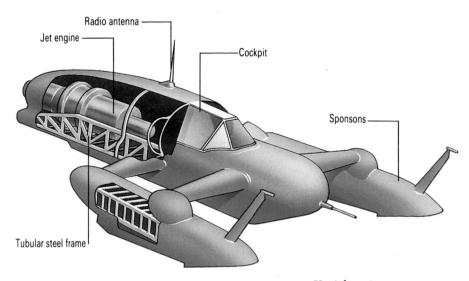

time Campbell was in no position to stop. The expense of building K7 had virtually ruined him, and he now had to try to cash in on his fame. When he was invited to Lake Mead in Nevada for a regatta he saw the chance of making some money, and accepted. There on 16 November 1955 he broke his own record, putting up the speed to 216.2 mph. He was now into a rhythm, inching up the record, with each attempt calculated to generate publicity and income.

Billy Butlin, founder of the holiday camps, offered a £5,000 prize for every new water speed record gained by a British pilot in a British boat—an open invitation to Campbell to continue annual runs, gaining the record each time but not by too much. In September 1956, at Lake Coniston, he put it up to 225 mph; the following November, also at Coniston, to 239.07. Both times Butlin was as good as his word, handing over cheques for £5,000. In 1958 Campbell reached 248 mph, in a boat originally designed for a maximum speed of 250 mph. On several occasions he had exceeded the design speed, producing a worrying tendency for the bows to lift. But Campbell was undeterred and in 1959 he increased the record to 260.35 mph. Now his ambition was to reach 300 mph.

Before that, however, he had set a new land speed record in July 1964 at a dry lake, Lake Eyre in Australia, reaching 403.1 mph to beat John Cobb's record. He became determined to do the double—the land and water speed record in the same year. With just eight hours to spare on 31 December 1964 he achieved a new record of 276 mph on Lake Dumbleyung in Western Australia. It was his finest moment. From that day, things began to go wrong.

By this time people had begun to tire of Campbell's record attempts. A sensible man would have retired K7, now ten years old and 30 mph beyond her design speed, and gone into some other business. He had nothing left to prove. But by now money was short, Campbell had no business left to return to, and record-breaking was all he understood. To reach 300 mph he acquired a new engine, a Bristol-Siddeley Orpheus with another 1,000 lb of thrust.

Bluebird arrived at Coniston in November 1966. The new engine's power was too much for the old air intake, sucking in pieces of metal and destroying the engine. A new one was fitted and the intakes modified. Still *Bluebird* refused to fly, ploughing into the water and putting out the engine just as it had at the beginning of its long

career. Villa fitted extra ballast to the aft, and finally Campbell was able to make a full-speed trial. Although he reached 250 mph, the boat kept tramping, and 300 mph seemed impossibly elusive. As Christmas came, the press and the timekeepers announced they were going home. Campbell sent his own team home and then, on Christmas Day, went out alone and ran the boat at over 280 mph in perfect conditions.

On 4 January 1967 conditions were finally right for a record attempt. The team assembled in the early morning while it was still dark and launched the boat. On his first run Campbell covered the kilometre at 297 mph. Villa, listening on the radio circuit, heard the figure announced and was then astonished when Campbell said "Stand by. Am making my return run". He had not waited to refuel, or for the wash from his first run to settle down.

As *Bluebird* came back down the course again at full speed, Campbell hit the swell, which was worse than usual because he had used a water-brake to slow him at the end of the first run. *Bluebird*'s bows lifted and she became airborne. She turned over, hit the water nose first and started somersaulting, flinging off parts of her structure at every contact with the water. When the spray subsided, the broken hull of *Bluebird* lay on its side in the water. Nearby floated Campbell's helmet, a mangled life jacket, a teddy bear mascot. But of Campbell himself there was no sign. Skin divers later located the wreck, lying in 50 feet of murky water, but Campbell's body was never found. His attempt to live up to his father's reputation had finally cost him his life.

K7 (above) was designed by Ken and Lew Norris and built of high-tensile aluminium alloy by a bus builders, *Salmesbury Engineering Ltd, in England. To increase his chances of winning the world speed record on water, Campbell decided K7 had to be powered by a jet engine, unlike its predecessor, K4, which was a prop-rider. Campbell had to mortgage his house and sell his engineering business to pay for K7. The boat was unveiled by Lady Wakefield and tested on Ullswater in the Lake District. It took some months to cure the tendency for K7's bows to nose into the water like a submarine.*

Bluebird on Lake Coniston in September 1958 during the attempt to reach 250 mph. Foul weather wasted many days but Campbell set a new record of 248 mph after having to cram three runs into one hour: rules stipulated that the two-way run had to be done within one hour and K7 had reached only 188 mph on the first.

The final moment on Coniston, 4 January 1967. At 320 mph, Campbell reported over the intercom that the bows were tramping: "Passing close to Peal Island and we're tramping like mad . . . full power . . . tramping like hell here . . . I can't see much and the water's very bad indeed . . . I can't get over the top . . . I'm getting a lot of bloody row in here . . . I can't see anything . . . I've got the bows up . . . I've gone . . . Oh."

Veteran Circumnavigator

FACT FILE

The fastest solo circumnavigation

Built: 1965/66

Length: 54 feet

Weight: 11½ tons

Sail area: 2,403 square feet

Francis Chichester was not a happy man when he sailed from Plymouth on 27 August 1966. His aim was to sail alone around the world with only a single stop, in Sydney, but instead of leaving on his great adventure with a light heart he was ill, depressed and far from confident about the sailing qualities of his 54-foot ketch, *Gipsy Moth IV*. The book he later wrote about the voyage begins with a sustained grumble. Unlike his predecessor Joshua Slocum, for whom sailing alone around the world was a long and enjoyable holiday, Chichester set out like a monk doing penance.

Chichester was not new to adventure. In 1929 he had learned to fly, bought an aircraft, and flown it single-handed to Australia. Other epic journeys were made, but in 1953 Chichester gave flying up in favour of sailing. When the first single-handed transatlantic race was organized in 1960 he entered, and won; he also completed the transatlantic races in 1964 and 1966. He began to believe that it might be possible to realize his dream of circling the globe alone, but in a boat, not an aircraft.

The more Chichester thought about the

Francis Chichester (1901–72) *aboard* Gipsy Moth IV *near Tower Bridge, London, before setting off on his circumnavigation. His intention was to follow much the same course as the tea clippers over the 14,000 miles to Sydney, which he hoped to reach in a similar time, about 100 days. Sydney was to be the only stop, to save time. After his voyage around the world, Chichester made a triumphant return to England (opposite). In 1971, he crossed the Atlantic alone in* Gipsy Moth IV, *but died the following year after becoming ill on a race.*

project, the more possible it seemed. He was not interested in simply completing the trip, as Slocum had—he wanted to do it faster than any other small boat had managed.

Chichester's ambition was to reach Sydney in 100 days, then sail on and complete the circumnavigation in another 100 days. To achieve that would need a boat that was both fast and manageable. For long periods it would have to sail itself, using self-steering gear, and the key to success would be Chichester's ability to select the right course and rig to make good progress while he was asleep. The sails must not be too big or unwieldy to be handled by a single man—particularly one who was just a few weeks short of his sixty-fifth birthday when he set off.

Yet Chichester allowed his judgement over the design of the yacht to be overruled. He had wanted a boat 48 feet long, but the designer John Illingworth asserted that *Gipsy Moth IV* would be so easy to handle that she could be longer, and thus faster. When launched, *Gipsy Moth IV* turned out to be so tender that she would lay almost on her beam ends in a modest blow. This, says Chichester, "put ice into my blood", for how would a yacht that could be blown flat in the Solent behave when she met the gales of the huge Southern Ocean?

To try to stabilize her she was put into dry dock, her keel removed, and more lead added. This increased her weight, of course, so that Chichester finished off with a boat both bigger and much heavier than he had originally wanted. Moreover, she still heeled to 35 degrees which could prove dangerous in big seas.

All this sapped Chichester's confidence, and things were made worse by an injury he suffered when he slipped on the saloon skylight and hurt his hip. He set off from Tower Pier in the Thames on 12 August, and sailed around to Plymouth with his wife Sheila and son Giles on board. The voyage proper began when he crossed the Royal Ocean Racing Club's start line off Plymouth Hoe as the gun fired at 11 a.m. on 27 August.

For the first couple of days he was seasick and found the sailing hard. The self-steering gear did not seem to work well and would not hold the boat on course if all sails were set. But in the first four days he sailed 556 miles, which cheered him up. He passed Madeira and in the warmer waters began to enjoy himself. Every time a serious

Veteran Circumnavigator

squall hit the boat, however, things went wrong. The self-steering would not hold the course and *Gipsy Moth IV* would tear off at great speed, but in the wrong direction. Under these circumstances it was very difficult to lower sails and regain control while trying to steer the boat.

Despite the problems, he was making good time. By his 32nd day out, he reckoned he lay only 40 or so miles behind the position of *Cutty Sark* at the same point on one of her voyages. By the middle of October, *Gipsy Moth* had rounded the Cape of Good Hope and was halfway to Australia. Ahead lay 7,000 miles of running down the winds along the clipper way, one of the greatest sails in the world. By this time Chichester had had a spell of calms and was well behind *Cutty Sark*'s timetable, but he felt more cheerful.

The roaring forties, however, proved tough sailing. When the wind really blew and Chichester attempted to flee before it under bare poles, he found *Gipsy Moth* would do nothing but lie broadside on to wind and waves. Only by hoisting a storm jib could she be persuaded to sail. Chichester was dumbfounded. All his earlier yachts had steered easily downwind under bare poles. Broaching to under a heavy sea was the fate that clipper captains feared most, for if the sails went into the sea they were likely to founder. *Gipsy Moth*'s chances were better than that, but it was still impossibly uncomfortable, and Chichester was making slow progress.

On 15 November, with 2,750 miles to go to Sydney, disaster struck. The self-steering gear broke, two steel plates 6 inches wide and $\frac{1}{8}$ inch thick sheering clean through. Chichester thought his dream was over and decided to put into Fremantle, which was much closer than Sydney. Without the self-steering, he would be lucky to be able to sail for more than ten hours a day, and the rest of the journey to Sydney would take three months.

But during the day he started experimenting with the sails, creating a jury rig which would hold *Gipsy Moth* nearly on course, as long as the wind was astern. To his delight, it worked, and he decided to head for Sydney after all. The hope of reaching it in 100 days was gone, but he would still make good time.

Ahead, however, lay a tough sail through the Bass Strait and north to Sydney Harbour. The weather was rough, the currents unfavourable and *Gipsy Moth* continued to sail badly. Chichester noted bitterly in his log "I fear *Gipsy Moth IV* is about as unbalanced and unstable a

The rounding of Cape Horn (above) presented nothing to compare with the seas Gipsy Moth IV *encountered during a storm on the first night out of Sydney. Chichester later estimated, from marks made by objects flung about the cabin, that the masts went between 45 and 60 degrees below the horizontal. It was pitch dark, and he had the feeling of the boat being on top of him as things rained down from every locker.*

boat that there could be". Finally he sailed into Sydney at 4.30 p.m. on 12 December after 107 days 5½ hours.

In Sydney Chichester took advice from a number of yachtsmen on how to improve the sailing qualities of *Gipsy Moth IV* before he left on 29 January 1967. Almost immediately he hit trouble. The next night, *Gipsy Moth* was hit by a freak sea, and virtually turned turtle. Slowly she righted herself without going completely over. The result of the upset was an appalling mess, the loss of several sails, winches and other gear, and a bilge almost full of water. But Chichester was still alive, and *Gipsy Moth* still afloat.

The rounding of Cape Horn was the part of the voyage that had most frightened Chichester before he set off. As he expected, he found fearsome seas and winds gusting to 60 knots, but no disaster befell. By 26 March he was around the Horn and halfway home, heading up through

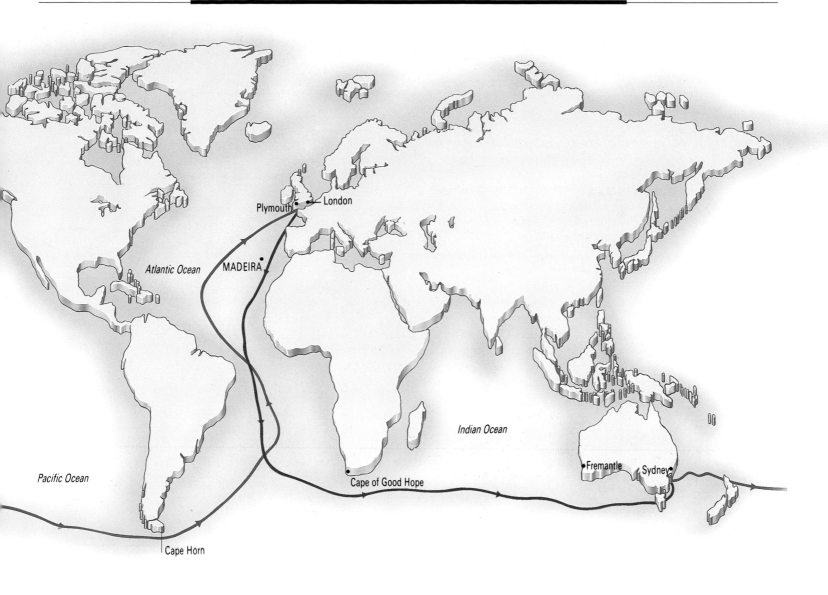

the South Atlantic Ocean with 8,000 miles to go.

Much of the way was easy, pleasant sailing, and even *Gipsy Moth* seemed to be enjoying herself at last. He reached Plymouth on 28 May, a passage of 15,517 miles in 119 days, at an average speed of 130 miles per day. He had completed the fastest ever circumnavigation of the world in a small boat, 9 months and 1 day, of which the sailing time was 226 days. He had also broken records for the longest passage and for a week's run by a single-hander.

After arriving in Plymouth, Chichester paid the price for the way he had driven himself, collapsing with a duodenal ulcer. This delayed his triumphal return to London until the beginning of July. He arrived at Greenwich on 7 July and was knighted by the Queen in the Grand Quadrangle of the Royal Naval College. Nearby, his yacht is preserved close to *Cutty Sark* whose great runs so inspired him.

As Chichester stepped ashore in Sydney, *he was faced by a press conference of over 100 journalists, quite a change from three months of his own company. The changes made to* Gipsy Moth IV *in Sydney proved beneficial. The yacht's handling improved, reducing her tendency to broach in a following sea, which had caused Chichester such concern while crossing the Indian Ocean.*

The Longest Journey under the Sea

The Arctic ice cap floats on top of a deep and unexplored ocean. Unlike the Antarctic, no land lies beneath the wilderness of broken ice, but until the development of the nuclear submarine the ocean remained as inaccessible as any place on Earth. Sir John Ross, the explorer, described the Arctic sea ice as "a floating rock in the stream, a promontory or island when aground, not less solid than if it were a land of granite". He exaggerated, but not by much; in reality the Arctic ice has the strength of rather poorly made concrete. But it is certainly tough enough to ensure that no surface ship will ever be able to plough its way through to the pole.

The idea of getting there under the ice, however, had been taken seriously by several explorers. The Australian Sir Hubert Wilkins had led an expedition to the edge of the ice in an old American submarine in 1931. In the 1950s, submarines had crept beneath the ice for a distance of several miles before retreating. In principle, there seemed no reason to suppose that the right vessel could not sail clean under the polar ice cap and emerge unharmed on the other side. Nobody really knew how far down the ice penetrated at the shallow edges of the ocean, so there was a risk that a submarine might find itself trapped between the ice above and the ocean floor below, isolated, out of contact and beyond rescue. The only way to find out was to try.

Ordinary submarines were really unfit for the journey. When submerged they depend on electric power, but the batteries that store it have only a limited life before the submarine must surface and recharge by running its diesel engines. Optimists like Wilkins believed there would be sufficient polynias—open stretches of water in among the ice—for him to surface at regular intervals to run his engines. Even if he were right, finding them would require luck.

The development of the nuclear submarine transformed the position. Here at last was a vessel which could realize Jules Verne's dream of 20,000 leagues under the sea. A nuclear submarine equipped with a system for reconstituting the air its crew breathes can stay down for months on end. Unlike a diesel submarine which constantly dives and surfaces, the nuclear submarine finds its natural habitat in the deeps.

This revolution in submarine technology was brought about largely by one man, the remark-able Admiral Hyman Rickover of the US Navy. In 1946 Rickover, then a captain, had studied nuclear physics and became convinced that a nuclear reactor could be squeezed down small enough to power a submarine. Many people laughed at him, for the first nuclear piles were just that—enormous piles of uranium and graphite as big as a couple of city blocks. Rickover refused to be daunted.

For three years he fought a bureaucratic guerrilla campaign to have his idea taken seriously. His master stroke was to get himself appointed head of the Nuclear Power Division in the Navy's Bureau of Ships and simultaneously chief of the Atomic Energy Commission's Naval Reactors Branch. He could now send memos to himself, approve his own ideas, and move ahead at startling speed. By January 1954 the first nuclear submarine, called *Nautilus* in honour of Jules Verne, was ready for launch. The following January she sailed for the first time.

Nautilus was a triumphant vindication of Rickover's ideas. Her performance was stagger-ing. She could cruise under water at more than 20 knots, was highly manoeuvrable, could go very deep and was reckoned to be 50 times as difficult for anti-submarine forces to catch as a diesel submarine. By the time she first needed refuel-ling, two years after her shakedown cruise, she had travelled 69,138 miles.

If any vessel had the capacities to cruise below the Arctic ice cap, *Nautilus* did. A number of

FACT FILE

The submarine that first sailed under the Arctic ice cap

Built: 1953/54

Length: 320 feet

Diameter: 28 feet

Maximum speed: 20 knots

Commander William Anderson (middle below) with Lt Commander Frank Adams (left) and Lt William Lalor, Jr., aboard Nautilus *after their successful voyage. Looking at the edge of the ice cap, the submarine's crew breathe their last fresh air before diving under it (right).*

The Longest Journey under the Sea

influential people, including Senator Henry Jackson of the State of Washington, had been pressing for the attempt to be made, and the US Navy agreed, although some admirals opposed risking their only nuclear submarine in such a hazardous operation. In great secrecy the captain of *Nautilus*, Commander William R. Anderson, prepared for the trip. No announcement was to be made in advance, in case *Nautilus* failed. Elaborate cover stories were prepared, suggesting that *Nautilus* was bound for Panama, and the crew packed their tropical gear. In fact the destination was to be Portland, in England, via the North Pole.

The first attempt to penetrate the ice failed. *Nautilus* approached the ice cap by navigating through the Bering Strait that divides Alaska from Siberia, reaching the shallow Chukchi Sea. To reach the deep Arctic Basin it was necessary to find a way through this sea without meeting any ice that came too close to the bottom to allow *Nautilus* through. They saw the edge of the ice and plunged beneath it, navigating in a shallow region with the seabed 40 feet below and the deepest ice 50 feet above them.

Suddenly the instruments showed a huge chunk of ice ahead, a mile wide and more than 60 feet thick. Beyond lay an even more formidable barrier, which swooped down and down toward the seabed. *Nautilus* crept forward, its officers certain that any moment they would hear the grinding sound that meant they were trapped between the ice ceiling and the seabed. They cleared the massive block of ice with a bare 5 feet to spare, and Anderson knew the mission had failed; to go on risking his ship in those waters would be foolhardy. He gave the order to turn south, and abandoned the attempt on the pole. *Nautilus* sailed for Pearl Harbor, its crew sworn to secrecy, for Anderson still hoped to make a second attempt later in the year.

They set off again on 23 July and returned to the Bering Sea in six days—an average speed of 19.6 knots, all of it spent deep under water where submarines cruise better, free from storms. This time, he found the ice had retreated, but it was still necessary to thread his way through the Chukchi Sea. Despite steaming to and fro, they failed to find a passage, and Anderson decided to turn his attention eastward to the Barrow Sea, where a deep valley ought to provide a gateway to the western Arctic Basin.

They found it and submerged with relief in an area that looked safe. The water was deep, the

ice far above, and Anderson increased speed to 18 knots and set course for the pole, 1,094 miles away. Beyond that another 800 miles would bring them to the Greenland-Spitzbergen edge of the pack ice.

From here on, the expedition was almost an anticlimax. *Nautilus* found places where the seabed rose almost vertically toward the ice, but there was always ample space to slip through. At the pole itself, reached on 3 August 1958 at 11.15 p.m., the sea was measured as 13,410 feet deep. *Nautilus* emerged from the ice within a few miles of where it expected, a tribute to good navigation under difficult conditions. The transit had taken 96 hours to cover 1,830 miles. Since then, operations by nuclear submarines beneath the ice have become almost commonplace.

A routine check of the torpedo tubes as the ship glides beneath the Arctic ice. The only technical problem was a leak in a water condenser, cured by a liquid made to plug leaking car radiators. Conditions aboard Nautilus *were quite luxurious, with a juke-box, ice cream and cola machines in the mess—which converted to a 50-seat cinema—a library with 600 books and a darkroom.*

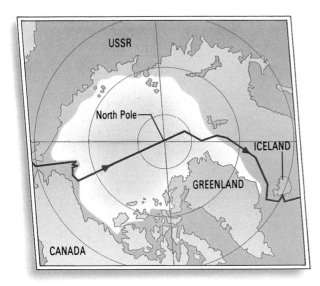

The route pioneered by Nautilus *might be of great benefit to commercial shipping if nuclear cargo-carrying submarines are ever built—or so Captain* Anderson *considered. It would cut 4,900 miles and 13 days off the route from Japan to Europe, a new submerged North-West passage.*

SIR HUBERT WILKINS

The first attempt to explore the Arctic by submarine was made by Sir Hubert Wilkins, an Australian adventurer. Sir Hubert, who spent most of his life in the US, persuaded the American government in 1931 to back his efforts to reach the pole in a submarine. For a fee of $1 a year for five years, the US Shipping Board let Wilkins have a 1918-built "O" class submarine, which he renamed *Nautilus*.

Wilkins expected to find open water every 25 miles or so, giving him a fair margin of safety with his 125-mile submerged range. If he was trapped beneath the ice, he planned to bring into use hollow ice-cutting drills mounted on top of the submarine.

From the beginning things went wrong: one of *Nautilus*'s two engines broke down in mid-Atlantic, through incompetence or deliberate sabotage. *Nautilus* was towed to Devonport dockyard in

Plymouth for repairs, which took three weeks. By the time she reached the polar ice it was too late in the year for an attempt on the pole.

Inside *Nautilus* conditions were horrible. It was cramped and so cold that ice formed on the walls. When they finally submerged, the grinding and tearing noises made by the hull scraping along the ice so terrified them that they promptly surfaced. In fact there was little damage, but even the toughest found these ghastly noises hard to bear, and after a few days Wilkins admitted defeat.

He limped into Bergen and was granted permission to scuttle her off Norway. The trip had been a disaster, but Wilkins remained convinced that a submarine would succeed where he had failed. He lived just long enough to see his prediction come true, dying on 30 November 1958.

Nautilus *enters Portland harbour in England to a rousing welcome on 12 August 1958, just nine days after reaching the North Pole. To release news of the success to the world as quickly as possible, it had been arranged that a helicopter would rendezvous with the submarine off Reykjavik, Iceland, and fly Captain Anderson to Iceland from where a plane would take him to Washington to report to President Eisenhower. A press conference was held, after which Captain Anderson was flown to England to rejoin* Nautilus *off Portland. The submarine would then enter the Royal Navy's submarine base. When the submarine returned to the United States, New York honoured the crew with a ticker-tape parade.*

Blue Riband-Winning Catamaran

In June 1990 the world's biggest catamaran, the *Hoverspeed Great Britain*, broke a record that had stood for 38 years. It covered the 2,800 miles between the Ambrose light-vessel, New York, and Bishop Rock off the Isles of Scilly in 3 days, 7 hours and 54 minutes. In doing so it broke the record set by the liner SS *United States* on her maiden voyage in July 1952, and won the Blue Riband for the fastest Atlantic crossing.

It was a victory that nearly caused a battle in court, for the US Merchant Marine Museum was reluctant to give up the Hales Trophy, awarded to the holder of the Blue Riband, to what it saw as a mere channel ferry. "Even if they come here and claim it, we're not going to give it to them," said Frank Braynard, curator of the museum. "The trophy was intended for great liners, not for toy boats, and this is a toy boat." On the other side of the Atlantic the captain of the *Great Britain*, John Lloyd, was equally certain that he and his crew had won the trophy fair and square. As it berthed in Falmouth, *Great Britain* flew a 30-foot blue ribbon. "The trophy is ours. No ifs and buts, it belongs to us," he said. "A trophy that collects dust is not a trophy; it is a souvenir and it is cheapened by not being competed for."

The catamaran had already come a long way before it began its record-breaking Atlantic run. Built in Hobart, Tasmania, by International Catamarans, it had sailed across the Pacific, through the Panama Canal and up the coast of the United States to Somerset, Massachusetts, where it entered a dock for some strengthening work to be done on the superstructure, to cure a problem of vibration. The Atlantic crossing was merely the final leg of a journey to Britain to begin work as a ferry capable of carrying 450 passengers and 80 cars between Portsmouth and Cherbourg, or on other Channel routes.

The catamaran, or SeaCat, was seen as a successor to the large hovercraft, which have been used as car ferries since the early 1970s, and as a pre-emptive strike against the Channel Tunnel, expected to come into operation in 1993. By halving the crossing time of a regular ferry, Hoverspeed hoped to attract and hold passengers in what is likely to be a tough battle in one of the world's busiest waterways.

The SeaCat is capable of a top speed of 42 knots, giving it a comfortable theoretical margin over the *United States*, which averaged 35.6 knots on its record trip in 1952. But Captain Lloyd did not attempt to drive the catamaran flat out. To begin with, indeed, it seemed that he was going too slowly to stand much chance of a record. "We started off doing 35 knots," he says. "At first, when we realized how slowly we were going, it was tempting to throw open the throttles but I knew if we simply sat tight the boat would pick up speed itself as it consumed the 217 tonnes of fuel on board. By the time we reached the UK, we were doing 38 knots, keeping the engines at maximum continuous rpm."

There were just 10 tons of fuel left when the boat reached Falmouth, having averaged 36.65 knots for the crossing, just over a knot faster than the *United States*.

Captain Lloyd had not lingered in New York waiting for good weather, but had set out as soon as the boat was ready. In fact, he was lucky. "We saw nothing that I would call big seas," he says, nor did they meet ice or much fog. Conditions for an Atlantic crossing were about as good as they could have hoped for.

As they approached the Scillies and the end of the course, Lloyd and the SeaCat crew held a meeting to discuss what to do if, at that late stage, something went wrong. Reluctant to break out the champagne until the moment the Bishop Rock was astern, Lloyd admits: "We could have celebrated the night before our arrival, but I knew that if we did the engines would play up. So that night we planned what to do if one of the four failed. Could we make it on three engines?" Fortunately for them, the situation never arose and the catamaran passed the finish line and reached Portsmouth with all four engines running strongly.

The SeaCat has more in common with the great ocean liners than meets the eye. They used the well-established principle of a long, narrow hull to get maximum speed through the water, and so does a catamaran. The difference is that a catamaran has two narrow hulls, with the accommodation arranged as decking linking the two together. The catamaran form has been in use for thousands of years in the Pacific and Indian oceans, and its name derives from a word in the Tamil language of southern India, *kattu-maram*, which means trees tied together. Sailing catamarans have proved that they are the fastest in many classes of racing, combining light weight

FACT FILE

The world's largest catamaran

Date launched:
January 1990

Overall length: 242 feet 10 inches

Power output:
20,000 horsepower of thrust

Maximum speed:
42 knots

with the ability to carry a lot of sail without capsizing. When they do capsize, however, they are much harder to right than a conventional hull, which has made some long-distance sailors wary of them.

A conventional ocean liner cuts straight through the waves with its narrow hull. There is little buoyancy at the bow, so a liner does not pitch, tending instead to plough through the waves. While this produces an easy motion, it means that seas can sweep right over the deck in rough conditions. The SeaCat's twin hulls are also designed to pierce the waves, but because

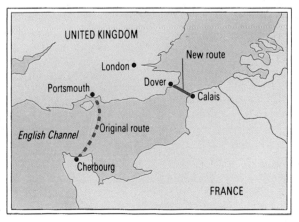

Hoverspeed Great Britain *beneath the New York skyline. The catamaran spent longer in the United States than anticipated, in dry dock at Somerset, Massachusetts, while the superstructure was strengthened to eliminate vibration.*

Blue Riband-Winning Catamaran

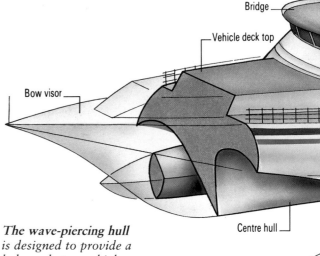

The wave-piercing hull is designed to provide a balance between high speed and passenger comfort. It took six years to refine the concept.

the passenger accommodation is carried high above them it stays dry.

The craft is very short in comparison to its breadth—242 feet 10 inches long by 84 feet 7 inches across—which means that the hulls must pierce the waves if pitching is to be controlled. On some early Channel runs, Hoverspeed did indeed find that the motion was unpleasant enough to cause seasickness, and shifted some ballast forward to try to correct the problem.

The hulls are linked by a bridging structure which is shaped on the underside like a third hull. In normal conditions this is lifted clear of the water, but in extreme weather it provides a third source of buoyancy. The shape of the underside is designed to reduce the shock impact of waves. The hulls and superstructure are made of welded aluminium, with access to the vehicle deck through the stern. The passenger saloon, 65 feet 7 inches wide, is fitted with airline-type seats, the centre section raised by 3 feet so that all passengers can see through the side windows. There is a separate lounge bar at the stern and an observation deck. The passenger area is mounted flexibly to reduce vibration.

Manoeuvring is facilitated by two water jets on each side, fitted with steering and reversing controls. The other two water jets are powered up when outside the harbour to bring the catamaran up to its maximum speed.

The *Great Britain* was not the first ship to break the record held by the *United States*. In 1986 Richard Branson crossed in three days and eight hours in his powerboat *Virgin Atlantic*

The welded aluminium hulls are joined by an arched bridge structure which incorporates a central third hull form. Above them is a vehicle deck, surmounted by a superstructure which contains air-conditioned passenger space. This is supported on anti-vibration mountings.

Challenger, but his claim to the record was disallowed by the Hales Trophy trustees because his boat was not built for commercial service. Nothing daunted, Branson commissioned his own trophy, a sculpture of Bishop Rock lighthouse, and when his own powerboat record was beaten in 1989 by an American, Tom Gentry, he handed over the sculpture.

The considerations that prevented Branson and Gentry from claiming the Hales Trophy did not apply to *Great Britain*. Although the catamaran was not on a scheduled run, and did not carry passengers, the British-based trustees of the trophy decided that it did in fact meet the

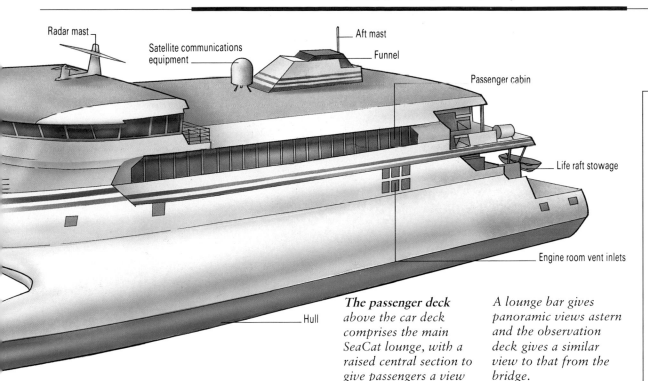

Radar mast
Satellite communications equipment
Aft mast
Funnel
Passenger cabin
Life raft stowage
Engine room vent inlets
Hull

The passenger deck *above the car deck comprises the main SeaCat lounge, with a raised central section to give passengers a view of the sea on both sides.*

A lounge bar gives panoramic views astern and the observation deck gives a similar view to that from the bridge.

The SeaCat's power is provided by four 16-cylinder Ruston diesel engines mounted in the wide hulls. Manufactured by GEC at Newton-le-Willows on Merseyside, the engines each produce 5,000 hp at 750 rpm. Medium-speed diesels have never before been fitted in a high-speed craft; it eliminates the need for gearboxes, since the engines are coupled directly to the largest water jets ever made.

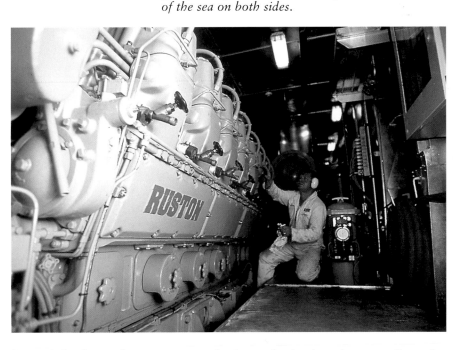

requirements. Commander Michael Ranken, secretary to the trustees, said: "We are a legally constituted trust and have the power to say who has won. The Hoverspeed vessel is eligible because it was built for commercial service. I wish there was a little less nostalgia about."

In fact, the trust deed of the trophy, originally commissioned by Harold Hales, MP for Hanley, Staffordshire, in England, to encourage "the craft of speed" in marine engineering, made no mention of a restriction to ocean liners. It was to be awarded to that ship which made the crossing at the highest average speed, without undue risk to the ship or her passengers or crew. The

trustees had no hesitation in awarding the trophy to Hoverspeed and the *Great Britain*, and the New York museum, faced with the prospect of going to court under English law, had no choice but to accept the verdict.

The Hales Trophy, a 4-foot-high silver and gilt sculpture showing scenes of Atlantic vessels from the fifteenth to the twentieth centuries supported by the god of the sea Neptune and his wife Amphitrite, was finally surrendered. In a ceremony in the pool of London in November 1990, it was presented to James Sterling of Hoverspeed by Lord Callaghan, Britain's prime minister from 1976 to 1979.

Until Harold Keates Hales first presented, in 1935, the trophy named after him, there had been no formal recognition of the vessel that held the record for the fastest crossing of the Atlantic. However, a notional trophy was the Blue Riband (or Ribbon) of the Atlantic. The first ship to hold it was one of the original Cunard wooden paddle steamers, the *Arcadia*, built in 1840. Fierce competition has since led to the Riband being held by all the great transatlantic lines. Hales himself was a self-made engineer with a passion for speed.

CHAPTER TWO

OVERLAND BY ROAD

One of the greatest but least remarked upon differences between our lives and those of the wealthier citizens of the eighteenth century is in the ease of transport. The middle classes then lived in houses no worse designed and often rather better built than our own, read good books and listened to music still enjoyed today. Until they set foot out of doors they lived a recognizably civilized life. When they embarked on journeys, however, they descended into an agony of discomfort and delay which had no respect for rank.

The Habsburg emperor Charles VI visited England in 1703 and set out from London to visit Petworth in Sussex, a distance of only 50 miles. The journey took three days, the imperial coach overturned a dozen times, and only by hiring labourers to walk alongside and help push him through the mud did Charles VI finally reach his destination.

It was the invention of the railway, the bicycle and, finally, the car that annihilated distance. Where once even the nobleman's coach could hope for no more than 4 mph, the lone cyclist by the end of the nineteenth century could bowl along at 10 mph, roads permitting. In 1884 the American cyclist Thomas Stevens cycled all the way around the world, a remarkable achievement for, as he himself was the first to admit, most of the journey was made over roads hardly improved since the Middle Ages.

Early in this century an even more dramatic improvement was brought about by the automobile, which proved in the Peking to Paris car race of 1907 that no part of the world was beyond its reach. Again, much of the success of the winning Itala was the result of a recognition by its owner, Prince Borghese, that the race would be won not on the roads but across mountains, along railway tracks and through rivers. The same applied more than 60 years later to the expedition that crossed the Darien Gap in Central America, a wilderness of forest and bog that had defeated many earlier attempts.

The car has become, of course, more than just a means of transport. It is an object of beauty and a sporting machine as well. In this section we explore a few episodes in man's love affair with the car which, in spite of pollution and congestion, shows no sign of diminishing.

Wheeling Around the World

Thomas Stevens, journalist, traveller and evangelist for the bicycle, set out in 1884 to ride alone around the world. His journey was not so much a ride as a pioneering essay in the sport now known as cyclo-cross, for Stevens carried his bicycle almost as often as he rode it. It was an 1883-model Columbia Expert, and singularly ill-suited to the task. It weighed at least twice as much as a modern machine, and riding it even on sound roads was hazardous. Downhill, it was easy to tip straight over the front wheel head first on to the road. Such accidents were known in cyclists' slang as headers, taking a purler, or coming a cropper, expressions which survive long after the bicycles have disappeared.

Despite these drawbacks, it was the penny-farthing (known as an "ordinary" to distinguish it from the new-fangled geared bicycles with their diamond-shaped frames which were soon to displace it) that created the first great boom in cycling in the 1870s.

The ordinary appealed particularly to smart young men who wanted to cut a dash. By 1883 the Cyclists' Touring Club of Britain had more than 10,000 members, and the first long-distance records had been established between Land's End and John o'Groats. Nobody, however, had yet crossed the United States, let alone ridden around the world, when Stevens set off from San Francisco in California on 22 April 1884.

Stevens carried pathetically little: no coat, or tent or sleeping bag, and nothing to eat or drink. He had a sheet of oiled cambric which could be worn as a poncho or draped over the bicycle as a kind of tent. In a small case he carried medicines, matches, a map, a notebook, a pen and ink, and his League of American Wheelmen badge. His bicycle had solid tyres, so he needed no puncture outfit, but he did carry a .38 Smith & Wesson revolver and ammunition as an insurance against some of the wilder folk he expected to meet. He was 29 years old.

What sort of man was he? Born in England, he had moved to the US as a child. To judge by the huge, two-volume account he later published of his exploits, he was tough and resourceful but not very sophisticated. As Stevens innocently blunders his way through Turkey, Persia, Afghanistan and China, the reader anticipates the difficulties long before they occur to the traveller.

His first challenge was the Sierras, the snow-covered mountains of California, which he covered on foot, walking along the railroad track and carrying his bicycle. Next came the wild country of Nevada, where only sagebrush flourished in the sandy desert. In the town of Carlin, he demonstrated the bicycle to people who had never seen one by riding it around the pool table in the hotel bar. In the Humboldt Mountains he came upon a mountain lion, and fired his revolver at it twice without doing it any harm at all.

He set his daily target at 40 miles, a considerable distance when two-thirds of a typical day involved walking. Through the Great Plains he passed the homesteads that were beginning to spring up in country hitherto occupied by buffalo and cattle, and found a few ridable roads, although it was a lucky day on which he did not suffer at least one header. By 4 August he had reached Boston, and he spent the winter of 1884/85 in New York, where he wrote some articles for *Outing* magazine. Next spring he set off once more, as their special correspondent, on his ride around the world.

First stop was Liverpool, where he disembarked from the SS *City of Chicago*. Riding to London he was astonished by the smoothness of

FACT FILE

The first journey around the world on two wheels

Model: Columbia Expert

Diameter of front wheel: 50 inches

Date of journey: 1884–86

Distance wheeled: about 13,500 miles

The penny-farthing was invented in 1870 by James Starley of Coventry, England. The pedals were attached to the front wheels, and each turn of the pedal took the rider forward 13 feet. The seat was set back too far to exert maximum force, yet the handlebars were too close for comfort.

Thomas Stevens, *as depicted in his two-volume account of his epic journey,* Around the World on a Bicycle.

The mountain paths through the Sierra Nevadas were so treacherous that after a few slides Stevens chose to walk through railroad tunnels. There was barely room for a man and bicycle to cower at the side as the trains rumbled through, their black smoke making the darkness more intense.

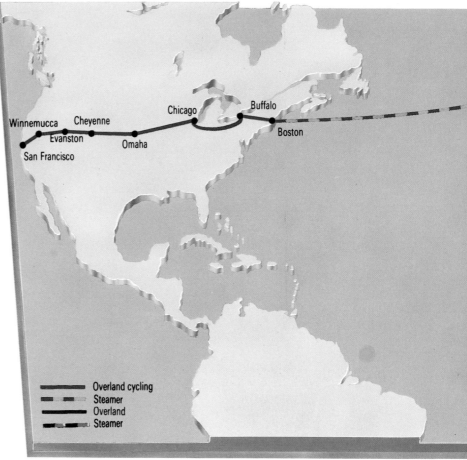

Overland cycling
Steamer
Overland
Steamer

the roads, and pleased that he did not have to dismount for horses, the English variety having long since got used to swells whooping by on their strange machines. When he reached Newhaven for the crossing to France, he realized that it was the first 300 miles of road he had ever covered without coming a cropper.

Through France, Germany, Austria and Hungary Stevens made good time. In Belgrade, the capital of Serbia, the last contacts with organized cycling died out. Close to the Bulgarian frontier a team of horses and a light wagon challenged Stevens to a race. The road was flat and Stevens went full speed, but the wagon kept up and they finally drew up together at the frontier post, the horses' sides white with sweat.

Stevens's greatest difficulty in Turkey and Kurdistan was to escape from the mobs of people anxious, indeed insistent, that he should show them how to ride. In narrow, crowded streets riding a penny-farthing was not easy, but he was given little choice. The Smith & Wesson came in handy when he was stopped by two would-be highwaymen, but in general Stevens found Turkish hospitality overwhelming.

In Persia, Stevens was summoned by the Shah to ride with him from Tehran to the summer palace at Doshan Tepe. Stevens was told to

The route Stevens took had to be altered radically on only two occasions. His arrest in Afghanistan compelled him to return to Constantinople to take a steamer to India. But it was in China that he encountered the most serious problems. He spent the first night in a Chinese village inn, amidst opium smokers and mosquitoes. The next night was worse. Pursued by hostile villagers, Stevens fled to an island in a river to escape them, then scrambled on to the next village. So it went on, the mutual incomprehension made worse by the lack of any means of communication. He was finally ordered to abandon his route through the country.

sprint, then to ride over rough stones, and finally to keep his balance when going as slowly as possible, in order to show what the first bicycle ever to appear in Persia could do. He spent the winter of 1885/86 in Tehran, sharing bachelor quarters with a group of staff from the telegraph office, and in March set off again, heading through Turkestan and southern Siberia.

He was arrested in Afghanistan and sent back to Herat, on the grounds that continuing would be too dangerous and that it would be impossible to guarantee his safety. Returning to Constantinople (present-day Istanbul), he took a series of ships to Karachi. From there he went by rail to Lahore, reasoning that it was as close as he could get to Furrah, in Afghanistan, where his journey had been so rudely interrupted.

In India Stevens found a magnificent road for cycling, "an unbroken highway of marvellous perfection from Peshawar to Calcutta," broad, level and smooth, and shaded on either side by trees. The only trouble was the appalling heat. A day or two's experience of the midday sun soon showed him that the Indian climate was not to be trifled with, and he even overcame his antipathy to alcohol when offered a "peg"—a big brandy and soda—by some servants of the Raj. Thus fortified, he reached Calcutta and took a boat to

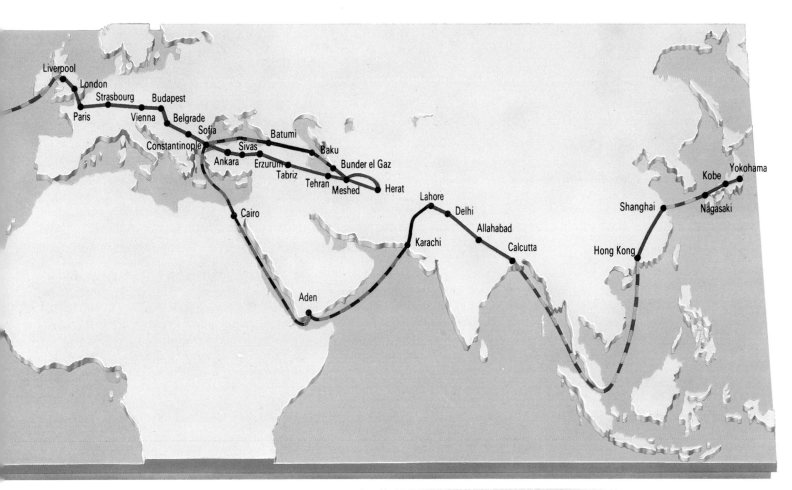

Hong Kong. Ahead lay the final stretch through China and Japan before crossing the Pacific back to his starting point in San Francisco.

Stevens's progress through China was less a bicycle ride than a series of arguments with bewildered officialdom. In Kingan-foo, a mob attacked Stevens who almost resorted to the Smith & Wesson before escaping in some peril into the Manchu quarter of the town, where the chief magistrate rescued him. At this point, it became clear even to Stevens that cycling across China was not really a practicable proposition, and at the insistence of the authorities he made the rest of the journey to Shanghai by riverboat, before catching a ferry to Nagasaki.

Japan proved a much more straightforward proposition. While life at a Chinese village inn had nearly unhinged his reason, the equivalent in Japan seemed close to paradise. Even the roads were good, so Stevens completed his journey to the port of Yokohama in high spirits.

There, on 17 December 1886, his journey by bicycle ended, and it remained only to cross the Pacific aboard the *City of Peking* for San Francisco. It had been an extraordinary journey and his fame was secured; others may bicycle around the world but nobody can take from Stevens the distinction of doing it first.

The return to Herat in the heat was exhausting for Stevens, in low spirits at not being able to reach India overland. One of his escorts kindly exchanged his horse for Stevens's bicycle for part of the journey, but soon fell off and broke two of the spokes. The bicycle was repaired in Herat.

Stevens warmed to Japan and its people. "The Japs are a wonderful race," he wrote. "They seem to be the happiest people going, always smiling and good-natured, always polite and gentle, always bowing and scraping." He was impressed by the awareness of Western dishes, when he was served beef and onions.

A Triumph for the Automobile

FACT FILE

The first
transcontinental car
race

Date: June–August
1907

Distance: 9,200
miles

Duration: 61 days

Winner: Prince
Scipione
Borghese/Itala

*Prince Borghese
undertook a
reconnaissance of the
first stretch of the race,
the Nankow Mountains
outside Peking. He was
convinced the cars
could get through, but
only by dragging them
up on ropes hauled by
porters and animals,
then lowering them
down the other side.*

On the morning of 31 January 1907, the Paris newspaper *Le Matin* issued what it called a stupendous challenge: "Is there anyone who will undertake to travel this summer from Paris to Peking by automobile?"

This was a bold suggestion. Cars were still in their infancy and for most of the distance there would be no roads to drive them on. Within a few days it was clear, nonetheless, that plenty of people were prepared to take the idea seriously. One of the first to respond was the Marquis de Dion, president of the de Dion-Bouton motor company and founder of the Automobile Club of France. In a letter delivered to *Le Matin* the same day, he declared: "The roads are abominable and often exist only as lines on a map. However, it is my belief that if a motor car can get through, the de Dion-Bouton will get through . . . I take up this challenge here and now, provided that I have one other car against me as competitor and travelling companion."

De Dion soon had his wish. In the first flush of enthusiasm there were at least a dozen entries, but these began to shrink as the difficulties became plain. *Le Matin*, meanwhile, changed its mind and decided the race should begin in Peking and end in Paris, rather than the other way around. Finally, five cars turned up in the Chinese capital on 10 June 1907 for the start.

Two came from de Dion-Bouton—standard lightweight 10-hp voiturettes, driven not by the company's founder but by professional drivers. There was a Dutch Spyker, a curious three-wheeled Contal, and an impressive 40-hp Itala, entered by Prince Scipione Borghese, an Italian diplomat and explorer who took the whole enterprise with great seriousness.

The cars they were driving were typical of the Edwardian era. The Itala was the biggest, a four-cylinder racer ordered by Borghese direct from the factory with minimal modifications. It had four speeds, right-hand drive, a conical clutch, magneto ignition, leaf springs, and could do about 8 miles to the gallon in favourable conditions. It was fast, able to reach 50 mph and heavy. The de Dion-Boutons, by contrast, were almost dainty, light 10-hp machines which their manufacturer believed would perform better on rough roads than the heavier Itala. The Spyker lay somewhere between the two extremes, with a 15- to 20-hp four-cylinder engine, extra low gears and larger than normal wheels to increase ground clearance.

All the participants agreed that they would travel in convoy through China and Mongolia, as far as Irkutsk in Siberia, offering each other assistance if needed, although this agreement seems to have been only reluctantly entered into by Borghese. Meanwhile, the Spyker's driver, Charles Godard, extracted enough money from a Dutch diplomat to pay for the petrol, which was being left at staging points along the way.

The five cars drove off in a line, led by one of the de Dion-Boutons and followed by a detachment of army officers on horses. All traffic on the northern side of the city had been banned as the cars accelerated through the Gate of Virtue Triumphant, leaving the cavalry behind. It was splendid, but short-lived, for two cars immediately took a wrong turning and were lost before they had even left the city. Borghese impatiently went on while the rest gathered themselves and followed. It began to rain.

The next day the first of the great passes over the mountains was tackled. Ropes were tied to the cars and porters urged into reluctant effort as they strained to drag the vehicles up muddy tracks between the rocks close to the Great Wall. Sometimes picks had to be used to clear away boulders, and coming down was even more

"Pékin-Matin."

LE PRINCE BORGHÈSE
premier du raid PEKIN-MATIN
sur sa voiture 24 HP ITALA
60 jours de voyage dont 44 de marche effective

A Triumph for the Automobile

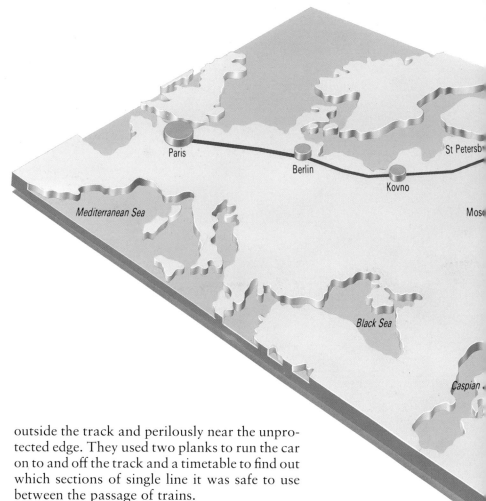

alarming, every man deployed to hold the cars back as the drivers stood on the brakes. Finally, seven days after leaving Peking the caravan reached the Mongolian border. They had covered 200 miles and had 9,000 to go.

Now at last they could drive, for the ground was flat even if it was not a road. Ahead lay a dash across the Gobi Desert, skirting around the whitened skeletons of oxen and camels which had tried, and failed, to make the same crossing. The three-wheeled Contal had been left behind, out of petrol, and its crew almost died before they were picked up by nomads and returned to Peking, claiming they had been betrayed.

To be fair, Godard had left some petrol behind for the Contal, a chivalrous gesture for it left him with too little to get across the Gobi himself. He believed that the de Dion-Bouton drivers, seeing his plight, would spare him enough of their fuel to get to the next staging-post at Udde. They did give him some, but not enough, and the Spyker coughed to a halt. The de Dions promised to send some fuel from Udde by camel while Godard and his companion, a French journalist named Jean du Taillis, waited. They had a long and agonizing wait, without food and water, before fuel arrived and they could escape. They, too, were lucky to survive.

The Italians, always anxious to press on, were the first to reach the Mongolian capital of Urga (now Ulan Bator). Meanwhile Godard and du Taillis in the Spyker drove nonstop from Udde to Urga, covering 385 miles in 24 hours, an astonishing performance for two men who a couple of days before were dying in the broiling heat of the Gobi.

Finally the great River Iro was reached. As the river was too deep to ford under the car's own power, the magneto was removed to avoid damage, the Itala hitched to yet more oxen, and dragged across, the water gurgling over the floor of the car and threatening to sweep it away. The magneto was refitted and the Itala was off, heading for Kia Khta and Russian soil. Here they believed that they had reached proper roads at last, for they had now reached the line of the Trans-Siberian Railway.

Unfortunately, the coming of the railway had led to a neglect of the roads. Vital bridges across rivers were down, and fording the rushing Siberian waters was impossible. There was only one option—to take the car on to the railway line and drive on the sleepers across the bridges, one wheel between the tracks and the other

outside the track and perilously near the unprotected edge. They used two planks to run the car on to and off the track and a timetable to find out which sections of single line it was safe to use between the passage of trains.

Behind Borghese came the two de Dions and the Spyker, enduring much the same difficulties. Instead of driving along the track, they put their cars in freight wagons and arrived in Irkutsk on the evening of 3 July, hard on the heels of the Italians who had left that very morning. By this time, Godard's car was very sick. The magneto was playing up and the rear axle had lost its oil after being holed by a stone. He plugged the hole

Prince Borghese's Itala *had few modifications: strengthened frame, stronger springs and wheels, and the largest possible tyres, made by Pirelli of Milan.*

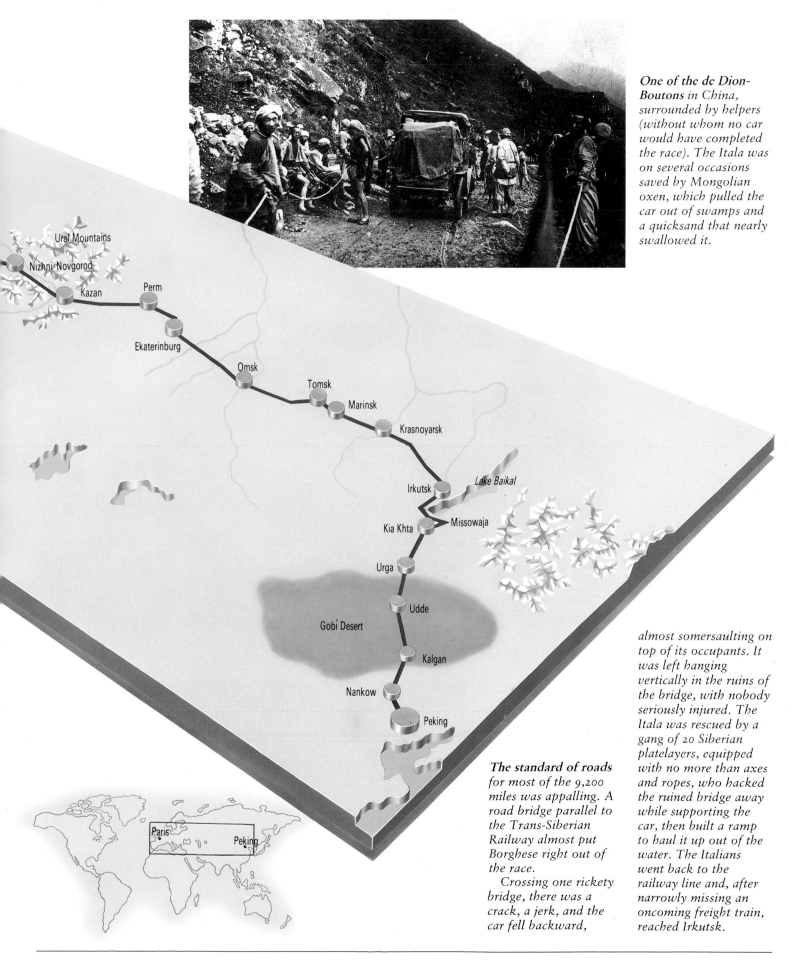

One of the de Dion-Boutons *in China, surrounded by helpers (without whom no car would have completed the race). The Itala was on several occasions saved by Mongolian oxen, which pulled the car out of swamps and a quicksand that nearly swallowed it.*

Ural Mountains

Nizhni-Novgorod

Kazan

Perm

Ekaterinburg

Omsk

Tomsk

Marinsk

Krasnoyarsk

Irkutsk

Lake Baikal

Kia Khta

Missowaja

Urga

Udde

Gobi Desert

Kalgan

Nankow

Peking

Paris

Peking

The standard of roads *for most of the 9,200 miles was appalling. A road bridge parallel to the Trans-Siberian Railway almost put Borghese right out of the race.*

Crossing one rickety bridge, there was a crack, a jerk, and the car fell backward, *almost somersaulting on top of its occupants. It was left hanging vertically in the ruins of the bridge, with nobody seriously injured. The Itala was rescued by a gang of 20 Siberian platelayers, equipped with no more than axes and ropes, who hacked the ruined bridge away while supporting the car, then built a ramp to haul it up out of the water. The Italians went back to the railway line and, after narrowly missing an oncoming freight train, reached Irkutsk.*

A Triumph for the Automobile

with a piece of bacon and refilled the axle with oil, but even a man with his innocence of motor mechanics knew this would not be enough. He cabled to the manufacturer of the car in Amsterdam for spares while the de Dions went on.

Help took some time coming, the spares being held up in Moscow for ten days by bureaucrats, but when Godard got going again he performed a miracle of driving. In 14 days he covered around 3,500 miles, a distance that had taken Borghese three weeks and the de Dions nearly five. Day after day he drove until his hands were raw. But even as he was doing it, a court in Paris was sentencing him to 18 months imprisonment for obtaining money under false pretences from the Dutch consular officials in Peking.

The Italians, marshalled by the superefficient Borghese, were now forging on toward Moscow. After a carriage-maker in Perm had rebuilt a collapsed wheel, they entered Moscow in triumph, the roads lined with Cossacks on horseback at 100-yard intervals to greet them. They stayed for three days of celebration before leaving on 31 July. Ahead lay only 2,500 miles of metalled road to the finish in Paris, covered with no difficulty. Borghese arrived in Paris to the sound of a brass band playing the march from Verdi's *Aida*.

Behind, the de Dions and the Spyker had become embroiled in political manoeuvres. While *Le Matin* had been obliged to accept that an Italian car had won the race, it could not face the fact that the two French cars still running might yet be beaten by the Dutch. In fact the three, reconciled after their privations, had agreed to finish in convoy. This was not good enough for *Le Matin*, which arranged to have Godard arrested in Germany on the false pretences charge. Du Taillis was disgusted at this and made sure that the Spyker and its driver got the recognition they deserved for a remarkable performance, for unlike the others the car ran the whole way virtually without a service.

The race had proved that the motor car could, indeed, go anywhere and that, all other things being equal, a large and powerful car will perform better than a small and light one. It was a triumph for the automobile, but it did little for the successful manufacturers. Itala, de Dion-Bouton and Spyker have long since joined the list of makes that have gone under in the tough competition of the motor industry. The memory of the great Peking to Paris race remains to make them immortal.

THE CHALLENGE OF 1908

Even at the time, the New York–Paris car race, sponsored by French and US newspapers, was regarded as a farce. The race began in the middle of winter. The seven contestants—a Protos from Germany; a Sizaire-Naudin, Werner, Motobloc and de Dion from France; a Zust from Italy; and a Thomas Flyer from the United States—struggled through the worst blizzards for 10 years on their way to San Francisco, sometimes covering just 7 miles a day.

Cars were shipped to either Japan or Russia, where the incompetent organizers changed the route and rules for the umpteenth time. Siberia was a sea of mud, and stops for repairs were frequent. Although the Protos had been disqualified by being railed to Seattle for repairs, it re-entered the race and was ahead for most of the way. Its entry into Paris was ignored; the popping of champagne corks awaited the arrival of the Thomas at the offices of the newspaper *Le Matin*.

The 60-hp Thomas Flyer (above) was built in Buffalo, N.Y. Captained by Montague Roberts and later George Schuster, the car returned to drive up Broadway. The victors were congratulated by President Roosevelt.

The departure from Broadway (right) on Lincoln's birthday, 12 February, was watched by 250,000 people. Bands played the four national anthems and the cars set off on the 21,000-mile, 170-day race.

Race to the Channel

In January 1930, a journalist named Dudley Noble carried off a very neat publicity stunt for the Rover car company, beating the famous Blue Train from the south of France to Calais. Soon the same feat had been achieved in a Vauxhall, and advertisements were placed in the British motoring magazines to celebrate the fact. The French authorities were not very amused, and nor was Woolf Barnato, chairman of the Bentley company and a well-known racing driver who won the Le Mans 24-hour race three years running in Bentley sports cars.

Barnato regarded beating the Blue Train as hardly worth bothering about. The train went from Cannes to Paris via Marseilles, which took it well out of its way, and then spent more than three hours wending its way across Paris from the Gare d'Orléans to the Gare du Nord. In a late-night argument with friends in Cannes, Barnato wagered he could do a lot better than either the Rover or the Vauxhall. His bet, he said later, was laughed off as a joke, for he asserted that not only could he reach the Channel before the train, but could actually cross it and be in England before the train pulled into Calais. "All right," he said, "we'll have no bet but I say I shall do it, just to prove my contention that beating the Blue Train deserves little merit."

The car Barnato planned to drive was a Bentley Speed Six saloon with very dashing coachwork by Gurney, Nutting & Co. of Chelsea, London. The car was based on the chassis of the famous Bentley Speed Six, normally an open car with a bonnet which went on for ever and coachwork in the familiar British racing green. The Speed Six is the classic Bentley, introduced in 1929 and winning at Le Mans for the next two years at the hands of Barnato. It also won the six-hour race at Brooklands in 1929 and the Double-Twelve and the 500 in 1930.

The car Barnato drove against the Blue Train was mechanically identical but had closed coachwork. He is said to have sketched the design on the back of the proverbial envelope for the coach-builders to copy. It was an early example of "fastback" styling, with the bluff Bentley radiator and bonnet followed by a sleek, low roof sweeping down at the rear.

Gurney, Nutting told Barnato that with a roof that tumbled so steeply they could not build a full four-seater, but were able to find room in the

back for a seat set sideways between two cocktail cabinets. It was a pioneer GT car, with all the dash of a sporting Bentley and the comfort of a saloon. It weighed some 2½ tons, did 10 miles to the gallon and was capable of comfortably more than 100 mph. The rear window was a mere 2 inches high, which must have made rear vision tricky, but Barnato does not appear to have been the sort of driver who spent much time looking backward. W.O. Bentley regarded him highly: "The best driver we ever had, and I consider the best British driver of his day . . . the only driver who never made a mistake."

He opted to take with him a friend, Dale Bourne, a well-known amateur golfer who could take over the driving if Barnato became too tired. They sat in the Carlton Bar in Cannes until they heard that the train had left, at 5.54 in the evening of 13 March 1930. They finished their drinks in no particular hurry, and left.

The trip had required a certain degree of planning, because Barnato had to be sure of finding supplies of petrol in the middle of the night, by no means as easy then as it would be now. He topped up first at Aix-en-Provence, after a mere 100 miles, providing enough petrol to reach Lyons, where he had arranged for a garage to stay open after midnight. The next fuel stop was at Auxerre, where a petrol tanker had been paid to wait on the bypass to fill the Bentley. Arriving in Auxerre a little behind schedule at 4.20 a.m., Barnato took a while to locate the tanker which had driven into town rather than staying on the bypass.

By this time it was raining hard, which slowed him down so much that he reached Paris three-quarters of an hour late. Soon after leaving Paris he had a burst tyre and, as he had brought only one spare with him, he slowed down a little to make sure of preserving it to the finish. He pulled into the quayside at Boulogne at 10.30 a.m., allowing an hour for breakfast and for his papers to be processed before catching the 11.30 ferry. Quickly through the customs on the other side, Barnato and Bourne were soon touring gently up to London. They had proved their point, for they were in England long before the Blue Train reached Calais and saw no reason to hurry.

"On getting to London," Barnato later wrote, "I noticed the clock at Victoria on the Vauxhall Bridge Road signified the time as 3.20 p.m. I said

FACT FILE

The Speed Six Bentley that beat the Blue Train from Cannes to the English Channel

Built: 1925

Engine capacity: 6.5 litres

Power output: 160 horsepower

Maximum speed: 100 mph

LE NOUVEAU TRAIN BLEU VERS LA COTE D'AZUR

to Dale: 'Do you know, we've got to London before the train has got to Calais?' So to confirm this we clocked into Bourne's club, the Conservative in St James's Street. Then I thought we ought to register our arrival with the Royal Automobile Club. The news of our successful run had apparently already preceded us, for the hall porter was waiting with the time clock message stamping machine to 'mark our cards'.''

Over the rough French roads of the day Barnato had driven between Cannes and Boulogne at an average of just over 45 mph. He might have been quicker but in case his elaborate arrangements for refuelling failed, he had filled the boot with spare cans of petrol, as a result of which he had so much weight in the tail that he could not do more than about 80 mph without

The oil painting by Terence Cuneo (b.1907) that illustrates a fictitious moment in the race between the Paris, Lyons and Mediterranean Railway 4-8-2 and Woolf Barnato's Bentley. "Le Train Bleu" (left) was even more luxurious than the Orient Express. It attracted the most fashionable clientele and was celebrated in paintings and by the eponymous ballet score by Milhaud.

Race to the Channel

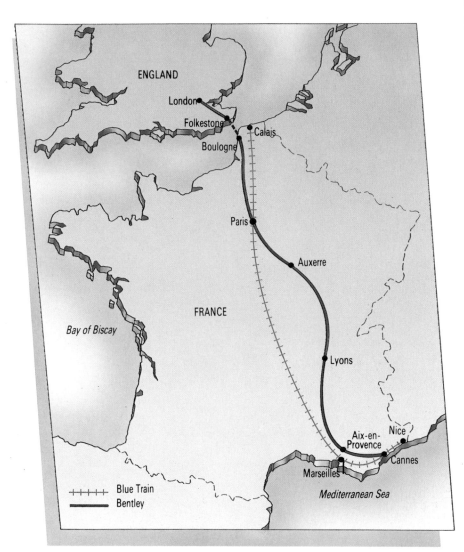

British passengers were conveyed from London to Calais by the Club Train, operated by Georges Nagelmackers's La Compagnie Internationale, which also ran the Blue Train and the Orient Express. In Paris the Calais portion was united with coaches from Berlin, St Petersburg, Warsaw and Vienna, allowing time for shopping before dinner in the train's Pergola Restaurant. From Marseilles the train swung east to run along the Riviera through Antibes to Nice. The train helped create the Côte d'Azur.

the springs bottoming. The average speed, very high by the standards of the day, only went to show, Barnato said, what a high average can be maintained over a long distance by not stopping for refreshments. He drove the whole way except for two hours near Pàris, where his eyes needed a rest from the strain of driving in fog and rain.

The French motoring authorities were incensed when they heard of the exploit, accusing Bentley of advertising an unofficial trial. In fact, no advertisements were placed, although the story was reported in the motoring press. The French Society of Motor Manufacturers banned Bentley from the 1930 Paris Salon and attempted to impose a fine of £160 on the Bentley company for racing on the roads of France without their permission. The fine was never paid.

Barnato did not hold on to the car for long, for later in 1930 it was advertised for sale in *Autocar* as a "Special Streamline Coupé" indistinguish-

able from new, an exceptional bargain at £345. Subsequently the car was owned by Lord Brougham and Vaux, and by racing driver Charles Mortimer before being sold in 1941 to Reg Potter, who stored it for many years in a garage in the Midlands.

Finally, in 1968, the car enthusiast Hugh Harben persuaded Potter to sell it. By this time it was looking sorry for itself but a complete rebuild restored it to more or less original condition. Harben made a few changes which today's restorers would frown at, fitting a sun roof and deepening the letterbox shaped rear window. But by the time he had finished, the car was once more in magnificent condition.

The Speed Six remains one of the most interesting cars from Bentley's great years. The irony is that it is remembered for a feat carried out by Barnato simply to demonstrate how insignificant it was to beat the Blue Train home from the south of France.

Hugh Harben bought the Bentley in 1968, by which time it was in a poor state of repair. With a good deal of work he restored the car almost to its original condition (left). It is now deep green below the waist line whereas before it was plain black. When Barnato sold the car in 1930, the advertisement (below) referred to him as "a world-famous racing motorist".

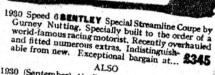

The Speed Six had a fixed-head long-stroke engine of six cylinders and 6.5 litres, capable of producing 160 hp at 3,500 rpm. The single overhead camshaft was driven by three coupling rods from the crankshaft and operated 24 small-diameter valves through rockers. The chassis was simple, with semi-elliptical springs front and rear. Later Bentley Continentals were to have a somewhat similar shaped roof, sweeping down to the rear. Woolf Barnato is seen here proudly standing next to his new car.

Across the Darien Gap

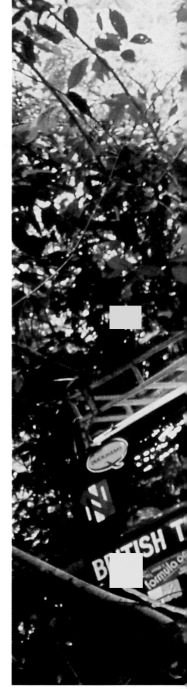

A narrow isthmus, coiling and twisting like a length of rope, joins together the two great landmasses of North and South America. At its thinnest, the neck of land provides the point at which the Caribbean is joined to the Pacific by the Panama Canal. To the south, straddling the border between Panama and Colombia, lies an area of swamp, jungle and mountain which is so impenetrable that no road or railway has ever been cut through it. For 200 miles the jungles of the Darien Gap prevent all movement and cut off South America from Central and North America as tightly as a cork seals a bottle. It is the only break in a highway that otherwise runs from the Arctic Circle to Tierra del Fuego.

In the early 1970s a group from the US, Panama and Colombia tried to prove that this gap could be bridged. They inspired an expedition which set out to be the first to drive all the way from north to south, taking specially prepared vehicles through the swamps and jungles of the Darien Gap, acting as pathfinders for the engineers who would one day build the road. A team of British servicemen and civilians, led by Major John Blashford-Snell of the Royal Engineers, set out to show that the gap could be crossed using a new model of vehicle, the Range-Rover, made by the Rover company.

Major Blashford-Snell and his party would not be the first people ever to cross the gap. That had been done on foot, and even in vehicles, but never in a single campaign. Previous crossings had been interrupted and resumed the following season, or had been abandoned altogether. The full journey, from Alaska to Tierra del Fuego, was 18,000 miles long. All but 250 miles of it was pretty straightforward motoring, although an accident in Canada raised doubts about the wisdom of using a new vehicle on such a demanding journey; it took 12 days for the parts to be sent from England to repair it. But much greater difficulties lay ahead.

Blashford-Snell had insisted that an advance reconnoitre should be done to assess the difficulties. A young Irish explorer, Brendan O'Brien, walked the course on foot, returning exhausted, covered in insect bites, and obviously ill. Once discharged from the Hospital for Tropical Diseases, O'Brien reported that the job might be possible but he wanted no part of it.

Only slightly daunted, the major assembled a large party, including 25 Royal Engineers, a Beaver aircraft and helicopters to provide air-drops during the crossing, 28 pack ponies, together with scientists, veterinarians and additional support from the armed forces of Panama and Colombia. It began to assume the proportions of a wartime task force: 59 men and 5 women linking up with 40 Panamanian and 30 Colombian servicemen in early January 1972.

Despite careful planning, the first few days of real jungle exposed the weaknesses of the equipment. As a form of mechanical packhorse the expedition had taken some "Hillbillies"—small vehicles like tracked wheelbarrows that in English conditions could carry a 500 lb load, steered by a man holding on to two handles at the back. In the swamps of Darien, the tracks were quickly clogged with mud which set solid in the heat. Unless the tracks were cleared out every 200 yards, progress was impossible. Eventually the Hillbillies had to be abandoned.

More serious were the problems with the Range-Rovers. Designed as a luxury road car with cross-country capability, the Range-Rover was not really up to the job of crunching through the jungle on non-existent tracks, and hauling itself and its considerable loads up steep hills. Within 25 miles both front and rear differentials on one vehicle had blown up, tossing gear teeth through the axle casings as they exploded. When the other vehicle tried to tow the wrecked one out, its differential also failed. It was an embarrassing way to discover a weakness in the vehicles, the more so when it took a month for spares to reach the jungle and they promptly failed again.

By this time Blashford-Snell was growing anxious. He knew that they had only 100 days to make the crossing if the weather were not to turn against them. Time was passing and very little progress had been made. Close to desperation, he bought a secondhand Land-Rover from a dealer in Panama. It had been in an accident and had a dented roof, but this was unimportant.

Fortunately the Land-Rover performed superbly, running for 70 days in four-wheel drive, and for almost the entire time in first gear. On impossible slopes—and some were nearly vertical—the winch was used to haul the vehicle up. The only problem was that at a certain point

FACT FILE

The most gruelling test of man and machine

Date: 1971/72

Distance: 17,000 miles

Duration: 190 days

the slope would become so steep that petrol stopped reaching the carburettor and the oil warning light came on. The drivers gritted their teeth and pressed on.

If the vehicles were finding the trip a bit of a strain, the same could be said for the participants. It was an endless slog, days of hard work and poor rations interrupted by nights of discomfort amid the ghastly noises of the jungle. Saws whining, axes swinging, the advance party hacked their way forward, creating a path wide enough for the Range-Rovers to drag themselves through. Dozens of bridges were built to cross streams and ravines. Every night Blashford-Snell made contact by radio with his far-flung party,

calling base camp to fly in spares and rations. Tempers frayed as the jungle took its toll. Several members of the party had to be flown out, unfit to continue the nightmare journey.

In front was a team of Gurkhas, tough men from the mountains of Nepal who have served with distinction in the British Army for generations. Behind them were the engineers with the Land-Rover, chain saws, axes, aluminium bridging ladders and tools. Then came a long caravan of men, women and horses, with the Range-Rovers bringing up the rear. The scientific party had scooted off to carry out their work.

Drama turned into tragedy. Captain Jeremy Groves, acting as reconnaissance officer for the

The two Range-Rovers were heavily overloaded at the beginning, contributing to the strain on the differentials. These were broken by the flywheel effect of the special tyres with which the vehicles were fitted to cross swamps. Five differentials failed and had to be replaced by Rover engineers flown out from Britain.

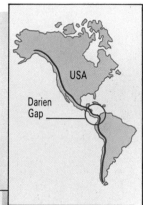

The Pan-American Highway stretches from the Arctic Circle to Tierra del Fuego apart from a 200-mile break where the jungles and swamps of the Darien Gap have prevented the construction of a road or railway.

main party, was being taken by boat with an officer and five Colombian marines to a gunboat which would carry them to the Atrato River. In rough water, their boat went down. Groves was carrying a briefcase full of vital documents and cash, and like the others was dressed in full kit, with boots, a revolver and a machete. Grabbing the briefcase he made for the shore, which he reached exhausted and nearly spent. Struggling to a nearby Shell depot to call for help, he found the Colombian officer, the only other survivor. When bodies of the drowned marines were washed ashore, they had been hideously disfigured by crabs.

By this time, the party was divided and discontented. Several were unhappy with Blashford-Snell's leadership, while those responsible for the Range-Rovers were worried that an expedition intended to provide good publicity would merely emphasize the vehicle's failings. Those unused to the Army command structure found it difficult to respond to Blashford-Snell's

orders when they thought them to be wrong.

But in reality it was too late to quibble. They would have to sink or swim with the leader they had; and it would have needed a man of superhuman qualities and saintly patience to keep this heterogeneous party happy. Blashford-Snell remained openly confident, not wishing others in the party to become aware of his doubts. Wearing a white pith helmet which made him look like a nineteenth-century British colonialist, he became the lightning conductor for the expedition's woes.

Two of the worst sections of the journey lay across Pucuru Heights and the Atrato Swamp. In both cases rafts were used to transport the vehicles around impossible obstacles and, using the edges of rivers as carriageways, the Range-Rovers drove through torrents of water pulling rafts behind them. On more than one occasion the vehicles slipped into the river, but by changing the oil three times, drying plugs and points, and flushing the cylinders out with petrol, the engines

Thousands of trees had to be felled in the Darien Gap by power saws to clear a path for the Range-Rovers. In Major Blashford-Snell's words, "Our prison, for that is what it was, was illuminated by a dull green light, which at times gave an almost translucent appearance to this eerie world. Great trees rose up like pillars reaching for the sun . . . day and night, the jungle resounded to the drip, drip, drip of the condensed humidity and the occasional crash of some giant tree at the end of its life."

were once again coaxed back into action.

Crossing the swamp, Blashford-Snell remembers, was really hideous. The rafts were used but could not move because the surface was covered with a dense mat of logs and water hyacinth. Machetes were useless against this tangle, and the answer was found in lengths of detonating cord, flung out ahead of the rafts and exploded to cut up the beds of weed. Using this method, the expedition could advance in 20-yard stages.

By this time, Blashford-Snell admits, common sense had ceased to exist. "Many had gone down with disease and mental stress. We were all suffering from trench foot, and one man went mad when he saw a Land-Rover being winched up a cliff, he was so sure it was going to crash down and kill somebody. We had got through nine back axles on the Range-Rovers, and a relief party of Colombian soldiers had been ambushed by guerrillas and killed."

All in all, things had not gone too well, but at last the end was in sight. On 24 April the expedition crossed the bridge into Barranquillita with flags flying. The inspector-general of the province met them, declared a public holiday, and the exhausted soldiers made straight for a well-earned beer in the local bars. It had taken them 99 days. By 26 April they were in Bogotá, and from here it was a simple enough drive to Tierra del Fuego, which they reached in the depths of winter, cabling to Blashford-Snell, now back in London: "Mission Accomplished".

The expedition had cost the princely sum of £19,000, not counting the contributions in kind, including rafts and vehicles. It had nearly been, in Blashford-Snell's words, "the biggest failure of all time". But in spite of the problems and the rows, in spite of the fragile vehicles, the snakes, the hornets and the horrors of the jungle and the swamp, they had got through. As far as creating a road across the gap, the expedition was a failure, for no road has yet been built. But it certainly has its place as an astonishing footnote in the annals of humankind's conquest of nature.

The Atrato Swamp would have been impassable without the Avon Rubber company raft, the only one of its kind in the world, which could carry a car. The 40-odd miles of swamp was a green morass of water covered with weed that was sometimes so thick that explosives or chain saws had to be used to clear a channel for the raft. Surveyors lowered a drum of concrete into the swamp; at 1,000 feet it had still not reached the bottom. Mosquitoes, snakes and alligators all added to the trials of crossing the swamp.

Mercedes and Moss: a winning combination

FACT FILE

The fastest time ever set in the Mille Miglia

Mercedes-Benz 300 SLR

Date built: 1954

Engine capacity: 3,000 cc

Power output: 290 horsepower

Maximum speed: 170 mph

1955 Mille Miglia

Distance: 998 miles

Duration: 10 hours, 7 minutes and 48 seconds

Average speed: 98.5 mph

Stirling Moss was born in 1929, the son of a racing driver who had competed in the Indianapolis 500. By the age of 14, Stirling Moss was already an accomplished racing driver, and he joined the Mercedes-Benz racing team in 1954 at the age of 24. He retired in 1961 after 16 Formula 1 wins. Few victories gave him as much satisfaction as the Mille Miglia (opposite).

Motor racing is a modern sport, but has quickly acquired its own legends. Among the most romantic is a race in Italy that was run 24 times between 1927 and 1957: the Mille Miglia. It consisted of a single lap 1,000 miles long, always beginning and ending at Brescia, although the route and distance varied slightly from year to year. On ordinary roads, the fastest cars of the day—and some of the slower ones—took part in an event that combined festival and competition. Hundreds of thousands lined the route, which wound over mountain passes and cut through historic cities such as Florence, Rome and Siena.

The drivers and co-drivers had to be ready and willing to change a wheel or carry out emergency repairs themselves, for their support crews were usually far away. When Juan Fangio came second in 1953, he did so in an Alfa Romeo which was steering on only one front wheel, the other track rod having broken. In 1947 Tazio Nuvolari, in a Ferrari, first lost a mudguard, then his bonnet. Finally, his seat broke loose from the chassis so he threw it away, grabbed a sack of oranges and sat on that instead.

The race went over roads that were rough and unprepared: blind corners, level crossings, manhole covers and other hazards made it exciting and also very dangerous. The only safety precautions, laughably inadequate, were straw bales lining the route in towns and villages.

The cars left from Brescia at one-minute intervals, with the fastest leaving last, which provided plenty of action along the way as the faster cars caught up and overtook the slower ones. All sorts of cars were entered, some of them hardly suitable for racing; in the later years there was even a class for bubble cars. But the real interest was focused on the fast machinery starting last, mostly Alfa Romeos before the war and Ferraris afterward.

Few foreign teams were prepared to make the trek to Italy to take part in so chancy an event, and non-Italian winners were therefore rare. The race was never won outright by a British or a French car, and only three times by German ones. The most celebrated of these wins came in 1955, when a young Englishman, Stirling Moss, drove a Mercedes-Benz to victory. The fame of Moss's win was ensured by an account of the race written by his passenger, Denis Jenkinson,

and published in *Motor Sport*. It instantly became a classic of sports writing, later inspiring a television play, *Mille Miglia*, by Athol Fugard.

Jenkinson and Moss had worked out that the only way a non-Italian could hope to win the race was by applying science. It was impossible to expect a driver to know every corner, brow, curve and level crossing on the course; even the top Italian drivers who had regularly competed in the race knew only a few sections perfectly. The answer lay in creating pace-notes, details of the course written down on paper from which Jenkinson could read as the race progressed. These are now commonplace in rallies, but were then a novel idea.

Moss and Jenkinson made several trips around the course (writing off one car and breaking the engine on another) and eventually acquired 17 pages of notes, which concentrated on places where they might damage the car, such as railway crossings, sudden dips in the road, bad surfaces and tramlines. The difficult corners were classified into three categories: "saucy ones", "dodgy ones" and "very dangerous ones", and where the road went over a brow Jenkinson made careful note as to whether it turned sharply or went straight on.

This meant that if Moss trusted him, he would be able to take blind brows at full speed, knowing that the road went straight on. A system of hand signals was arranged to convey the information, for it was impossible to converse in the car once under way. Jenkinson wrote down his pace-notes on a strip of paper 17 feet long, carried on rollers in a box with a window on the top; a handle turned the rollers.

A new Mercedes-Benz sports racing car, the 300 SLR, was the car that Moss and Jenkinson were to drive. There was a huge entry for the race that year—521 starters, who began leaving at 9 p.m. on the evening of 1 May. The turn of Moss and Jenkinson did not come until 7.22 a.m. the following morning when the silver 300 SLR, number 722, was finally flagged off. Ahead were Fangio, Karl Kling and Hans Herrmann in similar cars; behind were the Italians Eugenio Castellotti, Umberto Maglioli and Piero Taruffi in Ferraris. Denis Jenkinson takes up the story:

"We had the sun shining full in our eyes, which made navigating difficult, but I had written the notes over and over again, and gone

Mercedes and Moss: a winning combination

over the route in my imagination so many times that I almost knew it by heart, and one of the first signals was to take a gentle S-bend through a village at full throttle in fourth gear, and as Moss did this, being quite unable to see the road for more than 100 yards ahead, I settled down to the job, confident that our scientific method of beating the Italians' ability at open-road racing was going to work.

"Barely 10 miles after the start we saw a red speck in front of us and had soon nipped by on a left-hand curve. It was 720, Pinzero, number 721 being a non-starter. By my right hand was a small grab rail and a horn button; the steering was on the left of the cockpit, by the way, and this button not only blew the horn, but also flashed the lights, so that while I played a fanfare on this Moss placed the car for overtaking other competitors. My direction indications I was giving with my left hand, so what with turning the map roller and feeding Moss with sucking sweets there was never a dull moment.

"On some of these long straights our navigation system was paying handsomely, for we could keep at 170 mph over blind brows, even when overtaking slower cars, Moss sure in the knowledge that all he had to do was to concentrate on keeping the car on the road and travelling as fast as possible. This in itself was more than enough, but he was sitting back in his usual relaxed position, making no apparent effort, until some corners were reached when the speed at which he controlled slides, winding the wheel from right to left and back again, showed that his superb reflexes and judgement were on top of their form.

"Cruising at maximum speed, we seemed to spend most of the time between Verona and Vicenza passing Austin-Healeys that could not have been doing much more than 115 mph, and, with flashing lights, horn blowing and a wave of the hand, we went by as though they were touring. Approaching Padova Moss pointed behind and I looked round to see another Ferrari gaining on us rapidly, and with a grimace of disgust at one another we realized it was Castellotti. The Mercedes-Benz was giving all it had, and Moss was driving hard but taking no risks, letting the car slide just so far on the corners and no more. Entering the main street of Padova at 150 mph we braked for the right-angle bend at the end, and suddenly I realized that Moss was beginning to work furiously on the steering wheel, for we were arriving at the corner

The Italians' love of the motor car made the authorities more indulgent toward the idea of races over public roads than those in most countries. Ordinary traffic was banned from the roads, but the only safety measure was a line of straw bales in towns. A fatal accident in the 1957 Mille Miglia convinced people that racing cars and crowds should be separated.

much too fast and it seemed doubtful if we could stop in time.

"I sat fascinated, watching Moss working away to keep control, and I was so intrigued to follow his every action and live every inch of the way with him, that I completely forgot to be scared. With the wheels almost on locking point he kept the car straight to the last possible fraction of a second, making no attempt to get round the corner, for that would have meant a complete spin and then anything could happen. Just when it seemed we must go head-on into the straw bales Moss got the speed low enough to risk letting go the brakes and try taking the corner, and as the front of the car slid over the dry road we went bump! into the bales with our left-hand front corner, bounced off into the middle of the road and, as the car was then pointing in the right direction, Moss selected bottom gear and opened out again.

"All this time Castellotti was right behind us, and as we bounced off the bales he nipped by us, grinning over his shoulder. As we set off after him, I gave Moss a little handclap of appreciation for showing me just how a really great driver acts in a difficult situation.

"More full-throttle running saw us keeping the Ferrari in sight, and then as we approached a small town we saw Castellotti nip past another Ferrari and we realized that we were going to have to follow through the streets, until there was room to pass. It was number 714, Carini, so soon, and this encouraged Moss to run straight round the outside of the Ferrari, on a right-hand curve, confident from my signals that the road would not suddenly turn left.

"Approaching the Ravenna control I took the route-card board from its holder, held it up for Moss to see, to indicate that we had to stop here to receive the official stamp, and then as we braked towards the 'CONTROLLO' banner across the road, and the black and white chequered line on the road itself, amid waving flags and numerous officials, I held my right arm well out of the car to indicate to them which side we wanted the official with the rubber stamp to be. Just beyond the control were a row of pits and there was 723, Castellotti's Ferrari, having some tyre changes, which was not surprising in view of the way he had been driving.

"With a scream of 'Castellotti!' Moss accelerated hard round the next corner and we twisted our way through the streets of Ravenna, nearly collecting an archway in the process, and then out on the fast winding road to Forli. Our time to Ravenna had been well above the old record but Castellotti had got there before us and we had no idea how Taruffi and the others behind us were doing.

"Now Moss continued the pace with renewed vigour and we went through Forli, waving to the garage that salvaged the SLR we crashed in practice, down the fast winding road to Rimini, with another wave to the Alfa Romeo service station that looked after the SLR that broke its engine. I couldn't help thinking that we had certainly left our mark round the course during practice. Ever since leaving the start we had had the rising sun shining in our eyes and now, with the continual effects of sideways 'G' on my body, my poor stomach was beginning to suffer and, together with the heat from the gearbox by my left buttock, the engine fumes, and the nauseating brake-lining smells from the inboard-mounted brakes, it cried 'enough' and what little breakfast I had eaten went overboard, together with my spectacles, for I made the fatal mistake of turning my head sideways at 150 mph with my goggles lowered. Fortunately, I had a spare pair,

and there was no time to worry about a protesting stomach for we were approaching Pesaro, where there was a sharp right-hand corner.

"We were beginning to pass earlier numbers very frequently now, among them some 2-litre Maseratis being driven terribly slowly, a couple of TR2 Triumphs running in convoy, and various saloons, with still numerous signs of the telling pace, a wrecked Giulietta on the right, a 1,100 cc Fiat on the left, a Ferrari coupé almost battered beyond recognition and a Renault that had been rolled up into a ball.

"Through the dusty, dirty Adriatic villages we went and all the time I gave Moss the invaluable hand signals that were taking from him the mental strain of trying to remember the route, though he still will not admit to how much mental strain he suffered convincing himself that I was not making any mistakes in my 170 mph navigation. On one straight, lined with trees, we had marked down a hump in the road as being 'flat-out' only if the road was dry. It was, so I gave the appropriate signal and with 7,500 rpm in fifth gear we took off, for we had made an

Crowds were particularly dense at the start and finish of the race. Jenkinson described the start of the race at Brescia: "As the flag fell we were off with a surge of acceleration and up to peak revs in first, second and third gears, weaving our way through vast crowds lining the sides of the road. Had we not been along this same road three times already in an SLR amid the hurly-burly of morning traffic, I should have been thoroughly frightened, but now, with the roads clear ahead of us, I thought Moss could get down to some uninterrupted motoring."

Mercedes and Moss: a winning combination

error in our estimation of the severity of the hump. For a measurable amount of time the vibromassage that you get sitting in a 300SLR at that speed suddenly ceased, and there was time enough for us to look at each other with raised eyebrows before we landed again. Even had we been in the air for only one second we should have travelled some 200 feet through the air, and I estimated the 'duration of flight' at something more than one second. The road was dead straight and the Mercedes-Benz had a perfect four-point landing and I thankfully praised the driver that he didn't move the steering wheel a fraction of an inch, for that would have been our end."

By the control in Rome, Moss and Jenkinson were told they were in the lead by almost two minutes, leading Taruffi, Herrmann, Kling and Fangio. Their average speed to Pescara had been 118 mph, to Rome 107. Very soon after Rome they saw Kling's Mercedes off the road among the trees, badly wrecked, but it had no effect on Moss. On the next pass a brake grabbed, locked the wheels and the car spun. "There was just time to think what a desolated part of Italy in which to crash, when I realized we had almost stopped in our own length and were sliding gently into the ditch to land with a crunch that dented the tail. 'This is all right,' I thought, 'we can probably push it out of this one' and I was about to start getting out when Moss selected bottom gear and we drove out—lucky indeed!

"The approaches to Florence were almost back-breaking as we bounced and leaped over badly maintained roads and across the tramlines, and my heart went out to the driver of an orange Porsche who was hugging the crown of the steeply cambered road. He must have been shaken as we shot past with the left-hand wheels right down in the gutter. Down a steep hill in second gear we went, into third at peak revs, and I thought 'It's a brave man who can unleash nearly 300 bhp down a hill this steep and then change into a higher gear.' At speeds of up to 120–130 mph we went through the streets of Florence, over the great river bridge, broadside across a square, across more tramlines and into the control point.

"Up into the mountains we screamed, occasionally passing other cars, such as 1900 Alfa Romeos, 1100 Fiats and some small sports cars. Little did we know that we had the race in our pocket, for Taruffi had retired by this time with a broken oil pump and Fangio was stopped in

Florence repairing an injection pipe, but though we had overtaken him on the road we had not seen him as the car had been hidden by mechanics and officials.

"At the top of the Futa Pass there were enormous crowds all waving excitedly and on numerous occasions Moss nearly lost the car completely as we hit patches of melted tar, coated with oil and rubber from all the competitors in front of us, and for nearly a mile he had to ease off, the road was so tricky.

"On we went, up and over the Raticosa Pass, plunging down the other side in a series of slides that to me felt completely uncontrolled but to Moss were obviously intentional. Amid great crowds of people we saw an enormous fat man in the road, leaping up and down in delight; it was the happy body-builder of the Maserati racing department, a good friend of Stirling's, and we waved back to him.

"Down off the mountain we raced, into the broiling heat of the afternoon, into Bologna at close on 150 mph and down to the control point. We were away so quickly that I didn't get the vital news sheet from our depot. Now we had no

Jenkinson (centre) and Moss (right) at the end of the race talking to Daimler-Benz engineer Rudolf Uhlenhaut. It was usual to end a race with face blackened from fumes, road dust and dust from the linings of comparatively primitive brakes. Jenkinson recalled Stirling Moss's comment on their victory: "I'm so happy that we've proved a Britisher can win the Mille Miglia, and that the legend 'he who leads at Rome never leads at Brescia' is untrue—also, I feel we have made up for the two cars we wrote off in practice."

idea of where we lay in the race, or what had happened to our rivals, but we knew we had crossed the mountains in 1 hour 1 min, and were so far ahead of Paolo Marzotto's record that it seemed impossible. Looking up I suddenly realized we were overtaking an aeroplane, and then I knew I was living in the realm of fantasy, and when we caught and passed a second one my brain began to boggle at the sustained speed. Going into Piacenza we passed a 2cv Citroen bowling along merrily, having left Brescia the night before, and then we saw a 2-litre Maserati ahead which shook us up perceptibly, for we thought we had passed them all long ago. It was number 621, Francesco Giardini, and appreciating how fast he must have driven to reach this point before us, we gave him a salutary wave as we roared past.

"The final miles into Brescia were sheer joy, the engine was singing round on full power and after we passed our final direction indication I put my roller-map away and thought 'if it blows to pieces now, we can carry it the rest of the way'. The last corner into the finishing area was taken in a long slide with the power and noise full on

and we crossed the finishing line at well over 100 mph, still not knowing that we had made motor racing history, but happy and contented at having completed the whole race and done our best.

"From the finishing line we drove round to the official garage, where the car had to be parked, and Stirling asked 'Do you think we've won?' to which I replied 'We must wait for Taruffi to arrive, and we don't know when Fangio got in'. At the garage it was finally impressed upon us that Taruffi was out, Fangio was behind us and we had won. We clasped each other in delirious joy, and would have wept, but we were too overcome and still finding it hard to believe we had won."

Their final time for the 998-mile course had been 10 hours, 7 minutes, 48 seconds, an average of 98.5 mph. Fangio, driving alone, was half an hour behind, and then came Maglioli in his Ferrari and Giardini in his Maserati. Moss and Jenkinson had created a record that was never to be beaten, for an accident at the 1957 race, and the realization that fast cars and crowds do not mix, brought the Mille Miglia to an end.

The restored Mercedes 300 SLR which Moss drove to victory, now in the Mercedes-Benz Museum in Stuttgart. The car has a 2,982 cc, 300 hp version of the straight eight-cylinder engine that had proved so successful in Formula 1 racing in 1954, fitted into a space-frame chassis made from small-diameter tubes welded together to make a strong structure. Suspension was by double wishbones and longitudinal torsion bars at the front, and swing axles, also with torsion bars, at the rear. There were large drum brakes, mounted inboard, and a five-speed gearbox set behind the final drive.

Supremacy at Le Mans

When Jaguar first won the Le Mans 24-hour race in 1951, the winning XK120C had never been in a race before. There was no sponsorship, no racing budget, no car transporters—the winning car drove to and from the track—and racing success was incidental to the main business of making cars. Only the Jaguar team leaders (first Stirling Moss and later Mike Hawthorn) were full-time racing drivers. Between 1951 and 1957, in those days of innocence, Jaguar's competition department won a string of successes, including five wins at Le Mans and victories at the other great circuits.

By the early 1980s, however, these triumphs were becoming a distant memory. Jaguar had been absorbed into the British Motor Corporation and allowed to languish. The quality of the cars was poor and it seemed that Jaguar was doomed to join other British motoring names like Riley and MG in the graveyard. Three things saved the company: privatization, John Egan (who arrived as chief executive in 1980 at the nadir of Jaguar's fortunes) and Tom Walkinshaw, a Scottish racing driver and developer of racing cars who believed that Jaguar's XJ-S might win races with him at the wheel.

The new regulations for international touring cars introduced in 1982 provided the opportunity, with a new class for cars that were based on their road-going counterparts, with only small modifications to engines, transmission and braking systems. Walkinshaw persuaded Egan that the XJ-S could be competitive in this new class, but was told that he would have to organize the entire programme from his own headquarters at Kidlington, near Oxford.

With sponsorship from the French oil company Motul, Walkinshaw entered the XJ-S for the 1982 season and did well. The following year he had a close battle with the BMW 635CSi, losing the championship on the very last race. But in 1984 there were no mistakes: the XJ-S won seven of the first nine races, making Walkinshaw champion driver. He also won the Francorchamps 24-hour race, the touring car equivalent of Le Mans. At last it was possible to imagine Jaguar repeating its great wins of the 1950s at the apogee of sports-car racing, Le Mans.

That, however, would never be possible with the XJ-S, for in the intervening years Le Mans had changed dramatically. No longer was it possible to imagine driving a car to the track under its own power, or winning with a slightly modified road car. Today Le Mans is a competition for out-and-out racing cars designed and built in the same way as their Grand Prix cousins. They may bear the names of the great marques—Porsche, Mercedes, Ferrari or Jaguar—but they bear little relation to the showroom products that these companies sell.

In fact, by the time that Walkinshaw began to develop a Le Mans Jaguar, a similar car was running in United States events, developed by a company called Group 44. Its XJR-5, using the Jaguar V-12 engine and driven by Bob Tullius, enjoyed some success in North American events, and it appeared as a Jaguar at Le Mans in both 1984 and 1985. Walkinshaw also entered an XJ-S in those races—though in a different class—so there was the curious sight of two Jaguar teams, neither of them under the full control of the company and hailing from different continents, running in the same races.

Tullius finished 13th at Le Mans in 1985, but by then Jaguar had decided that his car, designed for American regulations, could not be a winner in Europe. They backed Walkinshaw and his company, Tom Walkinshaw Racing (TWR), who in turn hired Tony Southgate, a well-known and successful designer of racing cars, to produce a new car, named the XJR-6.

The car that Southgate produced was based on the same V-12 engine used by Tullius, the engine that powers Jaguar XJ-12 saloon cars and was originally designed by Walter Hassan and Harry Mundy in the late 1960s. At 7 litres capacity, the normally aspirated V-12 with a single overhead camshaft on each bank of cylinders produced 700 bhp at 7,000 rpm. Its drawback was its weight, and to make up for that Southgate used lightweight components to try to get close to the weight limit for the class of 1,874 lb. He used the Du Pont plastic Kevlar, reinforced with carbon fibre, to produce a strong mid-engined car, with the engine itself acting as a load-bearer carrying the rear suspension.

Although a 48-valve engine had been tried initially in one of Tullius's Group 44 cars, Walkinshaw and Southgate chose the 24-valve unit for the XJR-6. The car was completed in the summer of 1985 and made its first appearance in Mosport, Canada, in August. It immediately

FACT FILE

Twenty-four hours at the limit of car and driver

XJR-9
Date built: 1987

Engine: V-12

Engine capacity: 7 litres

Power output: 700 horsepower at 7,000 revolutions per minute

Length: 15 feet 9 inches

Maximum speed: 230 mph

A Jaguar at dawn in the 1989 Le Mans, which proved an interruption to Jaguar's wins, when a Mercedes took the chequered flag. The previous year three of the five Jaguars completed the race (left), with the car of Jan Lammers, Johnny Dumfries and Andy Wallace winning the race—the first Jaguar victory since 1957. Lammers drove 176 of the 394 laps.

Supremacy at Le Mans

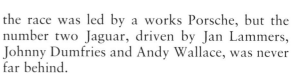

The Le Mans 24 hours can be lost in the pits, even if the pit stop is only for refuelling. In the 1988 race, the battle between the Porsche driven by Stuck, Bell and Ludwig and the leading Jaguar hinged on fuel, since drivers have a fuel allocation and incur penalties for exceeding it. Jaguar's success has been partly due to their superior fuel consumption: Lammers had $4\frac{1}{2}$ gallons left, Stuck less than half a gallon.

showed speed, sweeping past two Porsches, but suffered a wheel bearing failure, probably as a result of the exceptional downforce achieved by Southgate's design.

The first win for the XJR-6 came in the 1986 season, when Eddie Cheever and Derek Warwick drove the car to victory in the Silverstone 1,000 kilometres (621 miles). There was also a win at the Nurburgring, but none of the three cars entered at Le Mans was still running at the finish. A defiant mechanic from the TWR team spray-painted "We'll be back" on the deserted timing box by the pits before the disconsolate team left for home.

Over the winter of 1986/87, TWR made a number of improvements to the car, which began the 1987 season under the designation XJR-8. Several times during 1986, races had been lost due to engines cutting out as a result of fuel starvation, so for 1987 the three fuel tanks were reduced to one, with a better arrangement for picking up the last drops of fuel.

The 1987 season was a triumph, with Jaguar winning the World Sports Car Championship, which they had never contrived to do in their great days in the 1950s. They won eight of the ten races to finish well ahead of five different Porsche teams, but still the ultimate prize eluded them. At Le Mans, three Jaguars started, and one completed the course in fifth place.

For 1988 yet more changes were made to the car, which by now had become the XJR-9. Five Jaguars were entered for the race, but in practice the Porsche 962Cs proved quickest, taking the first three places on the grid with the first Jaguar occupying fourth place. For the first five hours

In motor racing tyre technology is tested to its limits, and sometimes beyond with tragic consequences. At the 1955 Le Mans a burst tyre caused a Mercedes to crash; the driver and 85 spectators were killed. An explosive tyre failure on a Sauber-Mercedes during practice before the 1988 race led to the team's two cars being withdrawn when no satisfactory explanation for the burst could be established.

the race was led by a works Porsche, but the number two Jaguar, driven by Jan Lammers, Johnny Dumfries and Andy Wallace, was never far behind.

The leading Porsche's engine blew up just before half time, and the race developed into a battle between the Lammers Jaguar and a works Porsche driven by Hans Stuck, Derek Bell and Klaus Ludwig. These three Porsche drivers had between them ten Le Mans wins, and Bell was going for his sixth win, and a hat trick.

Klaus Ludwig was unlucky enough to run out of fuel some two and a half hours into the race, losing a couple of laps as he limped back into the pits with the engine popping and banging, and some help from the starter motor. Refilled, the car went perfectly again and began to gain on the Jaguar, which had taken the lead. Though Hans

The winning XJR-9 in the 1988 race. After Ludwig's Porsche had lost time refuelling, he had to turn up the turbo boost to try and catch the Jaguar, running the risk of exceeding his fuel allocation. His only hope lay in a prolonged downpour of rain, which would slow all the cars and enable the Porsche to use less fuel. There was a localized half-hour of rain, but this only delayed the Porsche when it went into a major slide.

Andy Wallace, Johnny Dumfries and Jan Lammers (left to right) celebrate their famous 1988 win. It was a brilliant combination, although some were surprised at the choice of 27-year-old Andy Wallace who had never driven at Le Mans. He proved the wisdom of his selection. During practice he climbed his way up to being the 15th fastest driver.

Stuck drove as hard as he could, Lammers and his co-drivers were always ahead.

At the finish the Jaguar had just 2 minutes and 36 seconds in hand after covering 394 laps, or more than 3,000 miles, in the 24 hours. It was one of the closest finishes seen at Le Mans for many years, and the first time Porsche had been beaten in the race for six years. Porsches came second and third, with another Jaguar fourth, and Porsches occupying the next seven positions. Sir John Egan said: "Le Mans is part of Jaguar's heritage. I felt we had to win again in the 1980s to prove ourselves."

Nor was it to be Jaguar's last win in the race, for in 1990 they scored a one-two, after also coming first and second in the toughest endurance race in the United States, the Daytona 24 Hours. Nobody could now doubt that Jaguar was back.

The Fastest Set of Wheels

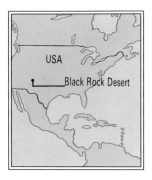

Richard Noble developed an ambition to break speed records when still a child, inspired by the exploits of John Cobb and Malcolm and Donald Campbell.

The appeal that appeared in several motoring magazines in September 1977 was brief and to the point. "Wanted—650 mph car designer" it said. The man who had placed it was Richard Noble, a young businessman with not much experience of fast driving but an ambition to gain the world land speed record. Among those who read the story was John Ackroyd, an engineer who thought he could do the job. It was to take them more than six years to prove they were right.

The car they built was a jet engine with wheels. The days when the land speed record could be won with a conventionally propelled car, using an engine driving wheels through a gearbox and transmission, disappeared in the 1960s. The record for this type of car is still held by Donald Campbell's *Bluebird*, at 429.3 mph. Much faster speeds require either a jet engine or a rocket, but the choice between the two is by no means straightforward.

A rocket car does not need an air intake, so it can be slimmer, proportioned like a pencil. By contrast, a jet car must be much broader to accommodate its air intake, increasing drag and reducing acceleration. In practice, designers of record-breaking cars usually make do with what is readily available and, in the case of Richard Noble's car, *Thrust 2*, that was a Rolls-Royce Avon engine from a Lightning fighter that had come to the end of its life with the RAF.

By the time Noble appealed for help to design a record-breaking car, he had already built a jet-powered car of his own, *Thrust 1*. This was a simple machine, based on racing-car practice and a Rolls-Royce Derwent engine that he had bought from a dismantler for £200. Its chassis he found lying disused in a factory.

Thrust 1 gave Noble some brisk rides before he turned it over at about 140 mph during a run at RAF Fairford in Gloucestershire. It bounced and rolled over three times, but Noble stepped out unhurt. To go any faster, he realized, the project would need to be professionally organized and backed. He started with just £175.

The first thing he needed was another engine. Oddly enough, engines are one of the easiest things for designers of record-breaking cars to find because there are always jet fighters being scrapped and their old engines, despite being in excellent condition, are worth little. Soon Noble acquired an Avon engine from the RAF for £500, and it formed the basis around which the car was designed. The engine was 25 feet long, weighed 3,700 lb, and in its final form produced 16,800 lb of thrust, using full reheat. That is equivalent to nearly 34,000 hp, or approximately the same as 40 Formula 1 Grand Prix cars.

It was during tests on a one-tenth scale model in the British Aerospace wind tunnel that Noble and Ackroyd realized that *Thrust 2*, initially intended merely as a stepping stone toward a record car, might itself be capable of breaking the record. By 1980 the car was making its first tentative runs at RAF Leconfield and at RAF Greenham Common. The car proved a handful, but its performance was impressive. *Thrust 2* accelerated to 100 mph in two and a half seconds, then up to 200 mph in a further three seconds. In order to stop in time, Noble had to release braking parachutes even before he reached the end of the measured mile, so that they would fill with air just in time to stop him before he ran off the end of the runway.

At Greenham Common he set six new British land speed records, including the flying mile at 248.87 mph, without using reheat. Any higher speed would have sent him off the airfield and wrecked the car. These records were achieved without the full bodywork, the car running down the runway like a jet-propelled bedstead.

By 1981 the bodywork was complete and it

The size and shape of Thrust 2 were dictated by the engine, which ran down the centre of the car. The cockpit had to be placed on one side, balanced by an empty cockpit on the other. The frontal view was dominated by the huge inlet for the jet engine, allowing a limited but adequate view forward for the driver.

The Fastest Set of Wheels

The chassis was designed by Ackroyd on the space-frame principle, a series of struts and beams welded together to form a rigid box over which the body panels could be mounted. The space-frame was made by Tube Investments, using the same tubing that is used to make racing bicycles. GKN agreed to make the chassis at the company's expense. The steering was by rack and pinion, Ackroyd finding a heavy-duty system normally used in Leyland buses perfectly suitable.

The state of the track in the desert was the crucial factor in the final attack on the record in 1983. Ackroyd's solid wheels were designed to rise and plane over the surface, rather than plough through it. If it had been too crumbly, the drag would have been enough to wreck the attempt. Solid wheels had several advantages: they could be smaller and lighter, were cheaper, impervious to punctures and blow-outs and did not need a large stock of spares.

was time for a real record attempt. To find a sufficient stretch of flat ground, record breakers have for decades made for the dried beds of America's great salt lakes, usually to Bonneville in Utah. For the record attempt, the conventional wheels with tyres which Noble had used in Britain had been replaced by solid aluminium wheels 30 inches in diameter. This was possible because the surface of the salt flats is not rigid but has some degree of give, making it possible to use a solid wheel.

Nobody had tried this before, so it was a step in the dark; but in reality there was little choice, as no tyre company could be found willing to develop tyres for the speeds envisaged.

Thrust 2 did just enough at Bonneville in 1981 to keep the project alive. A problem of low-speed stability and the tendency of the wheels to cut ruts in the salt limited speeds, but Noble managed a two-way average of 418.118 mph over the flying kilometre. It was a long way short of the 622 mph world record, held by Gary Gabelich, but it was progress. Unfortunately, just as these runs were achieved, the rain began and the salt was soon flooded and unsuitable for record breaking. The team came home.

In June 1982, Noble came close to wrecking the car, when he failed to deploy the parachutes soon enough in a test run at Greenham Common. Realizing he was not going to stop in

time, he put the car into a high speed swerve at 180 mph and slammed on the brakes. It skidded for 4,000 feet across the grass in a series of bounces, throwing dirt into the intake engine, before it finally stopped. A single error had done £22,000 worth of damage, but fortunately the engine had survived unscathed.

The car was rebuilt ready for a second attempt at the record, but it was late in the year before it was ready, and once again the weather intervened. Bonneville was flooded and in desperation the team sought an alternative site. They found Black Rock Desert in New Mexico, and put in some encouraging runs, reaching an average of over 590 mph for the measured mile. But Noble was still 30 mph short of the world record. There seemed to be insufficient power, the track was crumbly and several team members had to get home. The 1982 attempt was abandoned.

Noble knew that he had just one more chance; the sponsors who had financed the record attempt had been patient, but they could not wait for ever. During the winter of 1982/83, Rolls-Royce adjusted the Avon engine to produce more power, while Ackroyd altered the underside of the car, trying to smooth out the airflow. In September 1983, they were back at Black Rock ready for what everybody recognized would be their last attempt on the record.

The car performed well, but a series of

Tie-down tests at Reno airport in Nevada to check minor but vital modifications were made prior to the successful runs in September 1983. The tests in England had relied on the brakes to hold the car on full thrust from the engine until the reheat flame lit. The procedure in the desert was to measure speed over a flying kilometre or mile, in which Thrust 2 would take progressively longer run-ins to build up speed in steps. The car was always driven flat out for maximum acceleration. This used up 10 gallons of kerosene per mile. The smaller amount of fuel required by a jet engine compared with an even thirstier rocket was a major factor in the choice of engine. The amount of fuel required by a rocket weighs a car down at the start and makes it dangerously lively by the end of the run, at maximum speed.

niggling problems prevented Noble from beating the record. The engine refused to produce full power or the reheat failed to come on. They were close, but not quite there. They tried finding different tracks across the salt, even changing the 6-inch wide wheels for 4-inch ones, but that made things worse rather than better.

Finally, on 4 October, Noble managed a run in one direction of 624 mph, fractionally over the record, and turned for the return run. To gain a record, the speed is averaged over two runs in different directions and must exceed the previous record by 1 percent so the second run would need to be faster if Gabelich's 622.407 mph was to be beaten. On the return run, *Thrust 2* did everything that was expected of it, achieving 642.971 mph and peaking at a speed of just over 650 mph, its design speed. The two-way average was 633.468 mph—a new world record.

Across Africa on an Air Cushion

Late in 1969 one of the most unusual expeditions ever launched set out across the African continent. Its objective was to complete a journey of 5,000 miles through ten countries in less than three months, using a hovercraft to travel along the great highways of Africa, its rivers. It was one of the largest expeditions ever mounted in Africa, and the first time an air-cushioned vehicle had ever travelled on its own power south of the Sahara. The regions through which it went were among the most unexplored and undeveloped in the world, with some of the highest concentrations of disease. The purpose was to study the geography and wildlife, and to investigate how effective the hovercraft would be as a means of transport in a region with few roads.

The leader of the expedition was David Smithers, a journalist, publisher and explorer who knew Africa well and had, in 1968, led an expedition by hovercraft from Manaus on the Amazon through the Orinoco in Venezuela and finally into the Caribbean. The success of that expedition had convinced Smithers and his backers, the International Publishing Corporation and the Royal Geographical Society, that the hovercraft could accomplish things beyond any other form of transport.

The hovercraft had been invented in Britain in the early 1950s by an electronics engineer, Christopher Cockerell. His first experiments involved an old vacuum cleaner and a coffee tin, but he moved quickly to the first working model, a flying saucerlike craft that drew air in with a fan, and blew it out in the form of an annular ring around the periphery of the craft. He tried it over water, and it worked. With official support, patents were taken out and a full-scale hovercraft was built by Saunders-Roe. This was SR.N1, launched in May 1959, which demonstrated the feasibility of the principle. Later that summer it crossed the English Channel. It proved as effective over land as over water, making it the first truly amphibious vehicle.

By the time Smithers came to organize his expeditions, a much bigger and more practical hovercraft was available. The SR.N6, or Winchester class, was designed as a passenger ferry, able to carry 38 people at maximum speeds of 52 knots. The actual hovercraft, No. 018, was already four years old and had been used as a ferry and for charter work. To complete the journey it would have to travel through sea, swamp, sand, bush, rice fields, reeds, rapids and lakes, carrying at least 2 tons more than it was designed for. A total of 30 scientists, technicians, writers, cameramen and crew took part in the expedition, although not all of them were present all the time.

The journey began at Dakar in Senegal with a short sea voyage up the coast to St Louis, then on to the Senegal River. Shell had provided fuel dumps at 250-mile intervals along the route, mostly in fair-sized towns, and for the first section of the journey to Timbuktu in Mali, most nights were spent in comfortable lodgings.

On the very first day, after leaving the town of Richard Toll in Senegal, the hovercraft proved its value. They had decided to explore some swamps impassable to normal vehicles and travelled all day through empty country with not a soul in sight, disturbing enormous flocks of flamingos and pelicans, until the swamps dwindled and disappeared. Soon they were lost. Whichever way they turned, the water petered out and they could find no landmarks. Finally the pilot, Peter Ayles, opted to take to the bush. Ploughing majestically through grass taller than a man's height, the SR.N6 finally found its way back to the swamp and then to open water.

This side trip cost more fuel than planned, so an unscheduled stop had to be made at Kaedi, on the Mauritanian side of the Senegal River. At this small village the expedition was able to purchase 77 gallons of cooking kerosene—three months' supply for the village—and carry it back to the hovercraft in a selection of tin cans and other vessels. The Gnome engine ran happily enough on this fuel, producing a cloud of black smoke.

At Kayes in Mali, the first of the planned portages was carried out. One object of the expedition was to find out how quickly the hovercraft could be dismantled, loaded on to railway wagons, and then reassembled. The first problem at Kayes was getting the hovercraft out of the river and up 200 feet of steep bank on to the railway car. Ayles unloaded everything from the vehicle, took it back across the river, gave it full throttle and made a run for the bank.

"Everyone waited for the dull, rending crunch that would end our safari," Smithers wrote later. "Instead, completely obscured by clouds of

FACT FILE

The longest hovercraft journey

Built: 1968

Length: 48 feet 5 inches

Width: 23 feet

Power output: 900 horsepower

Weight: 10 tons

spray and dust, the giant craft roared up the bank and settled gently on its skirts as though it were an everyday affair." Next the engineers had to disassemble the craft, a job that took six men virtually the whole day in broiling heat. Finally it was in pieces small enough to attach to the railway flat-car with twists of rusty wire, all that the local agent for the railway could provide.

At Bamako the railway reached the Niger River and the hovercraft was reassembled. Here the expedition struck north toward the Sahara along the Niger, a river so broad that at times it seemed like a sea, until they reached Timbuktu, the golden city where the sand and water meet. Between there and Gao the hovercraft startled

The SR.N6 crosses the Benue River at Garoua in Cameroon. The captain of Garoua's only ferry was mesmerized by the hovercraft and crashed his boat, which sank. Traffic built up (above) and included the lorries ordered to take SR.N6 overland to the Logone River at Yagoua. David Smithers (left) in Kinshasa.

Across Africa on an Air Cushion

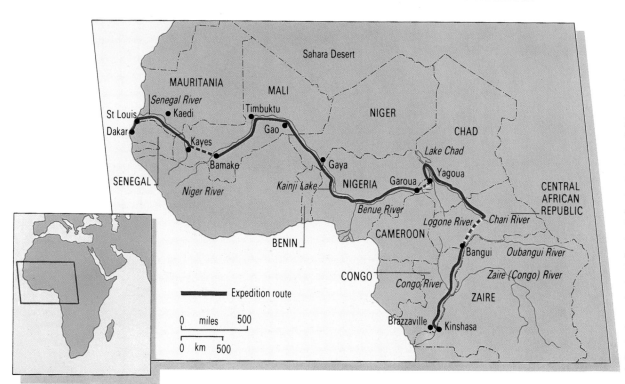

The route followed rivers wherever possible; the sections overland caused problems, but SR.N6 exerted so little pressure on hover that it could cross fields of crops without damaging them. For most of the journey, the expedition was overwhelmed by kindness; they were given messhui—a sheep roasted on spits—on 12 successive nights. President Bokasa of the Central African Republic and President Mobutu of Zaire were given a demonstration of SR.N6.

The hovercraft drawn up on the north bank of the Niger River, west of Timbuktu, during a stop for scientists to make observations. The team was made up of scientists of many disciplines—hydrology, parasitology, entomology, zoology and anthropology.

herds of hippo in the river, scattering them in panic. Although several submerged, fortunately none surfaced again directly beneath the hovercraft's skirts, and they all got clean away.

At the border between Mali and Niger lay the Labezanga rapids, hitherto uncrossed and with a fearful reputation. People asked with incredulity: "Are you really going to cross them?" to which the members of the expedition gave the answer "Yes, of course," as confidently as they could. In the event, it was all a bit of an anticlimax. There were one or two eddies and swirls, and a drop of a few feet, but in the hovercraft it was scarcely noticeable.

Near Gaya, a low bridge which did not appear on the maps blocked the river. To get around it the hovercraft had to cross rice paddies and sorghum fields, while Smithers and co-pilot Don Paterson held ropes to steady it. Finally, after edging under power cables, crossing a road and sliding down a bank, the hovercraft was back in the river the other side of the bridge. At Kainji Lake in Nigeria, a worse problem arose. Here there were supposed to be locks to drop vessels 100 feet from the top of a dam, but rats had eaten the cable insulation and the lock gates would not open. A 2-mile trail through the bush, followed by a descent into the river aided by some bulldozers manned by Canadian engineers, bypassed that obstacle.

After exploring Lake Chad, which involved a portage over the mountains by lorry, the expedition set off south again. Another portage was needed, again by lorry, to get from the Chari River to Bangui on the headwaters of the Congo. By now the two British Hovercraft Corporation engineers, assisted by the pilot and co-pilot and other obliging members of the expedition, were getting quite skilful at taking the SR.N6 apart and putting it together again.

Passing through the Congo, the expedition crossed the equator and celebrated with champagne. But soon disaster struck. Travelling along a channel between Congo-Brazzaville and an island the propeller hit an overhanging tree and one blade was broken. They began to drift as the engineers took a hacksaw to the other blades to

A bridge built over the Niger River by the French at Gaya on the border of Niger and Benin was built so low that few craft could pass under it. The plan was to use a gentle slope on the Benin bank of the river, but the prospect of war between the two countries made that impossible. A steep bank on the Niger side had to be negotiated instead, and a crop of 12-foot-high sorghum then had to be crossed before the river was rejoined.

re-balance the propeller. Going ashore things got awkward, for Congo-Kinshasa (Zaire) was in a state of near-war with Congo-Brazzaville.

Sensing danger, Smithers managed to get the expedition back on board and set off, although it was by now quite dark. By 11 p. m. they reached the confluence of the Congo and the Oubangui rivers and anchored, but then it became clear that the hovercraft had taken on a lot of water. They had to start the engines again and find somewhere safer to moor. Eventually, at 4. 30 a. m., they found a reed bed and hovered on to it, before collapsing exhausted.

From here to Kinshasa was relatively easy going, although the river was clogged with water hyacinth which would have prevented any other form of transport moving. The expedition entered Kinshasa accompanied by a flotilla of powerboats, sirens hooting, crowds cheering, flags waving. A Congolese guard of honour scattered in alarm as the hovercraft mounted the concrete slipway of the Lever plantation in a cloud of spray. The journey was over. It had taken 83 days, and provided the scientists aboard with unique opportunities for studying specimens. It had also demonstrated clearly how the hovercraft could go to places beyond the ken of any other vehicle. It had completed the last 300 miles with half a propeller, and throughout the expedition experienced no mechanical failures except for one ignition plug.

David Smithers hoped the success of the expedition would lead to hovercraft like the

SR.N6 being used in many ways in developing countries. The British government of the day was, however, reluctant to help and the African governments were too poor and too disorganized to help themselves. "The hovercraft could have done so many things," he says now, "it could have been a ferry, a bus service, an ambulance, or a flying doctor for many areas that desperately needed it." Even the successful SR.N6 that completed the trip did not survive long. The Ministry of Defence took it to the Ivory Coast for a demonstration, and wrecked it. Christopher Cockerell's invention had proved itself, but nobody seemed to care.

Transport over mountain watersheds on three occasions required the dismantling of the hovercraft, enabling it to be loaded on to railway wagons or lorries. Convicted murderers were loaned by the local prison governor to help the loading at Yagoua, Cameroon.

CHAPTER THREE

OVERLAND BY RAIL

The Duke of Wellington had no doubt that railways were a mixed blessing. They would, he said, "enable the lower orders to go uselessly wandering about the country". How right he was. The nineteenth century has often been depicted as an age when the working class was oppressed. It is true that factory labour was no picnic, but the same steam engines that made it possible also provided a means of escape. No longer need people be tied to the same hearth from birth to burial.

The duke was present at the opening of the first great railway, between Liverpool and Manchester. Its success, much greater than expected, led to a tremendous and uncontrolled boom in railway building. Lines were constructed everywhere and thousands of locomotives built to pull the trains. Many of them were memorable machines. *Rocket*, still the most famous of engines, pulled the carriages in 1829 to open the Liverpool to Manchester line. The "American" 4-4-0 type of engine, the most numerous ever built, helped develop the United States and played a major part in the Civil War. The underground railway civilized London—for a while—and then spread to a host of other cities. The Orient Express brought luxury and style to continental travel.

In the twentieth century the railways have faced stiffer competition, from cars and aircraft. In the 1930s this competition was met by designing fast and comfortable trains which attempted to establish a new image. The American and Canadian expresses and, in Britain, the trains pulled by the likes of *Mallard*, the fastest-ever steam locomotive, kept up for a while a pride and confidence in the future of railways.

A new round of the battle began with the Japanese Shinkansen and the French high-speed train, the TGV. At a time when many countries have come to accept the need to contain pollution from cars, the TGV is an example of what can be done with modern technology to provide faster journey times between city centres than cars or aircraft can match. If the TGV really represents the future of the train, the revolution begun by *Rocket* more than 160 years ago still has some way to go.

Trial by Steam

Seldom has the human imagination been so rapidly enlarged as in the month of October 1829, when the directors of the Liverpool & Manchester Railway held a public contest to determine what form of locomotion was best suited to their new line. People to whom 8 mph in a stagecoach had been a dizzying experience were overnight introduced to speeds three times as great.

The event responsible for this change was the Rainhill Trials, a spectacle that combined the excitements of science fiction with those of the race track. The six competitors were given their own colours and listed on a race card, grandstands were erected for the public to view the events, a prize was offered to the winner, and there were even allegations of "nobbling" from the unsuccessful.

Few had ever seen a locomotive before, or had any conception of the technical merits of the contestants. At the time, steam engines were regarded as plodding heavyweights, barely capable of outpacing a man. The astonishment of the crowd when the locomotive *Novelty* sped by at 28 mph was captured by the correspondent of the *Liverpool Mercury*: "It actually made one giddy to look at it," he wrote, "and filled thousands with lively fears for the safety of the individuals who were on it, and who seemed not to run along the earth, but to fly, as it were, on the 'wings of the wind'. It is a most sublime sight; a sight, indeed, which the individuals who beheld it will not soon forget."

Novelty, built in just seven weeks by the London engineers John Braithwaite and John Ericsson and named after a theatre, was the popular favourite. Lightly built and swift, it seemed to the eyes of the time the most beautiful of all the entries. Much less strongly favoured was the ultimate winner, George and Robert Stephenson's *Rocket*, the only entry which met all the demands of the trials successfully and was still running soundly at the end.

Two of the entries now sound like a joke. *Cyclopede*, entered by Thomas Brandreth of Liverpool, was powered by two horses walking on an endless platform like the tracks of a tank, running around gear wheels on the vehicle's axles which transmitted the drive. *Cyclopede* could manage 6 mph with its horses at full stretch, too slow to meet the requirements of the

trials, so it was not taken seriously by the judges. An even less likely competitor was the *Manumotive*, a manually propelled vehicle entered by a Mr Winans, which put in a brief appearance but stood no chance of meeting the requirements of covering 70 miles at a minimum of 10 mph and pulling a load three times the engine's weight.

The triumphant *Rocket* was largely the work of Robert Stephenson, son of the engineer who had laid out the Liverpool to Manchester line, George Stephenson. Between them, the Stephensons had both genius and long experience, for George had built his first locomotive at Killingworth colliery in Northumberland in 1814. It demonstrated that the weight of the engine could provide sufficient adhesion between iron wheels and iron rails to pull substantial loads, as long as the gradients of the track were not excessive. Later, in 1825, Stephenson had provided locomotives for the world's first railway to operate a scheduled passenger service, between Stockton and Darlington. The first of these, *Locomotion*, weighed 8 tons and could pull a train weighing 50 tons at 5 mph along a level track.

The Liverpool & Manchester Railway was aiming at much greater speeds, and as the line neared completion the directors seem finally to have asked themselves how they could be achieved. Would locomotives suffice, or should the trains be pulled by cables operated by stationary steam engines located at 21 points along the line? The trials were an opportunity for the locomotive engineers to show that they could do the job. The prize was £500, over and above the cost of purchasing the winner, for "a Locomotive Engine which shall be a decided improvement on any hitherto constructed," as Henry Booth wrote in an advertisement in the *Liverpool Mercury* calling for entries.

It was fortunate that Booth himself was not among the judges, or the cries of malpractice from the defeated would have been louder. It was Booth who seems to have been responsible for one of the novelties in the design of *Rocket*—the multi-tube boiler which enabled it to maintain steam pressure so well. This provided a large heating surface of 134 square feet, enabling *Rocket* to raise steam in around 40 minutes and to maintain it even when running at full power. Neither *Novelty* nor Timothy Hackworth's *Sans Pareil*, its main rivals, had such an efficient

FACT FILE

Prototype for the world's first class of successful passenger locomotive

Date built: 1829

Weight: 4 tons 3 cwt

Driving wheel diameter: 4 feet 8½ inches

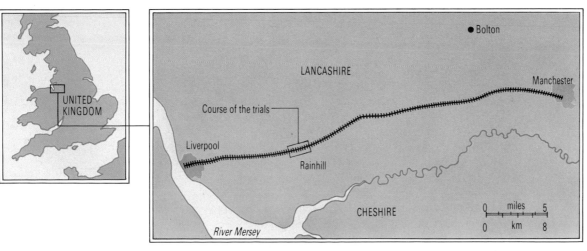

Rocket *passes a* **grandstand** *at the Rainhill Trials, followed by Hackworth's Sans Pareil and Braithwaite's and Ericsson's Novelty. Begun on 6 October 1829, the trials were watched by 10,000 to 15,000 people who lined the 1½ miles of track along which the competition was held.*

Trial by Steam

boiler. George Stephenson, a dour, ungenerous man, never gave Booth credit for suggesting this boiler design, which had been invented in France by Marc Seguin.

The Stephensons were able to run their engine at Killingworth before the trials, to sort out any small problems. It was then dismantled, taken by road to Carlisle and then by barge to Bowness on the Solway Firth, and finally by steamer to Liverpool, where it arrived on 18 September.

The rules stipulated that the engines were to be fuelled and watered and attached to trains three times their own weight. They were then to make a trip of 32½ miles by going to and fro along the track ten times, the distance chosen because it was equivalent to that between Manchester and Liverpool. The engines could then be refuelled before repeating the same task, the whole 65 miles—or 70 if the starting and stopping distances are included—to be completed at an average of more than 10 mph. On Thursday 8 October, *Rocket* duly completed this test, averaging 16 mph, and at one point reaching 29 mph. Despite several attempts and some good performances, neither *Novelty* nor *Sans Pareil* was able to match it. Both engines broke down more than once, and neither managed to complete the course.

There could be no doubt who had won the trials, and George and Robert Stephenson were immediately given orders for more locomotives. The first of these, *Meteor*, *Comet*, *Dart* and *Arrow*, were to be delivered within three months. During 1830 a series of excursions was run along the line to reassure the public that it was indeed possible to travel at 30 mph without giddiness or disturbances of vision while watching the scenery go by. The line was formally opened on 15 September, when eight locomotives, including *Rocket*, were made ready to carry 772 people from Liverpool to Manchester.

The first train, pulled by the locomotive *Northumbrian* and with George Stephenson driving, carried the prime minister, the Duke of Wellington, and members of his government. The high spirits of the morning were to be overshadowed by a tragedy: William Huskisson, MP for a Liverpool constituency, fell in front of *Rocket* which ran over his left leg. By early evening he was dead. As Frances Kemble, a young girl travelling on one of the trains, wrote: "The contrast between our departure from Liverpool and our arrival at Manchester was one of the most striking things I ever witnessed."

Rocket's driving wheels *were 4 feet 8½ inches in diameter to help the locomotive attain the speeds looked for by the judges. These large wheels were driven directly through cranks by two cylinders inclined at an angle of about 35 degrees and mounted high on the boiler. This caused an awkward swaying action at speed, compelling the driver to hold on to anything at hand to stay on his feet. The position of the cylinders was later altered. Exhaust steam from the cylinders was blown through the funnel which was as tall as possible to create a good draught through the firebox.*

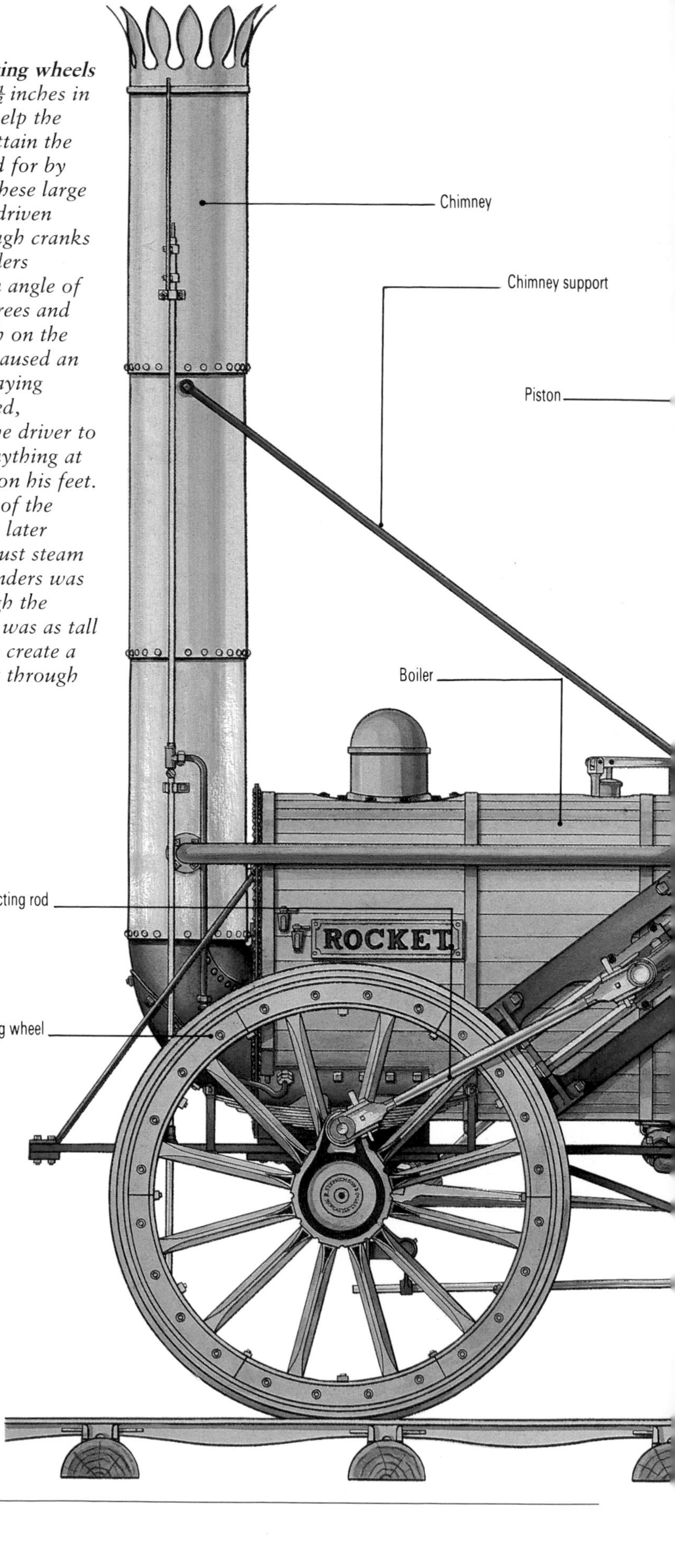

Chimney

Chimney support

Piston

Boiler

Connecting rod

Driving wheel

ROCKET

Rocket's cylinders were 8 inches in diameter, and the piston had a stroke of 17 inches. Their location high up beside the firebox was unusual; it was not long before nearly all locomotives had their cylinders mounted at the front close to the smokebox. But it was the boiler that gave the engine its revolutionary significance. The heating surface of the water was increased by replacing the usual 2 to 3 large tubes by 25 smaller copper tubes, which can be seen behind the wheel.

The Stephenson family by an anonymous artist, with George Stephenson (1781–1848) showing the miner's safety lamp he invented to his son Robert (1803–59). The mine to the rear may be Killingworth where George Stephenson completed his first engine Blucher in 1814. Father and son had equally illustrious careers, primarily as builders of railways, although a locomotive building company, Robert Stephenson & Co., achieved renown.

Cylinder

Control levers

Firebox

Footplate

Water barrel

Civil War Combatant

FACT FILE

The locomotive used in the Chattanooga railroad expedition

Built: 1855

Driving wheel diameter: 5 feet

Weight: 22½ tons

The American Civil War was the first great conflict in which the railways played an important part. On both sides, many of the locomotives used were 4-4-0-type engines, among the most successful wheel configurations ever built. Easily the most famous was the *General*, completed by Rogers Locomotive Works in Paterson, New Jersey, in December 1855. In 1862, *General* was involved in one of the most spectacular incidents of the war, when it was taken over by a group of Union soldiers in an operation behind Confederate lines which led to a hectic chase along the track.

The object of the raid was to disrupt Confederate communications, particularly along the 135 miles of track linking Atlanta to Chattanooga. A plan was devised to destroy bridges on the track by stealing a train, driving it along the track and setting light to the wooden trestle bridges. Unable to pursue the raiders because of the damaged bridges, the Confederates would also be prevented from reinforcing their lines.

It was an ingenious plan, made possible by the ease with which agents could be infiltrated behind enemy lines. Twenty-two men under Captain James Andrews were detached from the Union army and, dressed in civilian clothes, they slipped through the lines at night.

They split into several groups, arranging to meet at the town of Marietta. Among their number were several who had experience as train drivers. They slept the night at Marietta, arranging to catch the first northbound train in the morning, due in at daybreak. They bought tickets separately, so as not to arouse suspicion, and got on to the crowded train when it drew in. The plan was to seize the train when it reached Big Shanty, 8 miles from Marietta, where it stopped to allow the passengers to get off for breakfast, a normal practice in those days.

The train was full, and the line guarded along its length by armed men. Could it be seized by a mere 20 men (two had overslept and missed the train) and make its escape before anybody noticed? As one of the party, William Pittenger, wrote later with pardonable exaggeration: "The annals of history record few enterprises more bold and novel than that witnessed by the rising sun of Saturday morning, 12 April 1862."

When the train stopped, the driver, fireman, guard and most of the passengers got off. The raiders moved smoothly into action. All but three cars were uncoupled, four of the men got aboard *General*, and the rest of the party, who had been keeping guard, jumped into an open boxcar. At the order, the steam valve was opened and they were off. As the people on the platform gasped and leaped for their muskets, *General* clattered off into the distance.

It had all gone very smoothly, but soon there was a setback. *General*'s driver, knowing that the train was about to stop for breakfast, had allowed the fire to run down, and the raiders quickly ran out of steam. They stopped, threw more wood into the firebox and in three minutes they were away again. It was unfortunate that the track was a single one, for it meant that the raiders would have to adhere to the timetable to pass trains coming the other way in loops.

In addition, they would have to cut the telegraph wire, which ran along the track, to prevent signals being passed ahead of them. There was no telegraph at Big Shanty, but they did not know how quickly their pursuers might reach one, so they stopped again to cut the wire. At the same time, others tried to wrench up the line behind their train, although it was difficult because they did not have the right tools.

At the first station reached, Cass, *General* took on wood and water. The man who supplied them was told by Andrews that the train was a special, carrying ammunition, and that the regular train was coming on behind. So persuasive was his manner that he was believed. The first major station, at Kingston, was 32 miles from Big Shanty and was reached in two hours.

Here the raiders were given the unwelcome instruction to wait for the local freight, which was coming the other way and running behind time. When it came it carried a red flag, indicating that another was behind it—and when that finally arrived it, too, gave notice that yet another train must come through before *General* could advance. For more than an hour the raiders were forced to sit silent in their train.

Meanwhile the dispossessed driver of *General*, Captain William Fuller, had not been inactive. First he had run after it on foot with two other railway employees because he had the idea that the train had probably been seized by escaped convicts who would drive it only a mile or so before abandoning it. A few miles out of

James J. Andrews was from Kentucky, though born in the "panhandle" of western Virginia, and had worked as a "spy and secret agent" for the Union before the expedition. He was described by a high-ranking officer as "true as steel, and very smart". The locomotive chase between General *and* Texas *was to inspire many artists' impressions (opposite).*

Civil War Combatant

Big Shanty he saw the broken telegraph line and realized the matter was more serious.

But at that moment he also saw a party of workmen with a hand car, which he immediately mobilized for the chase. In a hand car, he reasoned, he might easily manage 7 to 8 mph, half the speed of the train, and stand some chance of catching it at Kingston. They set off as fast as they could, and almost immediately came off the track where it had been damaged, landing in a ditch. They were uninjured, put the car back on the track and continued the pursuit.

Fuller knew he had just one chance. The only locomotive on the track this side of Kingston belonged to an iron furnace, located up a private track 5 miles long. If it happened to be near the main line, he would take it over and use it to pursue *General*. As they approached the branch line, the exhausted pursuers, who by now had covered 19 miles, saw to their joy that the engine, *Yonah*, was on the main track, aimed for Kingston and already steamed up. Fuller and his men leaped aboard and set off in pursuit. They reach Kingston just 20 minutes after *General* had finally managed to leave, and here Fuller transferred to one of the waiting freight trains.

The crew of *General* continued to put obstacles in the way of their pursuers, throwing out rail ties and tearing up track, and eventually Fuller was forced to stop by a long break in the line. Once again he continued the pursuit on foot, and within a mile met a freight train coming toward him. This was a train that had been held up to allow *General* past. Fuller explained the situation and quickly resumed the pursuit in the freight train, whose locomotive was another 4-4-0, *Texas*. His luck was holding, while Andrews's was running out. Fuller left behind the freight cars at the next station and went off full tilt in *Texas*.

By now he was hard on the heels of *General*, whose crew could hardly believe it when they heard a train whistle behind them. Frantically they threw more ties on to the track, hoping to reach a bridge and set it on fire before Fuller could catch them. Both trains were flat out, doing 60 mph or more, and *General* attempted to slow its pursuers by detaching cars and allowing them to roll back. Each time Fuller slowed down in time, coupled on to the car, and continued.

The 15 miles to the town of Ringgold were covered in the quickest time Captain Fuller ever managed in 22 years as a driver. Soon he was within half a mile of the raiders, who in

Near Big Shanty, where the raiders took over the train, was a Confederate training camp. Captain Fuller, in charge of the train until it was seized, at first thought that it had been taken by deserters who had been reported as absconding from the nearby camp.

desperation set their only remaining freight car on fire, with the idea of releasing it on the next bridge. Fuller and his men quietly came up to it and pushed it off the bridge. By now *General* was almost out of fuel. Everything combustible aboard the train had been crammed into the fire, and there was nothing left to burn.

Reluctantly, Andrews and his party were forced to abandon the train and take to the woods. As they did so, they put the train into reverse, hoping to ram the pursuers—but they left the brake on the tender, and *General* did not

The Western & Atlantic Railroad *4-4-0 Texas was the best engine that Captain Fuller commandeered for the chase. Built by Danforth, Cook & Co. of Schenectady, New York, in 1856, it is now preserved in the Cyclorama Building at Grant Park in Atlanta, Georgia.*

General *was built in 1855 by the Rogers Locomotive Works in Paterson, New Jersey, for the Western & Atlantic Railroad. Later in the Civil War, General was the last W & A engine to leave Atlanta when it was evacuated by Hood's army.*

Survivors of the Union raiders in front of the memorial statue at Chattanooga cemetery. Front from left to right: John Porter, William Knight, Jacob Parrot, ?, Daniel Dorsey; rear: William Bensinger, ?. Of the 22 men, 8 were executed, including Andrews, 8 escaped and the remaining 6 were later paroled. General itself is preserved at Union station, Chattanooga.

have enough steam left to move. The raiders, who were unarmed, were pursued by Confederate forces and within a few days all had been rounded up.

There was a military trial, and eight of the party, including Andrews, were sentenced to death and executed. The rest were imprisoned, but eight contrived to escape in October 1862 from prison in Atlanta, Georgia. The remaining six were paroled the following year. The survivors erected a monument to their fallen comrades in the National Cemetery at Chattanooga; on the top is placed a small model of *General*.

Both *General* and *Texas* (or what is purported to be them) still survive. *General* is kept in the Union station at Chattanooga, and occasionally run, though not on wood. Oil is used, and the fuel tank is concealed under a huge pile of fake wood. *Texas* is kept in Grant Park at Atlanta. Many other examples of this remarkable American locomotive also survive in museums across the United States, but none is as famous as these two, which played their part in one of the strangest stories of any war.

Locomotives under London

FACT FILE

The pioneer
underground steam
railway

Date opened:
January 1863

Length: 3¾ miles

Traction: Steam

By the mid-nineteenth century, London's streets had become almost impassable. While transport outside the capital was being transformed by the railways, within the city there was congestion and squalor. A man could travel swiftly from Windsor or Oxford to a London terminus, but it then took him as long again to reach his office in the City.

Transfers between the great stations established by the rival railway companies were inconvenient, dirty and slow. The roads were clogged, the pavements filthy, public transport by horse-drawn omnibus was unreliable, and the cabmen were notorious for insolence and extortion. One physician declared with a straight face that a woman he knew had suffered a miscarriage "by incautiously venturing over the broken and rugged country that lies between Cavendish and Portman squares". The immemorial cry went up: "Something must be done!" But what?

Sir Charles Pearson, solicitor to the City of London, had few doubts. The railways, he declared, must be allowed to bring their lines right into the centre of the city, rather than decanting passengers at what was then the perimeter. He wanted a grand terminus at Farringdon Street, linked to all the railway lines to the north, northeast and northwest. This plan was never realized, but by the early 1850s two different schemes had been hatched: for a City Terminus Railway linking King's Cross to Farringdon Street and a North Metropolitan Railway running from King's Cross to Edgware Road, near Paddington.

In 1854 the two rival schemes were merged, and the House of Commons approved a railway to run underground over the whole route. It would link Paddington in the west to King's Cross and then go on to terminate at Farringdon Street in the City. It would be the world's first underground railway.

It was another six years before ground was broken. The railway companies were of several minds, the City was recalcitrant, private investors doubtful, and the Crimean War an inconvenient distraction. Finally, and largely thanks to the enthusiasm of the indomitable Pearson, work began at the end of January 1860.

The work of digging was done by teams of navvies who worked all night by the light of blazing flares. The line they created was covered by an elliptical brick arch, with a span of 28 feet 6 inches, over vertical walls three bricks thick and rising 11 feet. The load-bearing roof was made of cast-iron girders between 1 foot 6 inches and 2 feet 6 inches deep, spaced 6 to 8 feet apart. Where possible, the line was left open to the sky, for it was clear that ventilation was going to be a major difficulty.

In promoting the railway, the engineers had cheerily dismissed the problems of providing clean motive power as easily solved. Locomotives could be built that would emit no noxious smoke or steam, they declared, although no such design then existed. Early in 1860 Robert Stephenson was given a contract to build a smokeless locomotive and by October 1861 had produced a machine that seemed to fit the bill. The engine had a small firebox and a large mass of firebricks stowed away in a chamber in the boiler barrel.

The principle was to run at full blast in open sections of the track, generating enough heat to bring the bricks to white heat, so that they would supply enough steam to keep the trains moving in the closed sections. To reduce emissions still further, steam was condensed through a cold water tank under the boiler. The principle sounded fine, but the reality was rather different.

When tested in 1861 over a stretch of the Great Western's line near Paddington, the "Ghost", as it was known, performed poorly. It took three hours to raise steam, and once in motion steam pressure fell quickly before it came to an ignominious stop. The Ghost was quickly abandoned, and an agreement was reached that the service would open using locomotives of the GWR fitted with condensing devices to reduce the steam somewhat. With the death of the Ghost went the hope that the railway could be the pure, clean and comfortable experience its promoters had promised.

On 2 April 1862 the tunnels were virtually complete when the Fleet River took a hand. Along the retaining wall of the terminus at Farringdon it ran in a poorly built sewer pipe, 10 feet in diameter. This suddenly burst, filling the tunnel with sewage 10 feet deep as far back as King's Cross. The opening of the railway had to be postponed until January 1863, when a huge celebration was planned.

Seven hundred people were invited to travel

Baker Street station (above and left) was illuminated by daylight as well as gas lighting. This was made possible by the shallow depth of the railway, built throughout by the "cut and cover" method of construction. An open trench was cut, restraining walls were built on each side and the works roofed over. To avoid houses, the route followed roads almost entirely. The railway was built to accommodate the 7-foot gauge of the Great Western trains, as well as the 4 feet 8½ inches used by every other railway company in London. Three rails were laid for each line, with both types of train sharing the rail nearest the platform.

Locomotives under London

from Paddington to Farringdon Street where a banquet was laid out for them. The prime minister, Lord Palmerston, was expected, but declined to come on grounds of age, explaining in addition that he wished to remain above ground for as long as possible.

The next day the public had their first chance of sampling the railway and took it in their thousands. From 8 a.m. every station on the line was crowded with people, so many that for long periods they had to be turned away. The trains, built to the generous GWR proportions, were admired. They had carpeted floors, well-upholstered seats, panelling on the walls, and were lit by gas lamps fed from rubber bags contained in cylinders or boxes on the roof. There were three classes, but nobody was allowed to stand; the rule book, indeed, expressly forbade it on pain of being forcibly removed from the train.

Passengers generally seem to have found the ventilation acceptable, but the same cannot be said of the company's employees, who were forced to spend much longer underground. On the first day two men working at Gower Street station were overcome by the fumes and had to be taken to University College Hospital to recover. The success of the line meant that by the end of January trains ran every four minutes during the day, beyond the capacity of the ventilation system. On 7 March, when Princess Alexandra of Denmark arrived in London for her marriage to the Prince of Wales, 60,000 used the Metropolitan Railway in a single day as they rushed to see her. By April, more than two million people had been carried.

The company tried to minimize the effects of the sulphurous fumes in the tunnels, even persuading doctors to claim that they were therapeutic for those suffering from respiratory complaints. Guards, policemen and porters working for the railway petitioned the directors to be allowed to grow beards in the belief that the fumes might thereby be filtered, and their request, after discussion at a GWR board meeting, was granted. Eventually large fans were put into the tunnels to try to keep the air clear.

Soon after opening, the Metropolitan Railway fell out with the GWR, which was running as many of its own trains down the lines as it could, cutting the profits available for the company that actually owned the line. As the GWR had provided the rolling stock, it believed it had a stranglehold over the line and threatened to withdraw its trains. The Metropolitan quickly

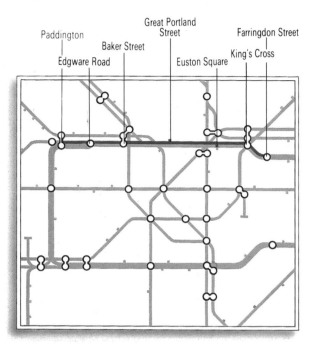

A trial run over the railway was organized on 24 May 1862 for dignatories, seen here at Edgware Road (below). The engineer of the Metropolitan Railway, John Fowler, is in the nearest wagon, wearing a pale-coloured suit and hat; on his right is the chancellor of the exchequer William Gladstone. The western end of the line was almost complete by the time this train was run. These dignatories were witnessing the creation of the first part of the London Underground system (above), which is still being enlarged.

Excavation at King's Cross, with the Great Northern Railway terminus beyond the workmen's hut. Engineers had many problems to overcome: keeping the cuttings buttressed to avoid damage to buildings above; underpinning walls; diverting sewers; and maintaining road traffic before the line was roofed over. East of King's Cross, along the old valley of the Fleet River, the railway cleared slum housing—an incidental benefit of much urban railway construction.

An "A" class 4-4-0 tank engine, one of the 24 original locomotives ordered from Beyer, Peacock of Manchester at a cost of £2,280 each. The engines were based on a design already supplied to the Tudela & Bilbao Railway in Spain, and were painted dark green. They had condensing apparatus to reduce steam in the tunnels and save water.

appealed to the other railway companies, who provided standard gauge trains, and ordered locomotives of its own from Beyer, Peacock & Co. of Manchester.

Unsatisfactory as steam power was bound to be, the underground's passengers had to put up with it until 1889, when electrification finally dispelled the dirt and smell. By then the Metropolitan had expanded into the District Line, a closely linked but technically independent company. Inevitably they fell out, arguing over the rights to different portions where the two lines overlapped, and the District acquired its own engines. Despite the disputes above ground and the smoke below, the public took to the new railways with enthusiasm, for they offered cheap, swift travel across the capital, something that no other form of transport has provided, before or since.

The Most Luxurious Train

Georges Nagelmackers was born in 1845 at Liège in Belgium. His father was involved with railway finance, and his family well placed to exploit royal connections to further his ventures. He died in 1905 at his chateau in Ville-preux-les-Clayes.

FACT FILE

Date: 1883–1977

Distance: 1,896 miles

Duration: 81 hours 40 minutes (1883)

It was an odd group that gathered at the Gare de l'Est in Paris on 4 October 1883. Among them were diplomats, journalists, bankers, a Belgian cabinet minister, a Romanian general, a distinguished French doctor, a writer from Alsace and a Dutchman named Jansson who appeared to be none of these things, but did not care to say what he was. Each man carried a revolver. They were greeted by flunkeys in eighteenth-century costume.

The party of 40 was the responsibility of a young Belgian, Georges Nagelmackers, founder of the Compagnie Internationale des Wagons-Lits et Grands Express Européens. The occasion was the inauguration of a new service which Nagelmackers had been trying to establish for more than a dozen years, and the VIPs he invited along were among the first to experience the joys of the freebie, travelling first class at somebody else's expense in the hope that they would bring lustre and publicity to the enterprise.

In that respect, the journey was a triumph, producing long articles in *The Times* and *Le Figaro*, as well as interviews and even books: just the kind of international reception Nagelmackers was seeking. The Orient Express was launched with a splash, a champagne-and-caviare experience at a time when most international train journeys were brutish and long.

Georges Nagelmackers's idea was to run a luxury train owned by him over tracks belonging to others, crossing frontiers without fuss while its passengers were cosseted by servants and insulated from the horrors of customs officials and the risks of brigandage. The inspiration had come to him in the 1860s, when as a 21-year-old fleeing from a disappointment in love—he was spurned by an older woman—he went to the United States.

There he experienced the mixed blessings of long-distance railway travel, rejoicing in the fact that a single train could take him right across the nation, but appalled by the crowding and discomfort involved. In those days trains had no toilets, and meals were taken in a hurry during brief stops. The food was usually awful and the train conductors were apt to blow the whistle for departure before you had had time to eat it. One British traveller, J.W. Boddam-Whetham, travelled in a Pullman sleeping car and reported that the horrors of the experience were indelibly impressed on his mind. The heat was intolerable, and the bunks so close together that it was not unusual to wake up with a stranger's feet resting on one's face.

Nagelmackers did, however, identify one overwhelming advantage in the cars operated by George Pullman—through running. Instead of having to change trains at a junction between different railroads, passengers could stay in the same cars while they were transferred to a different train. Although obvious in retrospect, this was not the usual practice at the time. Travellers between New York and Chicago had to make five changes of railroad, unless they chose to travel Pullman.

As Nagelmackers knew, the situation in Europe was even worse, with national borders adding to the confusion. He conceived the idea of a European network of trains, comfortable and well run, which passengers could make their home during the long journeys across the Continent. All that was needed was to persuade the railways of the benefits of the idea. They would collect the normal fares from anybody using the special cars, while Nagelmackers would cover his own costs and make a profit from the supplements he would charge.

For one reason or another this brilliant idea took a while to catch on. The Franco-Prussian War of 1870 put paid to the plan for a train between Paris and Berlin. And although Nagelmackers did well for a while running trains full of British empire-builders through Europe to Brindisi, where they boarded P & O ships for India, Ceylon and Australia, it was hardly what he had had in mind. That came to an end anyway when P & O cast in their lot with the French, who had built the first tunnel under the Alps and refused to let Nagelmackers use it.

His company faced bankruptcy, from which it was saved only by the timely intervention of an American, Colonel William d'Alton Mann. Frustrated by the Pullman company in his ambitions to set up a service of what he called "boudoir cars" in the US, Colonel Mann brought one to Europe. Nagelmackers was impressed, but had no money left, and Mann offered to go into business with him.

Mann was a rogue and a confidence trickster, whose source of money was never very clear, but he did Nagelmackers several good turns. He

The steamer journey from Varna was obviated by the opening of the last section of line to Constantinople in 1889, as advertised by the Wagons-Lits Company.

The Most Luxurious Train

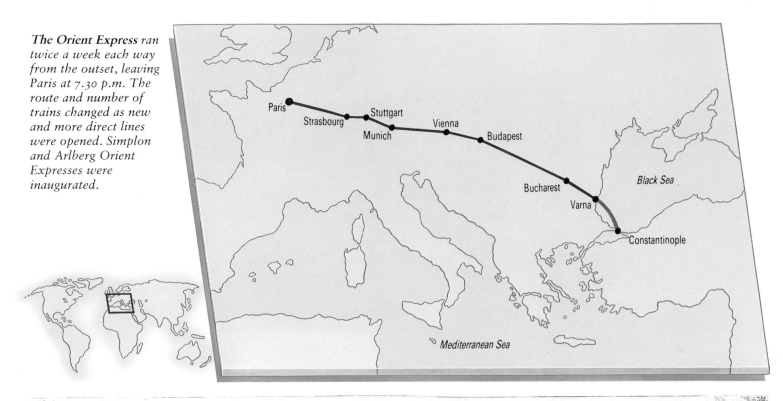

The Orient Express ran twice a week each way from the outset, leaving Paris at 7.30 p.m. The route and number of trains changed as new and more direct lines were opened. Simplon and Arlberg Orient Expresses were inaugurated.

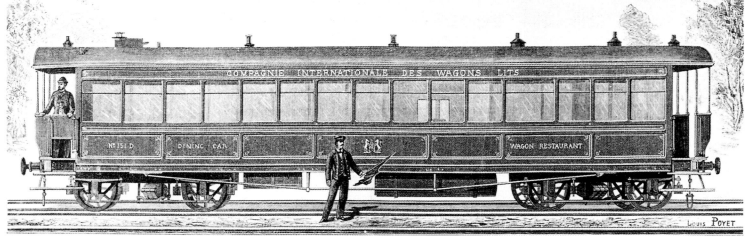

The first restaurant car of the Orient Express had a ceiling covered in embossed Cordoba leather, walls lined with Gobelins tapestries, and velvet curtains. The five-course dinner was cooked by a chef from Burgundy, "not merely of the first order but a man of genius", as one satisfied traveller put it.

saved the company from ruin and saw off, by the clever use of black propaganda, an attempt by Pullman to establish himself in Europe. The open Pullman cars, he told the European railway companies, were an invitation to debauchery. Respectable women would be importuned in their beds by strangers, while unmarried couples would use the cars for their liaisons.

Mann was persuasive, and his boudoir cars gained business while Pullman languished. But just as success was beckoning, Mann got bored. Nagelmackers, seeing his opportunity, raised fresh capital and paid off Mann, who returned to the US with $5 million in his pocket. Pullman tried to do a deal with Nagelmackers, and was

shown the door. The stage was finally set for the Orient Express.

To begin with, Nagelmackers had done no more than attach individual cars to existing trains, but the Orient Express was designed to be an entire train in itself. As his 40 guests clambered aboard in Paris in October 1883, they entered a world entirely under the control of Nagelmackers and his company. The compartments, called coupés, were like miniature sitting rooms, with two red plush armchairs, Turkish carpets on the floor and silk wall coverings. At night, a comfortable double bed folded downward out of the walls. Between each coupé was a bathroom, and in a coach at the rear of the train

A compartment prepared for sleeping (far left) could quickly be converted into use for passengers by day (left). The beds were originally covered with silk sheets, wool blankets and counterpanes filled with the lightest of eiderdown. The early toilet cabinets (middle) had porcelain basins set in Italian marble with vials of toilet water and lotions beside them.

The dining car was panelled in mahogany and teak inlaid with rosewood and decorated with carved scrolls, cornices and scallops. Diners could place small articles in the racks supported by gilded brackets that ran the length of the car on both sides. Gold-framed etchings by leading nineteenth-century artists hung on panels between the windows, and huge gas chandeliers gave a soft glow to the proceedings—the gas mantle had yet to be invented, and the naked flames had to be kept low to minimize the risk of fire. During the inaugural journey, a gipsy band came aboard at Tsigany in Hungary to give a concert of waltzes and czardas in a dining car temporarily cleared of furniture. As they struck up "La Marseillaise", the chef emerged from the kitchen, red-faced and eyes ablaze to lead the singing.

The Most Luxurious Train

King Boris III of Bulgaria (on the right) could not be restrained from driving locomotives of the Orient Express, especially inside his own country. On one occasion he stoked the fire too energetically and it blew back into the cab, setting the fireman's clothing ablaze. As the fireman leaped from the footplate to his death, King Boris urged the train on, alighting at Sofia to solicit the congratulations of the passengers for having arrived on time in spite of the accident.

ROMANCE AND INTRIGUE

Often exaggerated stories of skulduggery or illicit liaisons on the Orient Express have provided fertile ground for novelists and film-makers. *Stamboul Train* by Graham Greene was published in 1932, followed two years later by Agatha Christie's *Murder on the Orient Express*. In Ian Fleming's *From Russia, with Love*, the fight between 007 and a Soviet agent takes place aboard the train, and the plot of Eric Ambler's *The Mask of Dimitrios* is interwoven with its route. Alfred Hitchcock set *The Lady Vanishes* (1938) aboard the Orient Express.

Murder on the Orient Express was made into a film in 1974, starring Anthony Perkins, Vanessa Redgrave, Sean Connery, Ingrid Bergman, Albert Finney as Inspector Poirot, Rachel Roberts, Wendy Hiller, Michael York, Jacqueline Bisset and Lauren Bacall.

were shower cubicles. There was a smoking room, a ladies' boudoir and a library.

The destination of the train was Constantinople (now Istanbul), the Sublime Porte, capital of the Ottoman Empire and the point where Europe becomes Asia. To Victorians this was an exotic and dangerous place, for their concept of European civilization stretched no farther east than the borders of Hungary. Since rails had yet to be laid all the way to Constantinople, the journey was a complicated one, but it started easily enough.

From Paris the train crossed into Germany, through Strasbourg (then, of course, German), Stuttgart, Munich, Vienna and Budapest. At Augsburg, in Germany, there was a setback, for it was found that the dining car had an overheating axle box. Fortunately Nagelmackers had a spare ready at Munich, although it was an older type—a six-wheeler rather than a bogie car—and it ran so poorly that it became almost impossible to pour wine without spilling it.

In Bucharest, the journey took on a surreal quality. King Charles of Romania invited the entire party to visit him at his new summer palace at Sinaia, four hours away up a branch line in the mountains. Decanted at the station, they made their way to a hotel where a buffet had been prepared. Summoned into the presence of the king, they then had to walk up a mile and a half of muddy, unsurfaced road in pouring rain before arriving in a filthy condition.

Next the travellers entered Bulgaria, by crossing the Danube. No bridge existed yet, so they were forced to leave the train, cross by boat, and get aboard another train, operated by Austrian Oriental Railways, on the other side. It was five years before Nagelmackers's dream of a continuous track all the way became reality. Bulgaria was an eye-opener, a rather barren and melancholy country whose people seemed steeped in despair and hopelessness.

At Votova station, they were told that a fortnight before a gang of brigands had attacked the station, garotted the stationmaster, carried off his daughter and were about to set light to the place when they were disturbed and ran off, leaving their victims grateful to be still alive. The passengers on the Orient Express tightened their grip on their revolvers. Finally they arrived at Varna on the Black Sea, where a steamship was waiting to take them to Constantinople.

The return journey was relatively uneventful, enlivened when the train was joined in Vienna by fare-paying passengers, among them some elegant young women. The corridors of the train, wrote *The Times* correspondent de Blowitz, became like the pavement of the Rue de la Paix as the beautiful young ladies emerged from their compartments impeccably turned out to promenade under the scrutiny of the male passengers.

So the first journey of the Orient Express ended with precisely the impression that Nagelmackers had hoped to convey: glamour, comfort, elegance and a hint of intrigue and excitement. Who could resist it? Soon the train began to appear in novels, just as it later did in films. Extraordinary stories, not all of them untrue, began to gather around it. At least two government agents, one of them an American military attaché, either fell, jumped or were thrown to their deaths from the train.

King Boris III of Bulgaria, a train fanatic, could not be dissuaded from taking the controls when the Orient Express passed through his country. Wearing white overalls made for him in Paris, King Boris would spend long hours on the footplate, itching to get his hands on the controls. Firm instructions were given to drivers that he should not be permitted to do so, for his love of speed greatly exceeded his comprehension of the signalling system.

The Orient Express was never transport for the masses. Its fares were astonishingly expensive: £58 per person, or £160 for a couple with a servant. At that time, £160 would pay the annual rent for a substantial house in London, or keep a working-class family fed, clothed and supplied for a whole year. The people who could afford to travel on Nagelmackers's train were the truly rich, a class which did not long survive the nineteenth century. The arrival of high taxes on income and inheritance, World War I, and the depression of the 1930s transformed Nagelmackers's luxury train into a pale imitation.

After Nagelmackers died in 1905, his successor, Lord Dalziell, combined the Compagnie Internationale with Thomas Cook and Sons Ltd and the English Pullman Company, and catered for the beginnings of mass tourism. Rather than carrying a few extremely rich people, trains were filled with larger numbers, at lower fares and in less comfort. Thus was the Orient Express democratized, and its standards reduced; by the 1970s the train did not even boast a restaurant car for large parts of the journey.

Then, in the 1980s, a saviour emerged in the form of James Sherwood, an entrepreneur who

THE RESTORATION WORK

Restoration of the carriages for the Venice-Simplon Orient Express was undertaken in the 1980s by workshops in Belgium, Germany and England. The Pullman car *Audrey* (above) was once part of the Brighton Belle that ran to London Victoria. In all cars, marquetry panelling was restored or replaced, woodwork french polished, marble wash basins fitted, the electrics entirely rewired, new light shades made, based on a design by René Lalique, and new carpets woven in Yorkshire. No expense was spared to create a train that would measure up to the high standards of the original Orient Express.

had made his fortune running Sea Containers Ltd. Conspicuous consumption, long regarded as rather vulgar, was back in fashion as paper fortunes were made on the stock markets. Sherwood acquired and restored a series of carriages to create two trains, one to carry passengers from London to Folkestone, the other from Boulogne to Vienna, under the name Venice-Simplon Orient Express. Most of the sleeping cars are 50 years old, but magnificently restored, and the journey to Venice takes 30 hours. A second train, run by a Swiss entrepreneur, Albert Glatt, under the name Nostalgic Istanbul Orient Express, runs occasional trips from Paris to Istanbul and Bucharest, also using old rolling stock.

Goliaths of the Mountains

The great age of the luxury trains in the United States began in the days of the Depression and finally petered out during the late 1950s. In Canada, where the lines are longer and the scenery even more dramatic, the romance of the transcontinental journey survived, albeit unprofitably, until quite recent times. There has never been a better way to see the US or Canada than by train, a fact that railway managements exploited successfully until the greater speed of the airlines and the hurry even of modern tourism defeated them.

In the second half of the nineteenth century, both Canada and the US were united by railways that ran from shore to shining shore. In Canada it was possible to cover virtually the entire journey over the rails of a single company, which was never the case in the US. There, the railroads were regional rather than national, although by European standards they still covered huge territories. By 1900, more than 90 percent of the rail lines that would ever be built in North America were already in place. The pioneer era, when merely to cross the country by train was a kind of miracle, was replaced by the need to market the trains as an enjoyable experience.

Never was this more urgent than in the 1930s. In 1933, at the height of the Depression, trains in the US averaged only 43 passengers per run. The answer lay in new trains, with glamorous names and better standards of service. These great trains were powered both by steam and diesel, for it was a period in which the two prime movers were contesting supremacy.

The Pennsylvania Railroad used steam on the Broadway Limited—4-6-2 Pacifics of conservative design but great reliability. On some sections of the line, these K4 Pacifics could maintain average speeds in the region of 75 mph, making them among the quickest steam trains in the world. Often, in the great level stretches west, two K4s were coupled together to provide the motive power, their economical running making such prodigal use of locomotives feasible. Over the Allegheny Mountains, three K4s were needed to take the Broadway Limited up the 1 in 58 incline of Horseshoe Curve.

The rival Twentieth Century Limited also used steam, a fabled series of engines with a 4-6-4 layout known as the Hudsons. By 1938 the schedule for the New York to Chicago trip was down to 16 hours, giving an end-to-end speed of 59.9 mph, including seven stops totalling 26 minutes. In the fashion of the 1930s, some of the locomotives of both the Broadway Limited and the Twentieth Century Limited were given streamlined shapes, from the designers Raymond Loewy and Henry Dreyfus.

Any passenger reaching Chicago under the power of steam could continue by diesel, on one of the most glamorous trains of all, the City of San Francisco. In 1937, the Southern Pacific, the Union Pacific and the Milwaukee Road, over whose lines the train ran, bought from General Motors the world's most powerful diesel locomotives. The City of San Francisco exemplified the elegance of Art Deco, gleaming silver without and leather and chrome within. The power units, the longest locomotives that had ever been built, contained six 900-hp, 12-cylinder diesels, capable of pulling a 600-ton train at speeds of up to 110 mph. She made the trip in 39 hours; the cheapest ticket cost just $5, while the most expensive, at $22, provided a suite that slept four and had its own sofa and bathroom. Three meals a day cost an extra 90 cents.

On 12 August 1939 the City of San Francisco came off the rails near Harney in Utah, after a saboteur had damaged the track; 24 people died. The train went on running through the war, and in 1952 was trapped for five days by a blizzard in the Sierras. By careful husbandry, the crew fed 230 people with two meals a day, though by the time rescue came dinner was a frugal affair: spaghetti without sauce, a frankfurter, and half a cup of coffee per passenger.

Canadian railways, too, were noted for their spectacular trains. For many years the rival lines, Canadian Pacific and Canadian National, ran their cross-country trains in competition. It was possible to travel west by Canadian Pacific, covering 2,881 miles in 87 hours 10 minutes, and return by Canadian National, which had 2,930 miles to cover but much easier grades, so that its overall time was hardly different. That way, the traveller saw more scenery and had a taste of the different operating methods of the two railroads.

In the late 1920s Canadian Pacific introduced locomotives of its own design which were quickly recognized as outstanding. The 2-10-4 Selkirks were unusual among ten-coupled locomotives in being used for express passenger

FACT FILE

The heaviest engines ever built for the Canadian Pacific Railway

Selkirk 2-10-4

Date built: 1938–49

Number built: 36

Length: 97 feet 10⅝ inches

Driving wheel diameter: 5 feet 3 inches

service. Normally engines with ten driving wheels are ideal for freight trains because of their exceptional traction, but are limited in speed because a locomotive can only be so long if it is to get around curves, and that means that if ten driving wheels are used, they must be small. This in turn usually limits top speeds.

For most of the CPR's 2,881 miles from Montreal to Vancouver the going was easy, but there were two awkward sections—the northern shore of Lake Superior and the 262 miles over the mountains between Calgary and Revelstoke. To haul the CPR's flagship train—the Dominion, weighing 1,300 tons—up inclines as steep as 1 in

A parlour car of the 1930s reflects the attention paid to the comfort of passengers before the airlines began to erode the railways' supremacy. Rivalry was between railway companies rather than modes of transport. The advertising art of the 1930s (right) now commands high prices among collectors.

CANADIAN PACIFIC

CANADIAN PACIFIC STEAMERS CONNECT DIRECTLY WITH CANADIAN PACIFIC EXPRESS TRAINS TO EVERY PART OF **CANADA**

Agent:

Goliaths of the Mountains

45 required prodigious pulling power. Speeds on those sections were slow, no more than about 10 mph uphill and 25 to 30 mph down, because in addition to the slope the sharp curvature of the track had to be taken into account. To get the long 2-10-4s around these curves it was necessary to widen the track from 4 feet $8\frac{1}{2}$ inches by $1\frac{1}{4}$ inches and to provide the leading axle with nearly an inch of free play. On the flat, the big Selkirks could reach 65 mph.

In 1953, when American railways were beginning to sense the competition, Canadian Pacific resolved to modernize its two transnational services, the Canadian and the Dominion. It ordered from the American coachbuilding company Budd of Philadelphia a total of 173 new stainless-steel cars, to be pulled by diesel locomotives. Each train had dome cars, with windows in the roof to look up at the spectacular scenery, and the new timetable cut 16 hours off the journey between Montreal and Vancouver, although eastbound the reduction was a more modest $10\frac{1}{4}$ hours. The Canadian, the faster of the two services by half a day, quickly became one of the most famous trains in the world.

Canadian National retaliated by improving its own timetables, and buying from US railroads any luxury streamliner cars that were no longer wanted. The bold effort certainly increased traffic, but not enough to justify the expenditure, and by 1978 Canada's two railways operated a joint service over at least part of the track. Finally, in 1990 it was announced that the Canadian, a national institution since its introduction almost 40 years before, would stop running on a regular timetable.

In a declaration of faith in the future of rail, however, VIA Rail (the company that now operates all CN and CPR intercity trains) has refurbished the famous stainless-steel cars that caused such a sensation when they were introduced in 1955. At a cost of $200 million, air-conditioning, showers, interior design and the domes themselves have been restored and improved. The cars have been completely refitted from top to bottom, making them better than new, according to VIA officials. In the early 1990s, as all the cars are completed, new services are to be introduced. The first, in the spring of 1991, is the Western Transcontinental, between Vancouver and Toronto via Edmonton. VIA believes that the trains will uphold Canada's reputation for providing some of the most sensational railway journeys in the world.

THE SILK TRAINS

Unloading the silk at Vancouver began before the first passengers disembarked, so crucial was every minute in the race to transport it to New York—not only is silk perishable, but the shorter the transit time, the lower the cost of insurance. Longshoremen unloaded the bales in cargo slings or by conveyor, once achieving the unloading of 7,000 bales in three hours. The silk was wrapped in burlap and tied up in a bale weighing about 130 lb and measuring 3 feet by 2 feet by 1 foot. A 30-ton boxcar, lined with protective paper, could be loaded in 15 minutes. The value of the silk on the first CN special train was $2 million, at a rate of $9 per 100 lb.

The most precious cargo ever carried by the Canadian railways, to judge by the efforts made to run the trains to time on a fast schedule, was not passengers but silk. For almost 50 years the trains carrying the silk from Pacific ports to New York had the freedom of the tracks. Ordinary trains were shunted into sidings and elaborate security precautions introduced to protect the valuable cargo.

The silk trains were the result of a determined marketing drive by the president of Canadian National, Sir Henry Thornton. Silk is perishable, so any time that could be saved on its journey to the Silk Exchange in New York was worthwhile. Thornton, determined to wrestle the business away from Canadian Pacific, organized CN's first silk special on 1 July 1925. It was to be handled like a relay race; every 150 miles or so train crews and engines were to be changed and running gear lubricated.

Seldom have freight trains run faster than the silk specials. A typical time for the journey to New York was a fraction over four days. For speed, the locomotives were those normally used for passenger trains, and over some sections they reached 90 mph. Between 1925 and about 1936, competition for the business was intense, with CN, CPR and the Great Northern competing neck and neck. The best year was 1929, when the railroads shared revenues from half a million bales of silk, valued at $325 million. The largest silk train that ever ran was in October 1927. That consisted of 21 cars containing 7,200 bales worth $7 million—the product, somebody estimated, of two billion silkworms.

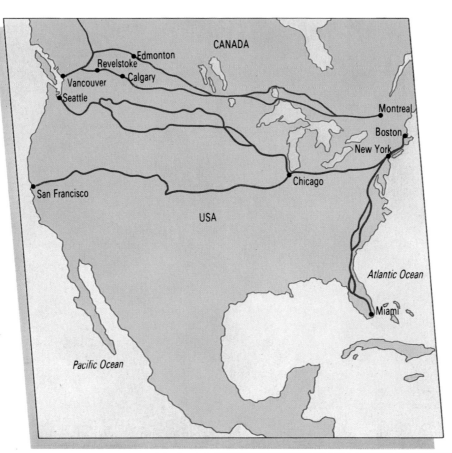

The new, named trains brought glamour and profitability to travel by long-distance expresses. Among the best known were the Twentieth Century Limited and its rival, the Broadway Limited, which both ran between New York and Chicago; the Empire Builder (Chicago to Seattle); the Canadian Pacific's Canadian (Montreal to Vancouver); the Orange Blossom Special (Boston to Miami); and the two rival trains that ran between Chicago and San Francisco, the City of San Francisco and the San Francisco Zephyr.

An eastbound Canadian Pacific train climbs the steep grade out of Field, British Columbia. The train has emerged from one of the two spiral tunnels designed to ease the gradient, and the lower portal can be seen beneath the first coach. The leading locomotive is a 2-10-4 Selkirk. The final example of the class, No. 5935, was the last steam locomotive to be built for the Canadian Pacific Railway, in 1949.

The Ultimate in Steam Power

The biggest, heaviest, most powerful steam locomotives ever built served the mountainous Wyoming division of the Union Pacific Railroad for 20 years from 1941. "Big Boy", as the class of locomotive was universally known, was a prodigy of steam power, able to pull trains weighing up to 4,200 tons up the 60-mile climb of the Wasatch Mountains unaided.

Before the arrival of Big Boy, this stretch of line had tested a long series of powerful engines. At first, helper engines were needed to shove the freight trains up the hill, but later the line acquired more powerful locomotives, with the idea of a single locomotive doing the job unassisted. No sooner were the new locomotives in service than the trains got bigger. Finally, in the early part of 1940, Union Pacific's Research and Mechanical Standards Department was ordered to design and construct an even more powerful engine. The result was Big Boy, by most reckoning the largest locomotive ever built and the one that combined the greatest pulling ability with an impressive turn of speed.

The order was for an engine able to pull 3,600 tons over the Wasatch unassisted. In just a year the first Big Boy was built and ready, a tribute to the excellence of American locomotive engineering. To do the job, Union Pacific estimated, an engine capable of 135,000 lb of tractive effort would be required. To transmit this amount of force to the rails would need sixteen 68-inch wheels in two sets of eight, and the engine's weight of more than 530 tons dictated at least four wheels for the lead and trailing trucks. Thus the 4-8-8-4 configuration was settled on.

To get around the curves along this awkward stretch of line, the engine had to be articulated—joined in the middle by a hinge, with one set of eight driving wheels each side of it. Clearly the boiler itself could not be hinged, so the bulk of its weight was borne by the rear set of driving wheels and on corners it slid across the front set on a support, hanging out by as much as 2 feet on a 10 degree curve.

The idea was not new, having originally been proposed by the French engineer Anatole Mallet in 1884. In Europe Mallet's principle was used mainly for narrow gauge railways, but in the US big Mallet articulateds were used for freight duties. Their speed was usually limited to 30 to 40 mph by vibration of the front frame, since at higher speeds great damage would be done to track and to wheels.

Improvements in the 1920s and '30s solved the vibration problem and better steam connections enabled high-pressure steam to be supplied to both sets of driving wheels—in the earlier engines only the rear set was fed with high-pressure steam, while the forward set operated at low pressure. In 1936, Union Pacific ordered forty 4-6-6-4 "Challenger" locomotives, which performed very well and provided the confidence to go ahead with the even bigger Big Boys.

The American Locomotive Company, of Schenectady, New York, was given the job of building the engines, sharing the design job with Union Pacific. Legend has it that the type got its name when a foreman at Alco chalked the name Big Boy on the smokebox of one of the early engines. Union Pacific had the idea of calling the type Wasatch, but publicity in the newspapers ensured that Big Boy was the name that stuck.

Everything about the engines was huge. The firebox was 20 feet long and 8 feet broad, plenty big enough for a family to sit down and have dinner. To toss the coal into its vast interior would have been beyond even the brawniest fireman, so a mechanical stoker was fitted which, with skilful operation, could be encouraged to throw the coal into the farthest reaches of the firebox. The tender could carry 28 tons of coal and 24,000 gallons of water, ample to get the big trains over the toughest sections of the track.

The main frames were huge castings, supplied by the General Steel Castings Company of Granite City, Illinois. The articulated joint between the leading unit and the main frame was designed so that it could transmit a load of several tons from the rear unit to the front one, thereby evening out the load carried by the driving wheels. In the Challengers, the joint had both horizontal and vertical hinges, so that the engine could adjust to humps and hollows in the track as well as curves. In the design of Big Boy the horizontal hinge was left out and the vertical hinge was designed to shift weight to the front wheels, helping to prevent slipping. To cope with humps and hollows, the wheels were mounted on individually sprung axles so that the suspension could accommodate uneven ground.

The cabs on the Big Boys were among the biggest on any steam locomotive, with room for

FACT FILE

The world's largest and most powerful steam locomotive

Date: 1941–44

Length: 132 feet 10 inches

Power output: 135,375 lb tractive effort

Diameter of driving wheel: 5 feet 8 inches

Weight: 539 tons 12 cwt

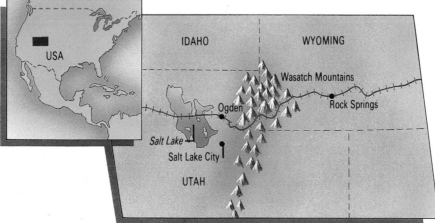

No. 4019 attacks the second part of the climb up the Wasatch Mountains after a stop for coal, sand and water. The engine was withdrawn from service in January 1962 after running 1,043,352 miles. The weight of the locomotives compelled Union Pacific to re-lay much of the route with 130 lb/ft steel rail.

The Ultimate in Steam Power

four people on seats and for a couple more standing. Even in the coldest winters the cabs were hot, but they rode very smoothly. For a huge locomotive, Big Boy ran well, able to reach speeds of up to 80 mph on straight and level stretches without rolling. But it really showed its mettle on the slow grind over the continental divide in the centre of the United States for which it had been designed.

Here the locomotives would pull steadily at about 15 mph, generating their maximum pulling power on the stretch between Cheyenne, Wyoming and Ogden, Utah, where on the notorious Sherman Hill a slope of 1 in 65 ran up to Sherman Summit at 8,013 feet. Leaving Ogden going east was a solid 60 miles of uphill grades, most of it around 1 in 88 as the rails climbed from 4,300 feet to 7,230 feet. Although designed to carry 3,600 tons over this section, the Big Boys showed that they could manage more and were regularly harnessed to 4,200-ton trains.

The huge publicity the Big Boys had enjoyed during their rapid construction ensured great interest in the first run, which took place in September 1941. A dormitory car was fitted behind engine No. 4013 for the run, to carry officials, test men and photographers. Behind that came a line of 100 fruit cars, all empty. With two long, moaning shrieks from its whistle and a black smudge of smoke from the short stack, 4013 started smoothly from Summit, in Omaha, attached to its first train.

Across Nebraska the stations were lined with people who had heard about the new engine. By late evening the train was in Sidney, Nebraska, and in the early hours of the morning it left Cheyenne for Sherman Hill, where an early fall of snow had dusted the lines. Between Tipton and Bitter Creek, Wyoming, it reached a speed of 72 mph and rode so smoothly it felt no more than 55. The following day saw an eastward run over the long climb the Big Boys had been designed to conquer, this time pulling a 3,500-ton train.

Again the line was crowded with spectators as the full power of the engine was unleashed. The smell of steam mixed with that of hot lubrication oil, and the sound of the thunderous exhaust combined with the clatter of cinders thrown out of the huge firebox landing on the cab roof as 4013 climbed the hill out of Echo, the toughest section. When the run was over, the weight of the train was recalculated and it was realized that 4013 had carried 3,800 tons, 200 more than the rated capacity.

The Big Boys proved highly successful engines, easy to run and reliable. With trains of regular weight and in normal conditions it was almost impossible to cause the wheels to slip, remarkable for articulated locomotives. Occasionally they were used on passenger trains, although their stock in trade was the less glamorous but profitable freight. They are recorded as producing 6,290 horsepower at 40 mph, consuming 100,000 lb of water and 44,000 lb of coal an hour in the process.

As time went by, experience allowed greater and greater loads, and the gradients were also trimmed by deviations, so that Big Boys could lift 6,000-ton trains up Sherman Hill by the end of their working lives in the early 1960s. The last were retired in 1962; six are preserved and can be seen at various locations in the US, from California to New Hampshire. None, alas, is still in working order.

The controls at the back of the firebox with the steam-operated butterfly firebox doors in the centre. The vertical lever on the right was the regulator, which determined the amount of steam being fed into the cylinders. The mechanical stoker fed coal into the firebox by a screw conveyor that passed underneath the cab footplate. The length of the firebox made it difficult to feed satisfactorily.

The boiler of the first Big Boy, No. 4000, *is lowered on to its frames at the American Locomotive Company's works in Schenectady, New York. The plates used in the boiler barrel were $1\frac{3}{8}$ inches thick and the boiler pressure was a high 300 lb/sq in.*

No. 4002 all set to go. The Big Boys were liked by both the crews and management. Union Pacific president Arthur Stoddard regarded them as "more than tools of an era—they were a symbol of the finest in transportation. Everyone on the line was proud of their performance and talked about it."

Streamlined Greyhound of the Rails

One Sunday in July 1938 the steam engine *Mallard* set a speed record that has never been equalled. Down Stoke Bank, south of Grantham in Lincolnshire, it pulled seven coaches weighing 240 tons at a speed of 125 mph—some say 126. It was the high watermark of steam, and one of the last records set in an era of intense competition on land, sea and in the air that came to an end with World War II. After the war steam lingered on British tracks for 23 more years, but the glory had gone.

The driver of *Mallard* on the morning of 3 July 1938 was Joe Duddington, who drove with his cloth cap turned back to front in traditional style. Her designer was the chief mechanical engineer of the London & North Eastern Railway, Sir Nigel Gresley, who had produced the first of a long line of 4-6-2 Pacific locomotives in 1922 and had steadily improved them ever since.

In 1935, the LNER introduced the Silver Jubilee service between London and Newcastle, promising to complete the journey in four hours at an average speed of 67.08 mph. It was competition with road and air travel, as well as the traditional rivalry with the London, Midland & Scottish Railway which ran over the west coast route to Glasgow, that inspired the LNER to introduce its new train. But there were also continental influences at work in Gresley's mind. In 1934, he had visited Germany and had been impressed by the "Fliegende Hamburger", an express service between Berlin and Hamburg. This Flying Hamburger, as we are unfortunately obliged to render it in English, was a lightweight diesel train of only three coaches which covered the 178-mile journey at an average speed of 77.4 mph. Impressed by the smoothness of the train at 100 mph, Gresley asked its designers to calculate how quickly a similar train would cover the London–Newcastle run. They quoted him four and a quarter hours for a three-coach train carrying 140 passengers.

Gresley and his board thought the train too cramped by British standards, and worked out that a modified A4 Pacific class locomotive might well achieve the same times with a train of much greater weight, capacity and comfort. To secure a sufficient margin of power, Gresley determined on a few modifications to cylinders and boiler and on streamlining to reduce wind resistance.

Gresley's streamlined A4 Pacifics were quickly put into service and the Silver Jubilee trains proved a huge success, attracting 100 percent loadings almost every day. The cost of the locomotives and the seven-coach trains was recovered from fare supplements alone within three years. *Mallard*, the 28th of the class to appear, emerged from the workshop in March 1938 at a cost of £8,500 and was given the number 4468.

At the time, the speed record for steam trains was claimed by the German railways for one of their own streamlined engines, No. 05.002, which reached 124.5 mph on 11 May 1936. On 27 August the same year, a Silver Jubilee train on a regular run south, pulled by No. 2512 *Silver Fox*, reached 113 mph, a record which still stands as the fastest ever reached by a steam engine on a normal service. Considerable damage was done to the engine during this run, including a broken big end on the middle of the three cylinders.

Fast running of the Silver Jubilee services depended on testing and improvement of the brakes, and it was during one of these tests that Gresley decided to go for the record. He selected *Mallard* and chose a quiet Sunday morning for the attempt, an out-and-out record run. Driver Joe Duddington was accompanied on the footplate by fireman Tommy Brae and locomotive inspector Sid Jenkins. Behind *Mallard* were a dynamometer car to measure the speed, an

Gresley's inspiration for the streamlining came from the racing-car designer Ettore Bugatti who had produced a streamlined railcar for Italian railways. Gresley claimed streamlining was vital to achieve the desired performance; some ascribed it to a concern with image. The side panels over the wheels impeded access for maintenance and were later removed. No. 4468 Mallard leaves the National Railway Museum at York (opposite) to work a train.

Streamlined Greyhound of the Rails

antique vehicle originally built in 1906, and seven coaches.

"I'd taken expresses along at, well—60, 70 or 80 mph," Duddington later told the BBC, "but this day we were going out to see just what we could do. I accelerated up the bank to Stoke summit and passed Stoke [signal] box at 85. Once over the top I gave *Mallard* her head and she just jumped to it like a live thing. After three miles the speedometer in my cab showed 107 mph, then 108, 109, 110—getting near Silver Jubilee's record of 113, I thought—I wonder if I can get past that—well, we'll try, and before I knew it the needle was at 116 and we'd got the record. They told me afterwards there was a deal of excitement in the dynamometer car and when the recorder showed 122 mph for a mile and a half it was at fever heat.

"Go on, old girl, I thought, we can do better than this. So I nursed her and shot through Little Bytham at 123 and in the next one and a quarter miles the needle crept up further—123½—124—125 and then for a quarter of a mile, while they tell me the folks in the car held their breaths—126 miles per hour. That was the fastest a steam locomotive had ever been driven in the world—and good enough for me, though I believe if I'd tried her a bit more we could have got even 130."

Back in the dynamometer car was a representative of the Westinghouse Brake and Signal Company, P.T.W. Remnant, who had managed to squeeze himself aboard for the record run even though no brake tests were planned. His account coincides pretty closely with that of Duddington. They began with a slight disadvantage, he said, because (as ever) the line was subject to Sunday maintenance and there was a speed restriction outside Grantham station. There were wry smiles as the speed fell back to 18 mph. But *Mallard* accelerated powerfully up the bank to Stoke summit, passing it at 75 mph according to the dynamometer record.

As the train was running at over 100 mph, Remnant walked back through the length of it. "There was a good deal of movement at the front; the middle gave one a floating impression, and the ride at the back was pretty rough. The guard looked as though he had had enough. Some of the more inventive newspapers the next day carried tales of the engineers 'having tea without a drop being spilt'. In fact, I believe there was a little broken crockery."

As the train approached a bend in the track at Essendine, with 123 mph recorded on the

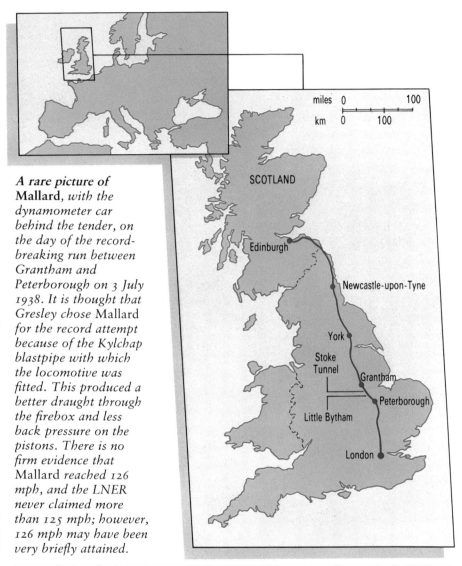

A rare picture of **Mallard,** *with the dynamometer car behind the tender, on the day of the record-breaking run between Grantham and Peterborough on 3 July 1938. It is thought that Gresley chose* Mallard *for the record attempt because of the Kylchap blastpipe with which the locomotive was fitted. This produced a better draught through the firebox and less back pressure on the pistons. There is no firm evidence that* Mallard *reached 126 mph, and the LNER never claimed more than 125 mph; however, 126 mph may have been very briefly attained.*

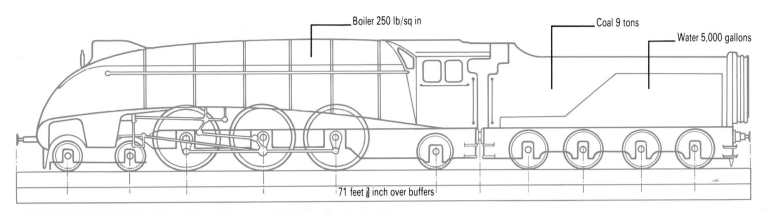

Boiler 250 lb/sq in
Coal 9 tons
Water 5,000 gallons

71 feet ⅜ inch over buffers

speedometer in the cab, the order was given to ease up. There were handshakes and smiles as people stuck their heads out of the window, to be greeted with a powerful smell. This was the "stink bomb", a device built into the centre big end bearing of A4 Pacifics to provide warning of the bearing overheating. In Peterborough station the fitters soon had the fairing off the driving wheels, to reveal that the big end bearing had indeed failed. The return to London was made behind an older and less glamorous engine.

After *Mallard*'s record run, Gresley made preparations for a further attempt to raise the record to 130 mph, but the war intervened. The smart trains of the 1930s made way for over-loaded troop carriers groaning out of King's Cross, and standards of maintenance suffered. The lines were soon no longer fit for record attempts, and the spirited competition between the old railway companies gave way to the uniformity of the nationalized British Railways.

In the 1950s things began to improve, and *Mallard* and her sister A4s ended their careers in the early 1960s in a blaze of glory. In May 1960, the failure of a diesel engine obliged *Mallard* to run the service to and from Newcastle every day for a week—a total of 3,750 miles. Renumbered by British Railways as 60022, *Mallard* ran its last scheduled trip on 25 April 1963, and retired to the Museum of British Transport at Clapham.

This was not quite the end. After the closure of Clapham in 1975, and the move of exhibits to the National Railway Museum in York, it was suggested that *Mallard* be restored to working order. By 1985 it was in steam once more. Since then it has been regularly seen pulling excursion trains, a remarkable survivor still as powerful and impressive as the day it was built.

Mallard at York station with a special train. The slight dip immediately behind the chimney was an accident. Gresley had intended to make the top of the boiler flat. A plasticine model was made in this shape for wind tunnel tests, but by accident somebody's finger made a small indentation behind the chimney. When this was tested, it was found that the smoke lifted away from the chimney more effectively, giving the driver better visibility, so this shape was used.

The Quest for Speed

From the time of the world's first steam-operated railways in Britain, speed has been a major factor in giving railways a commercial advantage over rival forms of transport. Even in the age of the aeroplane, railways in Europe are striving for ever higher speeds to extend the distance over which they can beat the airlines on city centre to city centre timings.

The TGV is only one of a number of high-speed trains that are being built to link the cities of Europe by a high-speed network. Proposals for similar schemes on the east coast of North America are under consideration. The need to counter the growing pollution caused by road transport has given an added sense of urgency to the development of fast, cleaner rail services.

During the 125 years that the steam locomotive was the dominant form of power on the railways, speeds built up steadily: 100 mph was reached in 1904, and the record was steadily increased during the 1930s to reach 125 mph. It took over 110 years of development to reach this speed by steam; it took just 36 years to raise the speed record for an electric train from 150 mph in 1954 to 319 mph in 1990. The record for diesel traction is 144.9 mph, set by a British high-speed train in 1986.

London Midland & Scottish Railway 4-6-2 No. 6222 Queen Mary *climbing to Shap summit in Westmorland with the Coronation Scot. Five streamlined Pacifics were built for this special service between London and Glasgow. They were a development of the "Princess Royal" Pacifics and intended for continuous high-speed running.*

A rare example of streamlining outside Europe or North America were the Japanese-built SL7 Pacifics, built in 1934 and used on the Asia Express of the South Manchuria Railway. This one is preserved at Shenyang, China.

The last streamlined steam locomotives *operating in commercial service are the WP Pacifics of Indian Railways. No. 7200, the first of a class of 750 locomotives, was built by Baldwin Locomotive Works in Philadelphia in 1947.*

Great Western Railway *4-4-0 No. 3440 City of Truro is reputed to have been the first engine to reach 100 mph, down Wellington bank in Somerset in May 1904. Now preserved, she is seen here at Haxby, Yorkshire.*

Train for the 21st Century

When the French high-speed train set off from the Gare de Montparnasse on 18 May 1990, the officials responsible were pretty sure it would prove an interesting trip. They were confident enough, anyway, to invite 150 journalists to watch and to carry aboard the Minister of Transport, Michel Delebarre. They departed ten minutes late because a roe deer had somehow vaulted the protective fences and found its way on to the track, but it was efficiently removed after being anaesthetized with a dart. French Railways (SNCF) was making a public attempt to beat its own speed record, set just two days before at 317 mph.

The train was France's latest candidate for the title of the world's fastest train. The Japanese bullet trains—pioneers of high-speed railways—have been left behind. The French "Train à Grande Vitesse", or TGV, has set new standards for fast rail travel, operating since 1981 between Paris and Lyons at speeds of 168 mph—37 mph more than the Japanese bullet trains. On 26 February 1981, the TGV set a record of 236 mph and won the title of the world's fastest train.

The pride of SNCF was dented, therefore, when on 1 May 1988 the West German prototype of its new InterCity Express set a new record of 252 mph on the Fulda–Würzburg line. But SNCF had another trick up its sleeve—a new line linking Paris to the Atlantic coast, and an improved TGV to run on it. On 6 December 1989, the TGV Atlantique (TGV A) reached 300 mph, recapturing the Blue Riband of the tracks. On 9 May 1990, it went even faster, reaching 317 mph on a stretch of line near Tours, before edging it up a fraction, to 319 mph, on 16 May. This is more than twice as fast as the fastest-ever diesel train (145 mph by a British Rail HST between York and Darlington on 9 November 1986) and half the speed of the fastest Airbus, the real competition for high-speed railways.

The TGV is an excellent example of how an old and apparently mature technology can be given a new lease of life. When research began in 1969 into trains capable of more than 150 mph, many assumed that such speeds would be possible only if the familiar steel wheels on steel tracks were replaced by the concept of magnetic levitation—trains hovering a few inches above the track on a cushion of magnetism. But the levitation experiments were not very successful. According to François Lacôte, SNCF's chief engineer in charge of TGV programmes, "It was the failure of our experiments with magnetic levitation that needled us into developing the TGV at the outset. Twenty years later, we still feel we have the right formula."

That formula consists of light, streamlined, high-powered electric trains running on a purpose-built track. Only passengers are carried, leaving the track clear of slow-moving goods trains, which can use the older tracks. The high power means that gradients steeper than those on conventional railways can be tolerated, with slopes of up to 1 in 30, which reduces the distance the lines must cover. Here speed itself is an advantage because the kinetic energy stored in a train travelling more than 150 mph carries it up hills on momentum alone.

The lines have no level crossings—no tunnels, even, on the original TGV line to Lyons—and there are no height restrictions under bridges. Modified signalling equipment, sophisticated design of bogies and carriages, and a special two-stage pantograph to collect the current from an overhead wire at 25,000 volts complete the package. No breakthroughs and no radical new technologies were needed to create a railway faster than anything that had gone before.

The driver of the train on the morning of 18 May was Michel Massinon, aged 45, a man whose childhood dream was to join SNCF and drive trains. During the run on 9 May he had been the first driver ever to exceed 310 mph. With him in the cab on both occasions was Daniel Vigneau, the engineer who had organized the record-breaking runs. Behind them were two ordinary TGV coaches and three buffet coaches converted into electronic laboratories and staffed by 40 technicians. The entire train weighed 258 tons. The record run began at Dangeau, 71 miles from Paris, where the railway divides, one line heading to Le Mans and the other to Tours.

By mile 76 the speed was up to 186 mph, and 248 mph was passed 7½ miles later. 260 . . . 267 . . . 280 . . . 290 . . . 307, the speed crept upward as Massinon crammed on full power. The train swooped into the new station at Vendôme at 307 mph. If it had wings it would long since have taken off, but instead it had been given a special skirt to create down force and keep it on the

FACT FILE

The world's fastest train

TGV Atlantique

Date built: 1985/86

Length: 781 feet

Power output: 12,000 horsepower

Maximum speed: 320 mph

Gauge: 4 feet 8½ inches

Weight: 472 tons

track. Screens in the technicians' coaches showed that the wheels were indeed lifting a fraction from the rails, but fortunately not all were doing so at the same time.

In the cab the driver had his eyes firmly on the track—"never look sideways" is his technique for driving at very high speed. The motors were at full power, alarms designed to sound in case of danger were silent and the camera installed on the roof showed that the pantograph was remaining in perfect contact with the catenary wires carrying the current.

At mile 101 the speed crept past 310 mph. The final downward stretch of line beckoned, where the record would be won or lost. At mile 103.6, everybody held their breath. In a cloud of dust the train shot by the watchers at the track-side at

320 mph, a new record. "We were flat out, using all the power," said M. Vigneau later. M. Massinon said: "I was so busy that I didn't have time to think of the record. I had to stick to all the parameters we had set in advance, the speed at certain points, and to remember that some of the curves had speed limits . . . Our idea was to reach the maximum speed at a very precise point because after that the slope is less helpful. As soon as I passed that section, I put on the brakes. This was everybody's success, everybody in SNCF."

To set up the record attempt, SNCF engineers had adjusted a few details on the train and the track, for they knew that they were approaching the absolute limit of the TGV's performance. The slope was gently downhill, and the driving

The Train à Grande Vitesse Atlantique is a development of the earlier orange, grey and white sets for the first high-speed line to Lyons. The number of trailer cars was increased from eight to ten, the interiors were redesigned with extra facilities, more powerful and compact motors enabled the number to be reduced from twelve to eight and more powerful disc brakes were fitted.

Train for the 21st Century

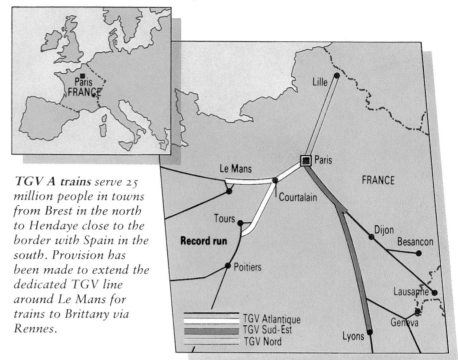

TGV A trains serve 25 million people in towns from Brest in the north to Hendaye close to the border with Spain in the south. Provision has been made to extend the dedicated TGV line around Le Mans for trains to Brittany via Rennes.

wheels of the train had been increased in size by 1 inch to 3 feet 6 inches, marginally increasing the gearing. The catenary cable was under more tension than usual—3.3 tons instead of 2.8—to diminish the curve of the wire and reduce the danger of the pantograph losing contact with it, and with only five coaches instead of ten, the power to weight ratio was doubled. The wind was favourable, blowing at 11–14 mph.

After the record run, there was only one word of disappointment from an SNCF official. He had been hoping to beat the 321 mph achieved by an unmanned Japanese vehicle using magnetic levitation. There is, however, little comparison between a proper train, albeit one prepared for a record attempt, and a pre-prototype Japanese vehicle. The SNCF therefore felt quite justified in claiming that the TGV possessed a greater potential than other forms of ground transport.

The record represented the culmination of a long process of development. When the TGV studies began, it was assumed that traction would be provided by gas turbines, but the energy crisis of the early 1970s changed the plans. France invested heavily in nuclear power stations, using indigenous sources of uranium, so it was logical to electrify the TGV.

As speed rises, so does wind resistance. The smooth shape of the train and the design of the bogies are therefore particularly important. The TGV has fewer bogies than a conventional train, each being shared by neighbouring coaches. As well as reducing wind resistance, this "articulated" system makes it possible to arrange the seating in between the bogies, so that no passenger actually sits over the wheels.

At very high speeds, the shock when the train runs into a tunnel or passes another going the other way can be considerable, enough even in extreme cases to dent the bodywork of the train, and certainly to make passengers' ears pop. Unlike the line to Lyons, the TGV A line does have tunnels, some of them with speed limits. Railways in west Germany have solved this problem with pressurized trains, like aircraft, which work well but are heavier and more costly to build and run. SNCF believes an adequate and much cheaper answer can be found in careful aerodynamic design and hermetic door seals.

Because trains run to the centre of cities, they can compete on journey times with aircraft even if their average speed is lower. Paris–Lyons takes just two hours by TGV, a time which cannot be matched by airlines. In addition, the train uses

The ten trailer cars have seats for 116 in three first-class cars and 485 in six second-class cars; the tenth car provides a bar and buffet. New facilities include a nursery with bottle warmers and changing table, three telephones, a kiosk for groups of up to 17 people, and tables with greater privacy for meetings. Fares are the same as those on other express trains.

far less energy—the equivalent of $3\frac{1}{2}$ pints of oil per passenger per 60 miles covered on the original TGV, now cut to just over $2\frac{1}{2}$ pints by the TGV A. That compares with the 12 pints used by an Airbus on the same basis. Every TGV saves France 100,000 tons of oil a year.

With the success of the TGV, the future now looks bright for high-speed railways. New lines are to be built from Paris to the Channel Tunnel and to Brussels, and another line to Strasbourg is under discussion. The line to Lyons could be extended to the Mediterranean coast. A total of 13 new lines have been proposed by SNCF, some of which would require government subsidy. France, a large and still relatively underpopulated country, is ideal for railway building, with empty rural areas through which the noisy TGV

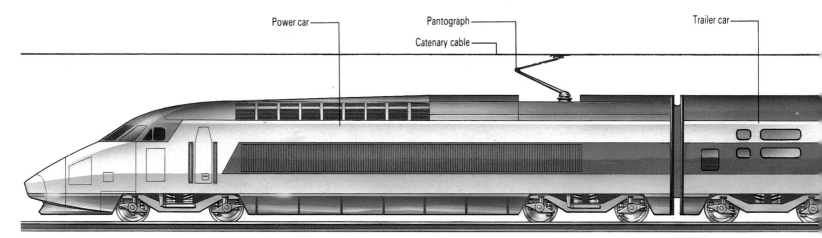

Power car — Pantograph — Trailer car —

Catenary cable —

The traction units, or *power cars,* of the TGV A trains – one at each end of the train – produce a total of 12,000 hp from their eight self-controlled synchronous motors, which are also used for braking. The steel disc brakes can bring a TGV A train running at 186 mph to a stop in 2 miles. This provides a margin of safety to run a train every 5 minutes. Experiments now being carried out with carbon fibre disc brakes, similar to those used on the European Airbus, may reduce the distance needed for stopping, which would permit closer spacing of trains.

lines can be routed with a minimum of protest. Some French towns have even campaigned vociferously to be included on a new TGV line. In much more crowded Britain, fear of noise and disruption tends to be greater than the enthusiasm for faster, cheaper and cleaner travel.

SNCF has so far failed to persuade its German opposite number, the Deutsche Bundesbahn (German Federal Railway), to collaborate on the TGV, so the French and German systems are in rivalry for the new lines proposed to link western Europe together. Although the Germans began before the French, it will be 1991 before the InterCity Express trains come into operation, linking Hamburg to Munich on two routes via Würzburg and via Frankfurt and Stuttgart. Like the TGV, the ICE has two power units, with 12

coaches between them. The goal of the programme is to develop a train capable of travelling twice as fast as a car, and half as fast as an aeroplane—an objective achieved in the experimental run in May 1988 which reached 252 mph.

There is much at stake in the contest between the two systems, and there is the prospect of competition from the Italians, the Japanese and perhaps the Canadians. The European Commission is working on plans for a Europe-wide express rail system, using 11,800 miles of existing, updated and new lines. This could involve the building of between 400 and 500 trains in the next ten years, a market worth up to £4 billion. Small wonder that a battle is going on to establish the prestige that comes from running the world's fastest trains.

The risk of drivers missing signals at normal operating speeds of up to 186 mph necessitated provision of a display on the control panel in the train's cab. If the driver fails to respond to a signal advising a reduction in speed, the brakes are automatically applied. The TGV A routes are controlled from a signal centre in Paris which is in radio contact with all trains.

CHAPTER FOUR

THROUGH THE AIR

Everybody has heard of Icarus and his doomed attempt to escape from Crete which ended when the Sun melted the wax holding his wings. Fewer may know of a Chinese legend about the emperor Shun, who lived from 2258 to 2208 BC. He understood the laws of aerodynamics and put them into practice when a granary that he was building burst into flames while he was on the top floor. "He donned the work clothes of a bird and, flying, made his escape," the story goes.

Fantasies about flying are clearly common to all cultures, but it was not until the eighteenth century that they became reality. It must have been extraordinary to be present when men first defied gravity in a lighter-than-air machine. Only in this century have we finally learned to fly—not by donning the work clothes of a bird but in machines that carry us faster, higher, and in greater comfort than any bird has flown.

It was the Montgolfier brothers who discovered the remarkable properties of hot air and another set of brothers, Wilbur and Orville Wright, who first flew a powered aircraft. Sensational as it seemed, the Montgolfiers' invention proved a dead end until revived for fun in the 1960s, although the gas balloon which first flew only a few days later had much greater promise before the crashes of R101 and the *Hindenburg* destroyed confidence in airships.

The Wrights' invention, by contrast, transformed travel and warfare within half a century. The demonstration by Alcock and Brown, and later by Lindbergh, that aircraft could fly the Atlantic opened the way to international air travel, which from small and hair-raising beginnings has become a huge industry. Faster, higher, bigger; the history of our conquest of the air has been marked by superlatives, some of which are chronicled here. At the end, we come full circle, to a hot-air balloon carried by the winds across the Atlantic and the Pacific oceans, using exactly the same principles that the Montgolfiers demonstrated more than 200 years ago.

Up and Away

FACT FILE

The first successful
hot-air balloons

First Montgolfière

Date built: 1783

Width: 35 feet

Volume: 28,000
cubic feet

Third Montgolfière
(in modified form)

Date built: 1783

Height: 75 feet

Width: 46 feet

Volume: 60,000
cubic feet

The age of flight began on 4 June 1783 in the Place des Cordeliers in Annonay, a French market town not far from Lyons. As the people of the town began gathering there late in the morning, two brothers, Joseph and Etienne Montgolfier, directed four workmen who were assembling a wooden platform. Two masts held with ropes were erected on each side of the platform, each with a pulley at the top. Over the pulley ran two ropes, attached at one end to an eye on a large piece of fabric which lay in a heap on the platform. By pulling the ropes, the fabric was raised so that it hung between the poles. It was made of sackcloth lined with three thin layers of paper, and at the base it had an open mouth about 8 feet square.

When all was complete, the brothers waited for the members of the local Diocesan Assembly, who were holding their annual meeting in Annonay. The Montgolfiers were keen to ensure that what happened next was seen by officials who could vouch for it. A brazier filled with burning shreds of wood and dry straw was placed under the mouth, and as the hot air filled the fabric it rose, straining on the ropes. Etienne gave the order to let go, and the balloon soared straight up to 3,000 feet, carried a mile and a half by wind, until it settled again to earth, landing on a stone wall. The brazier tipped over, set light to the fabric, and the whole affair was destroyed.

No person had been carried on this first flight of a hot-air balloon, but the principle had been clearly demonstrated. The next day the Montgolfiers petitioned the members of the assembly to record their approval of the experiment, thus making clear who had been the first to conquer the air. To this day, a hot-air balloon is called in French a Montgolfière.

The two brothers who had devised this extraordinary spectacle were the sons of Pierre Montgolfier, a paper-maker. It was Joseph, the dreamer, who was without doubt the progenitor of the hot-air balloon. There are many stories about how he devised the idea. One says that he watched a girl blowing soap bubbles, and saw them rise; another, that one day he was drying his wife's petticoat over a fire, and saw it fill with hot air and billow upward.

Joseph was well aware of the recent advances in chemistry, including the discovery by Henry Cavendish in 1766 of "inflammable air"—hydrogen. He knew, too, that hydrogen was a very light gas and had considered the idea of filling a balloon with it in order to fly. He dismissed this possibility because of the expense of acquiring the gas, but others did not, and while he and Etienne were experimenting with their hot-air balloons, other pioneers in France were trying to make the hydrogen balloon a reality. The bid to be the first men to fly was a race between the proponents of the hot-air balloon and those of the hydrogen balloon.

After the successful demonstration in Annonay, Etienne went to Paris to publicize the balloon and carry out further demonstrations. While he was there, the first test of a hydrogen balloon was carried out in the Champ de Mars by the French physicist J.A.C. Charles, who had contrived to generate sufficient hydrogen to fill a rubberized bag 12 feet in diameter. The "Charlière" worked well, rapidly ascending to 1,500 feet and disappearing over the Seine. It came down about 12 miles north of Paris near Ecouen, where terrified peasants attacked it with pitchforks. Etienne now had a serious rival.

He had meanwhile constructed a second Montgolfière, 70 feet tall and 40 feet in diameter, which he intended to demonstrate to the royal family at Versailles. It was made in the wallpaper factory of a friend, Jean-Baptiste Reveillon, who added some colourful touches in the form of brilliant strips of wallpaper. Unfortunately the first attempt to demonstrate it coincided with a rainstorm, and the balloon soon collapsed, looking hopelessly bedraggled. It did just enough, however, to encourage Etienne to proceed, but this time he resolved to make a balloon which would be resistant to fire, wind and water. To ensure that the Versailles demonstration was really impressive, he decided to jump one step ahead of the Charlière by sending animals aloft.

Etienne and his friends built the balloon in just four days and nights. Made of taffeta coated with varnish, it was smaller than the one destroyed by the rain, but had a lifting force of almost 700 lb, quite sufficient for the sheep, duck and rooster which had finally been chosen as crew. The demonstration, on 19 September 1783, was a triumph. The balloon lifted off and, despite losing some hot air when it was tilted by the wind, continued on its way for eight minutes before landing gently with its animals still alive.

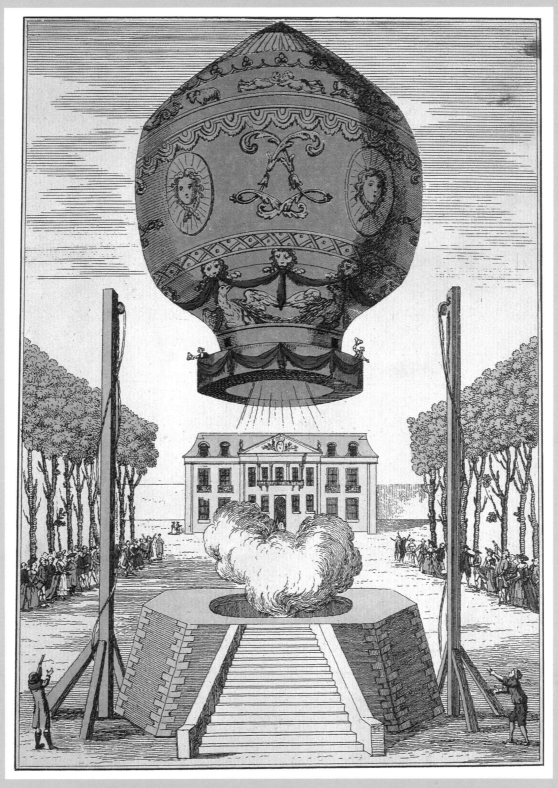

The first manned free flight, on 21 November 1783. Etienne Montgolfier had hoped that the event would be kept secret, but it proved impossible and a large crowd gathered at the Château de la Muette on the western outskirts of Paris. It was the home of the two-year-old dauphin and his elder sister; Benjamin Franklin was a near neighbour and an engraving was made of the first flight as seen from his terrace.

Up and Away

The third Montgolfière was built in four frantic days and nights. The urgency was caused by the imminent date for the royal demonstration at Versailles on 19 September 1783 and by the destruction by rain of the second balloon. A large platform was built with a circular opening 15 feet in diameter which contained an iron stove. The king watched the flight with his field glasses and sent people to check on the condition of the animals when the balloon came down just over 2 miles away.

King Louis XVI and his court were impressed.

Next, Etienne determined to try a manned flight. He modified the Versailles balloon, increasing its capacity by 50 percent. The burner was suspended below the balloon, within reach of the passengers who could toss fresh fuel into it with a pitchfork, but far enough away so as not to set the fabric alight.

The public demonstration set for 21 November was preceded by several tethered experiments, in at least one of which Etienne himself may have gone aloft. This demonstration is generally taken to be the first manned flight, and indeed it was the first in which the tethering ropes were disconnected. The crew consisted of a young scientist, Jean-François Pilâtre de Rozier, and a nobleman, François Laurent, the Marquis d'Arlandes. Both had been keen to take their chances in Etienne's balloon.

This time the launching place was the garden of the Château de la Muette, on the western outskirts of Paris, where the infant dauphin lived

under the care of the Duchesse de Polignac. The first attempt at a tethered test failed when wind tilted the balloon and brought it ignominiously to the ground. Repairs took an hour and a half, by which time the wind had abated. It took eight minutes to reflate the balloon, and at 1.54 p.m. it was off.

As he looked down, d'Arlandes was struck most by the silence of those on the ground. They seemed immobilized and, thinking they needed reassurance, he waved a handkerchief. De Rozier soon complained that d'Arlandes was not doing enough to keep the fire burning, so they both fed it with fresh straw. The wind was carrying them along the Seine, so they stoked the fire again, and d'Arlandes gave it a poke with his pitchfork. As it blazed up, he felt himself lifted as if by the armpits. "Now we're really climbing," he shouted, but at that moment there was a popping noise high in the rigging.

Looking upward, d'Arlandes saw that part of the fabric was smouldering, creating small holes.

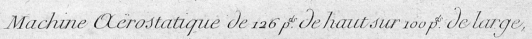

Machine Aérostatique de 126 p.ds de haut sur 100 p.ds de large,

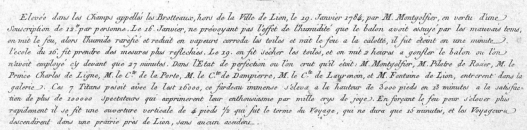

The Montgolfier brothers—*Joseph (1740–1810) (top) and Etienne (1745–99)— were opposites in temperament. Joseph was ingenious, interested in science but impractical in everyday life. His brother was businesslike and had trained as an architect, but was recalled to his father's paper mill when the eldest brother died. Joseph was later created a Chevalier de la legion d'honneur.*

Le Flesselles, the fifth Montgolfière, was designed by Joseph for Jacques de Flesselles. It took off from Lyons, after rivals for a place in the balloon drew pistols to enforce their claim, on 19 January 1784, watched by 100,000 spectators. The fabric tore, causing a harsh landing.

They were right over Paris, so they could not put down. Fortunately d'Arlandes put out the flames with a sponge attached to his pitchfork.

Once past the Port Royal, open ground appeared and d'Arlandes was all for putting down, but de Rozier warned that they were approaching two windmills. De Rozier threw on another bale as the balloon went between the mills. It cleared a pond and landed with the windmills a hundred yards on either side. They had been in the air 25 minutes and had travelled 5 miles. Most of their fuel remained unburned.

Etienne had launched his balloon just in time. Only ten days later Professor Charles and Marie-Noël Robert took off in their Charlière for a flight of more than 25 miles, lasting two hours. When they landed Robert alighted and Charles went on for a second solo flight, rising to 10,000 feet and making a series of observations of temperature and pressure. After 35 minutes he opened the valves and settled slowly down again, landing gently near La Tour de Laye. In less than two weeks, not one but two flying machines had been successfully demonstrated.

The Monoplane that Hit the Headlines

The moment when Charles Lindbergh finally came down to earth after his epic flight alone across the Atlantic was when he met King George V at Buckingham Palace. The king, who insisted on seeing Lindbergh alone, leaned forward and said: "Now tell me, Captain Lindbergh, there is one thing I long to know. How did you pee?" It was, said Lindbergh, a question that put him at his ease. He explained that he had carried an aluminium container for the purpose, and had dropped it when he was safely over France and no longer needed it. "I was not going to be caught with the thing on me at Le Bourget," he explained. In some remote hedgerow it may rest to this day, for aluminium does not corrode. The rest of Lindbergh's aircraft, *Spirit of St Louis*, is in the Smithsonian Institution in Washington, the only survivor of the planes that raced to be the first to fly from New York to Paris nonstop.

It was Lindbergh who won that race, and his the name that is remembered. Nobody now recalls his rivals, who came so close to denying him the prize. Some have even forgotten that the Atlantic had been flown before, by Captain John Alcock and Lieutenant Arthur Whitten-Brown, in a Vickers Vimy bomber in 1919. The two-man team departed from Newfoundland, and ended nose-first in an Irish bog. It is the glamour of the lone aviator, who set off from a proper

FACT FILE

The first solo flight across the Atlantic

Date built: 1927

Wingspan: 46 feet

Length: 27 feet 8 inches

Power output: 237 horsepower

Maximum speed: 129 mph

airfield and landed at another, that has lasted.

Lindbergh began his career as a barn-storming pilot in the early 1920s, touring the farm lands of the Midwest. The technique was to raise interest by flying low over a town, showing off a few stunts, then to sell tickets at $5 a ride. Lindbergh grew skilful at standing on the wings, even when the pilot threw the plane into a loop. But it was a precarious life, and in 1924 he enlisted in the US Army as a flying cadet. A year later he got his wings, went on the reserve list, and found a job as a pilot flying mail from St Louis to Chicago.

Within a year he had twice had to parachute from aircraft that had run out of fuel in poor weather. The day after the first of these mishaps,

he took a day off and went to the cinema. On a newsreel he saw a report of a huge new aircraft designed by Igor Sikorsky to carry a crew of four across the Atlantic to Europe. Flown by a French pilot called René Fonck, the Sikorsky was aiming to win a $25,000 prize for the first crossing from New York to Paris or the shores of France, or vice versa. The prize had been put up in 1919 by a Frenchman, Raymond Orteig, who ran two hotels in New York.

Lindbergh immediately began to take an interest in the race. He found Fonck's plans poorly conceived. Why take four men to fly a single plane? Why carry two radio sets, when one would do? Why decorate the interior of the plane

The crowd waiting to welcome Lindbergh at Croydon Aerodrome near London was so great that police lines broke and people ran on to the runway just as he was about to land, compelling him to take off again. Lindbergh had flown from Paris to Brussels and come on to England on 29 May. King George V awarded Lindbergh the Air Force Cross.

The Monoplane that Hit the Headlines

with red leather, and even provide a bed? To an aviator of Lindbergh's experience, raised in simple planes that cut out every frill, this seemed wasteful. It would be better to strip the machine to its limits, carry a single man, and use the extra space for fuel. His doubts proved justified when Fonck set out for Paris on 20 September 1926, failed to get airborne, and crashed into a gully at the end of the runway killing two members of the crew. It was at this point that Lindbergh realized he could do better.

He determined to fly the Atlantic alone, in a single-engined plane. He had some trouble explaining the wisdom of this idea to potential backers, but he was a persuasive young man and had soon raised $15,000 from St Louis business-men, sufficient to buy the aircraft he needed. Fokkers refused to sell him one, and the Wright-Bellanca company, who made a suitable mono-plane, would only let him have one if they were permitted to choose the crew. Guessing they would not choose him, Lindbergh turned them down. The only company that was prepared to help was the Ryan Aircraft Company of San Diego, California.

By luck, Lindbergh had stumbled on the best men in America to make his dream come true. While the rivals in the race suffered crashes, the Ryan company worked flat out on Lindbergh's

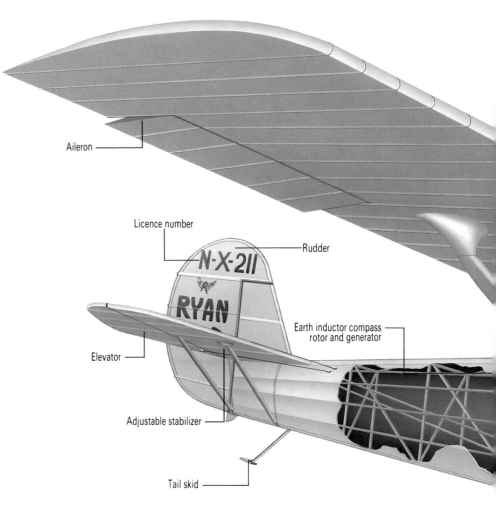

Aileron

Licence number

Rudder

Earth inductor compass rotor and generator

Elevator

Adjustable stabilizer

Tail skid

Lindbergh was impressed by the people at the Ryan Aircraft Company in San Diego, although their premises were in a dilapidated building on a waterfront reeking of dead fish. Hours of overtime were needed to construct the new design in less than two months. On the test flights the plane exhibited good reserves of power. These would stand her in good stead when laden with fuel for the Atlantic crossing; some rivals had crashed on takeoff due to lack of power. The Wright "Whirlwind" J-5C engine produced 220 hp at sea level, turning over at 1,800 rpm.

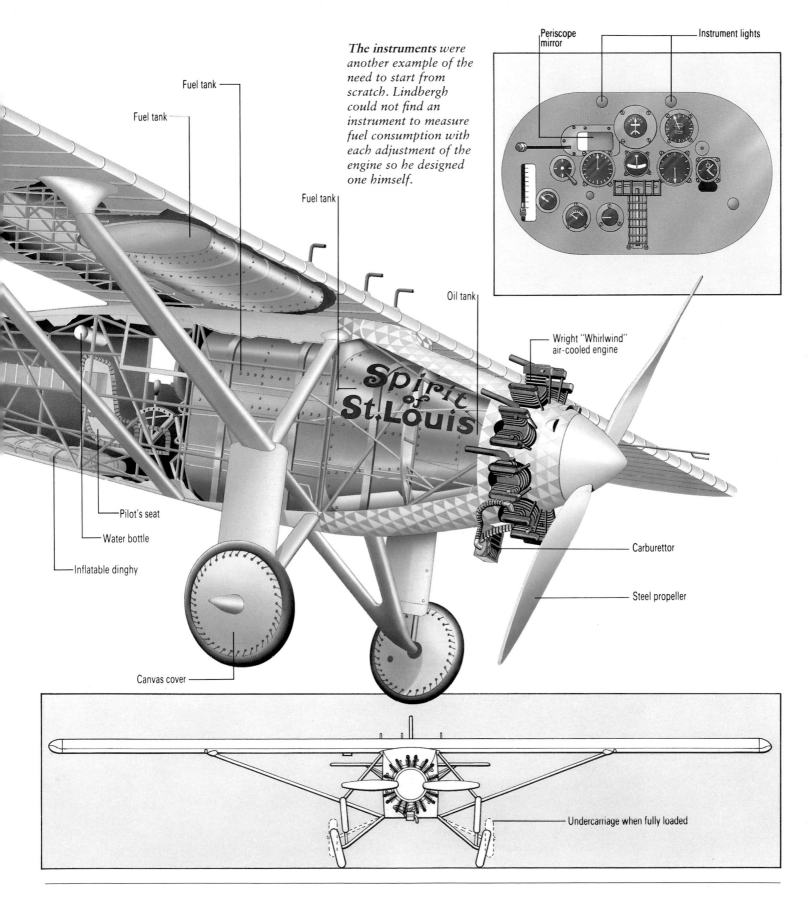

Fuel tank

Fuel tank

Fuel tank

The instruments were another example of the need to start from scratch. Lindbergh could not find an instrument to measure fuel consumption with each adjustment of the engine so he designed one himself.

Periscope mirror

Instrument lights

Oil tank

Wright "Whirlwind" air-cooled engine

Pilot's seat

Water bottle

Inflatable dinghy

Carburettor

Steel propeller

Canvas cover

Undercarriage when fully loaded

The Monoplane that Hit the Headlines

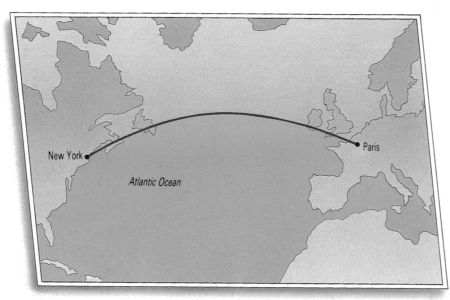

Lindbergh rightly considered lightness a key to success. As a result, safety and personal equipment were kept to a minimum. He did not even take a parachute. The list comprised an air raft with pump and repair kit, a canteen of water (8 pints), an Armbrust cup that condenses moisture from the breath, a knife, ball of cord, ball of string, large needle, flashlight, four red flares from a railroad sealed in rubber tubes, match safe and matches, a hacksaw blade, five cans of army emergency rations and five ham sandwiches. During the flight, he drank most of the water but ate little of the food, thinking that it increased his desire to sleep.

plane, the *Spirit of St Louis*. The chief designer was Donald Hall, and the monoplane he created had some novel features.

In most aircraft of that era, the pilot sat behind the engine but in front of the fuel tank, a position Lindbergh considered very dangerous. He decided to put the tank in front of him, which meant that he had no view forward, except by leaning out of a side window. Lindbergh explained that this was no serious disadvantage, since during takeoff the pilot could not see forward anyway, because of the engine high in the nose ahead of him. During normal flight he would not need to look ahead, because he would not be in any normal air lanes; for landing, he could see out sufficiently to get down safely. He wanted no night-flying equipment, and no parachute, in order to save a few pounds in weight. (He did take a rubber dinghy, in case of ditching in the sea.)

In order to speed up the building process, he agreed to let Hall use tail components from an existing Ryan model, although they would diminish the stability of the aircraft. It would not matter, Lindbergh argued, on an aircraft that was designed to be flown by an experienced pilot who would spend all of his time with his eyes on the compass and trying to steer a course above the waves.

Lindbergh decided to fly a great circle route, the shortest distance between two points on the Earth's surface. He drew the route on maritime charts of the Atlantic, and flew along it as best he could judge, setting his course by compass and making allowance for the wind by watching the spray from the waves below. It was a rough and

ready method but, as he explained, it would be accurate enough to ensure that he reached the European coast, and that was what mattered. He could still win the prize as long as he landed in France, and the design of the aircraft gave it a theoretical range of 4,100 miles—500 miles more than his great circle route. That ought to be enough to ensure a landfall even if his calculations were out.

The *Spirit of St Louis* made its maiden flight on 28 April 1927, just over two months after the order had been placed with the Ryan company. By 8 May Lindbergh was ready to fly to New York, when news came that two French airmen had set off from Paris on their bid to cross the Atlantic the other way. It looked as if all Lindbergh's efforts would be in vain. But Charles Nungesser and François Coli came down somewhere in the Atlantic in their Levasseur biplane, *L'Oiseau Blanc*, and were never seen again. Hope of finding them alive had not receded before Lindbergh took off for France, and he received requests to search for them in the area where it was thought they may have come down.

Once in New York, Lindbergh became obsessed by weather reports. As an experienced mail pilot, he knew he dared not try to make the trip in unfavourable weather, but also that he could trust the forecasters to give him advance warning of when the weather would improve. On the evening of 19 May, the good news came. Just after daybreak the next morning, weighed down with a full fuel load, the *Spirit of St Louis* was ready to go. It had never taken off fully laden, and the weather in New York was miserable, whatever the forecasters had said. In rain and over a muddy runway, Lindbergh opened the throttle and began to gain speed. He felt the tail go up, but then come down again. The plane splashed through a puddle, skimmed the next one, and was up. He cleared a set of telephone lines at the edge of the field by a bare 20 feet, and was gone.

Although he had laughed at the suggestion of carrying a periscope to see out, he nevertheless took one. For much of the journey he flew low over the sea, at an altitude where the greatest danger was colliding with the masts of ships. Peering through his periscope, which he lowered from the left side of the fuselage, he looked out for landmarks. But for most of the time, his eyes were on his chart, which lay on his lap, and a compass by which he steered. To conserve fuel, he cruised at a speed of 100 mph, which would

Landing at Le Bourget *(above) was made difficult by the lack of feeling induced by exhaustion. Thousands of people greeted Lindbergh and the plane was damaged by the pressure of the crowd and by those wanting a souvenir. Two companies of soldiers and countless police could not restrain the crowd. It was 4.15 a.m. before Lindbergh got to bed—63 hours since he had last awoken. Dressed in full flying kit, Lindbergh (left middle) poses before leaving for home.*

give him 50 hours of flying on what ought to be a 36-hour flight.

Eleven hours saw him over Nova Scotia, and heading across the Atlantic. There followed a long night of fighting off sleep and trying to keep on course. In the morning, he saw some trawlers, and seeking directions flew low above them. They ignored him, so rather than waste fuel, he flew on. An hour later, he saw land, and recognized it from his charts as the southern coast of Ireland. People waved to him from the ground.

He was next seen over Cornwall and then over the French coast at Cherbourg. By 9.52 p.m. he saw the Eiffel Tower and began to look for Le Bourget airport. The first time he missed it, but he turned round and tried again, landing to a huge welcome from an ecstatic crowd that had been warned of his arrival. He had flown from New York to Paris in 33 hours 30 minutes. He was the most famous man in the world.

Flying Farther and Faster

The great distinction of being the first to fly in a heavier-than-air machine was achieved by Orville Wright, at Kitty Hawk, North Carolina, on 17 December 1903. Between 1896 and 1902, Orville and Wilbur Wright learned enough about aerodynamics from experiments with gliders to begin work on a powered aeroplane. They built their own four-cylinder engine which drove two propellers by chain drives. Scepticism about the chances of success was reflected in the fact that just five people turned out to witness the first flight of 12 seconds.

Since that momentous day, aviators and aeroplane companies have worked to break new ground, either in terms of endurance and average speed over a long haul, or by raising through steady increments the speed of the world's fastest aircraft. Records in the first category were being established throughout the 1920s and '30s; after World War II, the target was the sound barrier and then Mach 2 and 3.

Amelia Earhart (above), *born in Kansas, was the first woman to fly the Atlantic as a passenger, in 1928. Four years later, she became the first woman to fly alone across the Atlantic, in a monoplane. The flight took 13¼ hours. In 1937, she set off around the world in a twin-engined Lockheed Electra, but went missing over the Pacific.*

Amy Johnson, *born in Hull, England, flew solo to Australia in 19½ days in 1930, just three days short of the record. Her epic flights to Japan via Siberia in 1931 and to Cape Town in 1932 set new records. She is seen here (right) just before setting off for Cape Town. On a flying mission in 1941 she disappeared over the Thames Estuary.*

The Wright brothers *were refused recognition or financial help for their aviation experiments in the United States, so in 1908 Wilbur Wright went to France to try to obtain support there. This time large crowds watched the flights in their* Flyer *biplane. A vast improvement on earlier models, in which the pilot lay prone on the lower wing beside the engine, in this* Flyer *both pilot and engine were upright. Wilbur flew from Hunardières-Le Mans (above) and achieved a flight of 2 hours 19 minutes, winning the Michelin Cup and securing many orders for the Wright biplane. He returned in triumph to the US and the brothers turned over their bicycle factory to the manufacture of aeroplanes. After Wilbur died in 1912, Orville sold his interest and went into research.*

The Schneider Trophy was first presented in 1913 by Jacques Schneider for success in a speed competition between seaplanes of any nation. The award stimulated aircraft development and had a major effect on World War II, since the competition led to the development of the Spitfire fighter that helped the RAF win the Battle of Britain. The Supermarine S.6 (above) was powered by a Rolls-Royce R type engine of 1,950 hp, which was a precursor of the Merlin engine fitted to the Spitfire. The S.6 won the 1929 race and set a world speed record with a speed of 357.7 mph.

The Lockheed SR-71 Blackbird (left) was put into service with the United States Air Force in the early 1960s and was the fastest military plane in the world. Able to cruise at Mach 3 (1,865 mph) and reach an altitude of 15 miles, most of the SR-71's airframe was built of titanium and coated with a heat-radiating black paint that could also absorb radar waves. Used as a spy plane, the SR-71's cameras could focus on a golf ball from a height of 14 miles. The plane's operating costs were so great they were taken out of service in 1990.

The Doomed Airship

Rigid airships represent one of the most fascinating dead ends in transport history. During the 1920s many saw them as the aerial equivalents of the great liners, gliding silent through the night sky as their passengers slept. They offered space, comfort and—by the standards of the time—speed. Britain, France, the US and Germany all built airships in the conviction that they represented the future. It took seven disasters and the loss of 266 lives between 1921 and 1937 to show them how wrong they had been. Of these accidents none was more profoundly shocking than the loss of the R101 in October 1930.

The R101 and its sister ship, R100, were Britain's attempt to catch up with the German lead in rigid airship design, which had begun in 1900 with Count Ferdinand Zeppelin's LZ-1. A rigid airship was more than just a bag full of gas or hot air with a basket hung below. It had a metal or wooden framework covered in fabric, with passenger accommodation inside the envelope. The lightweight hydrogen gas was contained in bags made of goldbeaters' skin, inside the cover and harnessed to the structure.

Also attached to the structure were engines, with propellers, capable of driving the airship at speeds of up to 70 mph. The rigid airship seemed particularly safe, because it did not depend on forward motion—and hence on unreliable engines—to keep it aloft, as aircraft did. It floated on the air like a liner on the ocean, the very image of soundness and security. This was a terrible illusion.

In Britain, the airship's greatest champion was Lord Thomson, a successful soldier who in 1924 became secretary of state for air in the first Labour government. He had no doubt that one day the British Empire would be linked together by airships and he quickly launched a programme to build two of them. No ideologue, he arranged for R100 to be built by private industry, while R101 was entrusted to the Royal Airship Works at Cardington in Bedfordshire.

Both had the same specification: a gas capacity of 5 million cubic feet, sufficient in theory to carry 100 passengers with 8 tons of mail and cargo for 3,135 nautical miles at a speed of 55 knots. Five million cubic feet of hydrogen gives a theoretical gross lift of 151.8 tons, from which must be subtracted the weight of the airship,

engines, fuel and ballast to calculate the payload.

Unfortunately, but perhaps inevitably, the weight of both airships turned out to be considerably greater than their designers anticipated. Consequently, when R101 was completed in June 1929, its disposable lift was only 46.8 tons, instead of the 63.3 tons intended. By the time fuel, ballast, crew and food were loaded, that left just 9.3 tons available for passengers, mail and cargo, instead of the 24.2 tons intended.

In spite of these problems, R101 was an impressive sight as it was walked out of the huge shed at Cardington by 400 men holding on to ropes. It was the biggest airship ever built—732 feet long, 140 feet high, and with an outer cover that was almost 5 acres in area. R101 was by quite a margin the biggest vessel in the world.

The lack of lifting capacity was, however, a serious embarrassment. One problem with airships was the need to carry a large amount of deadweight in the form of ballast, for there was no way of replenishing the gas in mid-flight. If leaks in the gas bags or an increase in temperature caused the craft to sink, the only way of correcting the situation was by dumping water ballast overboard. An airship flying without adequate amounts of ballast was dangerous and hard to control, so arrangements were made to collect rainwater falling on the cover in flight to replenish the ballast tanks.

It is clear that in spite of its apparent security, the airship operated in a very narrow safety envelope. Apart from the risk of fire there was the danger of the fragile gas bags puncturing, of loss of lift because of changes in temperature, or of damage from severe weather. Violent storms could carry airships upward like the leaves in autumn, as R100 found on a visit to Canada in 1930 which nearly ended in disaster. Navigation instruments were primitive in the extreme.

With the benefit of hindsight, it is hard to share Lord Thomson's conviction that airships had a future. Yet his ambition was to inaugurate a regular service to India, via Ismailia in Egypt. The trip by R100 to Canada, although hair-raising to the participants, had ended in apparent success. Now it was necessary to fly R101 to India with the secretary of state for air aboard. Lord Thomson wished this pioneering journey to take place while the Imperial Conference of 1930 was meeting in London, so that he could

FACT FILE

The ill-fated journey of Britain's largest airship

Date built: 1929

Length: 732 feet

Width (max): 140 feet

Volume: 5 million cubic feet

return in triumph and address the delegates. Many have subsequently blamed the disaster on Thomson's impatience, although that was only one element in the tragedy.

To prepare for the journey, R101 had been modified in an attempt to increase lift. An extra bay had been added to its length, and the network of wires that held the gas bags in place had been let out to increase capacity. This meant that the bags were now rubbing against the actual structure of the airship, which they were not supposed to touch. A huge number of holes were made in the bags, which needed patching. To prevent the same thing happening again, sharp edges on the structure were covered in soft wadding to protect the bags. Frederick McWade, the airworthiness inspector at Cardington, reported that he was unhappy with this solution and could not grant R101 a permit to fly; his objections were overruled and were not brought to the attention of Lord Thomson.

All was made ready for the departure to India. In addition to Lord Thomson, the passenger list featured all the leading airship designers from Cardington, including the director of airship development, Wing-Commander R.B.B. Colmore. It now seems rash in the extreme to fill an experimental flight with so many top brass, but there was complete optimism, bordering on complacency, that all would go well.

R101 beside the docking tower at the Royal Airship Works. Excessive weight was a key factor in R101's loss: it weighed 113.4 tons instead of the intended 90 tons. Lord Thomson was not warned about the need to restrict luggage and brought an Axminster carpet weighing almost half a ton as well as 254 lb of trunks and champagne.

The Doomed Airship

The Beardmore Tornado diesel engines which powered R101 were a major reason for the miscalculation of the airship's weight. Although diesel engines are reliable and economic to run, they are heavy in relation to other engines. However, the higher flash point of diesel fuel compared with petrol was a safety factor.

The lounge of R101 was 60 feet long by 32 feet wide and was on the upper accommodation deck, along with a dining room for 50 people and the cabins. On the lower floor were a smoking room, electric kitchens, crew's quarters and further cabins. The total floor area available to passengers and crew was 7,780 square feet, the size of a large country house.

Lord Thomson's timetable, already delayed by the alterations to R101, made a departure early in October vital if he were to return in time to address the conference. It was the first time R101 had left the British Isles, and ahead lay two long legs, from Cardington across France and down the Mediterranean to Ismailia, and then by way of Baghdad and the Gulf to Karachi. The first, some 2,235 nautical miles, was scheduled to take 48 hours, the second, 2,135 nautical miles, another 46 hours.

Departure was set for the evening of 4 October 1930, and the luggage was loaded. By the time all was ready and the secretary of state was on board, delay became impossible even though the weather forecasts for France were bad and becoming worse. R101 set off into the teeth of the fiercest gale it had ever experienced, though such was the cheerful spirit of those on board that it did not fail to make its customary tour of Bedford after leaving the tower. Flying barely 600 feet above the houses, it weighed 160 tons—the greatest load ever lifted by any aircraft at that time. After its farewell circuit the airship set off toward London.

As it flew over London, people came out into the streets to watch. Looking up they could see faces silhouetted in the large windows of the passenger cabin. As it crossed the Kent countryside just south of Hawkhurst, R101 sent a radio message to the Met Office asking for further weather forecasts. It passed over Bodiam Castle and crossed the coast 4 miles east of Hastings.

As R101 crossed the Channel, calcium flares were dropped from the control car into the sea, igniting to produce a brilliant light. By watching

the flares, R101's navigators could estimate their drift. By mid-Channel the wind was up to 44 mph, with fierce gusts, and R101 flew at no more than 800 feet. The passengers had eaten and were now smoking in the special room set aside for that purpose. Across the Channel R101 made only 24.8 knots into a rising headwind.

By midnight it was west of Abbeville and flying at 1,500 feet to clear high ground; but in gaining height it had spilled gas, at the same time as adding more than 5 tons of weight as a result of rain absorbed by the cover and collected in the ballast tanks. At this point, R101 was almost certainly flying about 4 tons heavy, sustained in the air by the aerodynamic effect of its motion.

Over the wooded country between the Somme and the Bresle R101 flew on, with just the crew on watch awake. By now the wind was blowing

The fire that devastated R101 was started when the calcium flares used to aid navigation ignited in the wet undergrowth. The fire started just below the passenger accommodation and quickly spread to the gas bags. R101 was a mass of twisted metal in minutes. Amongst the passengers were Air Vice-Marshall Sir Sefton Brancker, director of civil aviation, and the best of the design engineers, Squadron Leader Michael Rope.

The Doomed Airship

at 50 mph, but all five engines were running well. The speed over France was down to 23.6 knots as R101 battled against the wind, constantly blown eastward off its course to Orly airfield.

By 2 a.m., the change of watch, R101 had almost reached the Beauvais Ridge at a ground speed of no more than 20 mph. Seven minutes later the ship suddenly dipped, pointing toward the ground before righting herself. She then dived again and nosed quietly into the ground. Within seconds R101 was in flames. In less than two minutes it had gone, consumed by a terrible fire that killed 46 of the 54 on board, including the secretary of state for air and all the leading British airship specialists.

What had happened? The most scrupulous analysis of the accident, carried out by Sir Peter Masefield for his book *To Ride the Storm*, has revealed the most likely course of events. He believes that in battling against the storm R101 had almost certainly damaged its outer cover, a known weakness in the design. Much of it had been replaced when it had been found to be rotten, but a critical section near the front had been retained. There had been no full-speed trial after the repairs and before the flight, so the cover had never been fully tested. R101 had flown into the worst storm of its life, and had ploughed on at full speed, in order to meet the secretary of state's timetable.

There had just been a change of watch, and the new coxswain had not had time to get used to the handling of the ship in the difficult conditions when it hit a region of turbulence. The chances are that the cover was damaged, and the fact reported to the men on the wheel, who reacted by throttling back the engines in order to spare the cover further damage. But R101 was flying heavy and needed speed to maintain height. As it slowed, it lost dynamic lift, went into a dive and brushed gently into the ground at hardly more than 10 to 15 mph.

The destruction of R101 spelled the end for British airships. R100 never left the shed at Cardington again, and plans for R102 and R103 were abandoned. The Germans continued their work until 1937, when the *Hindenburg* burst into flames at its mast in New Jersey. After that, all the high hopes that had inspired a generation of designers lay in ruins. The first vehicle to meet R101's specification—to carry 100 passengers more than 3,000 miles—was a heavier-than-air machine, the Bristol Britannia series 300 turbo-prop airliner, in 1956.

LEVIATHANS OF THE SKIES

Within 18 months of the Montgolfiers' flights, a hydrogen-filled balloon had crossed the English Channel and seemed to point the way forward. The military used them in the American Civil War (1861–65), and the first powered dirigible was built in Germany in 1872. Their potential was developed most notably by Count von Zeppelin. His 420-foot-long LZ 1 flew for 1¼ hours in 1900. Competition between Britain, France, Germany and the United States to develop the airship was intense, despite serious accidents and losses. The loss of the *Hindenburg* ended enthusiasm for the airship.

LZ 129, the Hindenburg, *under construction at Friedrichshaven. Completed in March 1936, the* Hindenburg *was the largest airship ever built, with a length of 813 feet and a capacity of 7 million cubic feet. She exploded in May 1937 while docking at Lakehurst, New Jersey.*

Professor Salomon Andrée and two companions attempted to reach the North Pole by balloon in 1897, setting off from Spitsbergen, Norway, aboard the specially built Eagle. With a capacity of 170,000 cubic feet, the Eagle was fitted with sails which were intended to direct it. The three were not seen again until their frozen bodies were discovered 33 years later. A diary found on Andrée revealed that the balloon had been abandoned three days after departure because it continually struck the ice. Then began a 200-mile trek across the frozen wastes.

The Graf Zeppelin *was the first commercial airship to cross the Atlantic, on 11 October 1928, flying from Friedrichshaven to Lakehurst in New Jersey. The next year, the Graf Zeppelin accomplished the first around-the-world airship flight with passengers and mail. Thereafter it operated a regular service between Germany and Rio de Janeiro. With accommodation for 20 passengers, the Graf Zeppelin was 772 feet long and had a capacity of 3.7 million cubic feet. It was broken up for scrap in March 1940.*

Opening up the East

No experience in flying is quite the equal of taking off and landing on water. While an airliner must operate from a busy airport, with its crowds, queues and tiresome delays, a flying boat can make use of any stretch of water. It can pick up its passengers from a beach or a harbour, taxi out between the yachts and speedboats, gain speed to the heady scent of hot oil and the spatter of salt spray against the windows, and translate itself into another element. This is flying with the magic put back in. Unfortunately, there are only a few flying boat services left, mostly in holiday areas like the US Virgin Islands, so few people have a chance to enjoy a wonderful experience. There was a time, however, when flying boats were thought to hold the future to aviation.

In the 1930s, before war brought down the curtain, it was possible to fly all the way to the Far East in a flying boat, making stops in dozens of exotic places and taking two weeks over the journey. The airline, Imperial Airways, stopped at places that are hardly places at all: Rutbah Wells and Sharjah, Gwadar in Baluchistan, Kanpur, Akyab, and the islands of Lombok, Sumba and Timor.

The journey was accomplished in aircraft that were laughably slow, though by the last years of the 1930s the route was served by a magnificent flying boat, the Short S-23, better known as the Empire class. Until recently, it was possible to meet old colonial officers whose eyes would grow misty at the mention of *Canopus*, or *Coriolanus*, or *Caledonia*, or *Corsair*—four of the Empire class boats, built by Short Brothers beside the River Medway at Rochester in Kent.

It was in 1928 that Imperial Airways first planned its long-distance routes to destinations in the Empire. For services to India and Africa, Short Brothers provided the S-8 Calcutta, an all-metal biplane flying boat with three engines. The Calcutta carried a crew of 4 and 15 passengers, and could cruise at 80 mph.

A couple of years later Short produced the Kent, also a biplane, which was used by Imperial on the Mediterranean stretch of the run to India. The Kent had four engines, the first ever passenger aircraft so equipped, and could cruise at 105 mph. Only three Kents were ever built. Each had space for 16 passengers in a roomy saloon with comfortable armchairs.

In 1935, Imperial Airways' ambitions began to widen, as they contemplated passenger services throughout the Empire, and across the Atlantic. Imperial issued to British companies a request for an aircraft, and Short Brothers once more came to their aid.

They produced a design for a large flying boat, able to carry 24 passengers, with a single high wing. It was bigger, faster and more powerful than any plane built in Britain, and Shorts suggested it might be sensible first to build a prototype to see how well it flew. Imperial responded by saying there was no time for that, and ordered 28 of the new boats off the drawing table. So was born one of the most handsome aircraft that ever flew, the Short S-23 "C" Class Empire flying boat.

The prototype, *Canopus* (named after an ancient Egyptian city), was launched at Rochester on 4 July 1936. Its four 920-hp Bristol Pegasus engines gave it a top speed of 200 mph and a cruising speed of 165 mph. It weighed 18 tons, but the design of its deep hull enabled it to "unstick" from the Medway in only 17 seconds on its maiden flight. The major advantage of the Empire type was its 700 mile range.

Canopus went into service on the Mediterranean run in October, and on 12 December *Centaurus* left with the first of the air mail bags to Egypt, and *Caledonia* departed on an experimental flight to India. The boats were rolling out of the Rochester plant at the rate of two a month. By June 1937, a total of 14 had been delivered and the first proving flight to Singapore had been undertaken. By February 1938, enough Empires were available to start a regular service to Singapore.

Travelling east by flying boat was not without its awkward moments. During 1938 one boat collided with an Italian submarine; *Ceres* was forced down on to Lake Dingari in Tonk, India, and became solidly bogged down in mud. In 1939, *Centurion* was written off by a gust of wind while landing on the Hooghly at Calcutta, and *Connemara* was burned at Southampton. In August *Challenger* crashed in Africa.

Even one of these accidents today would cause a tremendous furore, but airline passengers of the 1930s were a phlegmatic lot. It was a great adventure and, like all adventures, involved an element of risk. To those used to small, draughty

FACT FILE

The world's longest flying boat service, operated by Short S-23 "C" class Empire flying boats

Built: 1935/36

Wingspan: 114 feet

Length: 88 feet

Power output: 4 × 920 horsepower

Maximum speed: 200 mph

The first of the Empire flying boats, Canopus, takes off from the River Medway with Rochester Castle, Kent, in the background (above). She left Rochester on the first route-proving flight, to Rome and Alexandria, in October 1936, returning on the first scheduled flight. Imperial Airways promoted the exotic nature of many of the places on the Empire route (left).

Opening up the East

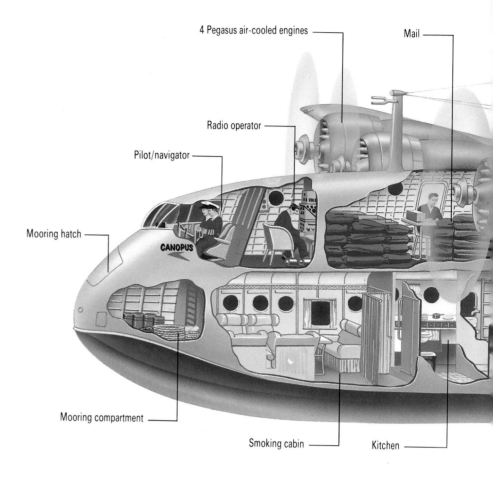

4 Pegasus air-cooled engines

Mail

Radio operator

Pilot/navigator

Mooring hatch

CANOPUS

Mooring compartment

Smoking cabin

Kitchen

and uncomfortable aircraft, the Empires were a revelation. One anonymous passenger, who wrote for *Imperial Airways Gazette* an account of his flight aboard *Calypso* to Singapore in March 1938, arrived at Southampton with a cabin wardrobe-trunk, a set of golf clubs, a suitcase, a heavy dispatch case and a typewriter. *Calypso* on this trip carried 3 tons of mail, 2 tons of cargo, and a few passengers, a couple of them young men going on their first contract to the newly opened oil fields in Bahrain.

From Southampton *Calypso* flew at 11,500 feet toward Marseilles. At this height it was chilly, so the steward gave out blankets and came round with cups of hot Bovril. Lunch consisted of soup, hot or cold meat and vegetables, sweet, cheese and dessert. At Marseilles the landing was made at Lake Marignane, a few miles from the city, after a flight of almost five hours. Here passengers spent their first night, before taking off again at 6.45 the next morning for Italy, landing this time on Lake Bracciano, 30 miles north of Rome. After refuelling, *Calypso* flew on to Brindisi, for more fuel and oil. Here the passengers were taken off in launches for customs examination before reboarding and flying on to Athens, landing in Phaleron Bay.

After a second overnight stop in Athens, *Calypso* took off again at 8.30 a.m., and landed for fuel in Mirabella, a landlocked bay on the northeast coast of Crete. Here Imperial Airways had moored the motor yacht *Imperia*, a floating depot and wireless station where the passengers took tea. After another 400-mile hop, *Calypso* landed on the harbour at Alexandria and taxied to her mooring between local craft.

After takeoff at six the following morning, *Calypso* flew over Port Said and Haifa, before landing on the Sea of Galilee near Tiberias. The passengers watched in amazement as the altimeters went down below sea level, for the Sea of Galilee lies 700 feet below the Mediterranean. After refuelling, it was off over the desert to Lake Habbaniyeh in Iraq, for more fuel to take *Calypso* as far as Basra. Over the marshlands between the Tigris and Euphrates rivers the local Marsh Arabs were known sometimes to take pot shots at passing flying boats, at least once with fatal results. That night was spent at Shatt-el-Arab, where *Calypso* met *Clio*, homeward bound, and *Calpurnia*, which had brought the King of Iraq to open a new airport and hotel.

An early start the following day called for the use of flares in the waterway to mark the takeoff path. Stops were made in Bahrain, Dubai, Gwadar and Karachi, where *Calypso* landed among the shipping in the harbour. The run to Calcutta the next day involved stops at the sacred Lake Raj Samand in Udaipur, and the reservoir at Gwalior—reputed to be the hottest place in India. A final stop at Allahabad, then to Calcutta, where a porpoise jumped out of the water a few yards ahead of the flying boat as it landed on the Hooghly. From Calcutta the route took *Calypso* on to Akyab on the northern end of the Bay of Bengal, then over southern Burma to Rangoon, and on to Bangkok. One more day, and a single stop at Penang, finally brought the flying boat to Singapore.

Few air routes have ever been so romantic, and although the journey may seem endless to those familiar to modern jets, it was fast compared to the only alternative, steamers. But hardly had the Empire service become fully established than it was brought to an end by the war, and never resumed. Those unique craft, half boat, half plane, had only a brief and brilliant flowering before being replaced by something altogether more mundane.

The interior layout provided two decks forward of the wing spar. The upper flight deck had stations for captain and first officer at side-by-side dual controls, storage for mail bags and a purser's desk. There were also places for a radio operator and flight engineer on longer hauls. On the lower deck, the mooring compartment in the bow contained anchors; aft was a smoking lounge with seats for seven passengers, two toilets, the steward's galley and a midship cabin with seats that converted into bunks for three passengers.

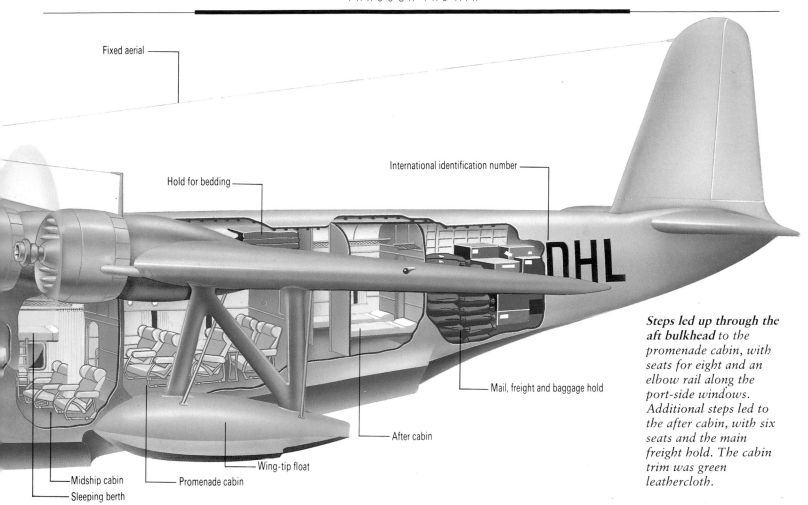

Fixed aerial

Hold for bedding

International identification number

Midship cabin

Sleeping berth

Promenade cabin

Wing-tip float

After cabin

Mail, freight and baggage hold

DHL

Steps led up through the aft bulkhead to the promenade cabin, with seats for eight and an elbow rail along the port-side windows. Additional steps led to the after cabin, with six seats and the main freight hold. The cabin trim was green leathercloth.

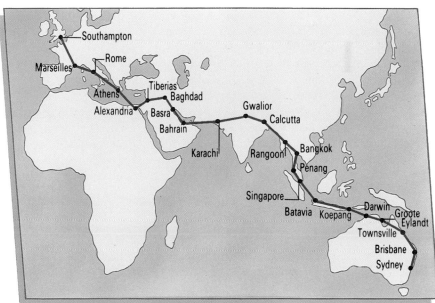

Southampton
Rome
Marseilles
Athens
Tiberias
Baghdad
Alexandria
Basra
Gwalior
Bahrain
Calcutta
Karachi
Rangoon
Bangkok
Penang
Singapore
Batavia
Koepang
Darwin
Groote Eylandt
Townsville
Brisbane
Sydney

An air service from Britain to Australia *began in late 1934, but until the introduction of flying boats in 1937/38, Imperial Airways planes operated the leg to Singapore and Hong Kong only. The regular* *flying boat service to Karachi began in 1937, and from July 1938 it went on to Darwin in Northern Territory. The thrice-weekly service, run by Imperial Airways and Qantas Empire Airways, was* *subject to repeated delays. Connections on to Sydney were provided by conventional aircraft. After World War II, the service resumed with Sunderlands and Sandringhams.*

Rescue from the Skies

From the waters of northern Norway to the Bay of Biscay, Europe's western seaboard is patrolled by helicopters which have achieved a series of near-miraculous rescue operations. Men, women and children have been snatched from ships, oil rigs, life rafts, mountain tops and vertiginous crannies high in cliffs. No two rescues are quite the same; all they have in common is the immense relief of the victims as they see the familiar profile of the Westland Sea King coming into sight and their anxiety as they wait to be hauled aboard.

The Sea King, with its long range, big cabin, legendary reliability, and instruments which enable it to locate a tiny life raft 250 miles from base in the dead of night and thick fog, has become the champion at search and rescue missions. Hundreds of people owe their lives to the remarkable helicopter which first flew as the Sikorsky S61 in 1959.

One of the most dramatic rescues of all happened when the 1979 Fastnet race was devastated by a freak storm. A highlight of the yacht-racing calendar, the Fastnet that year had 300 entries. Winds gusting to force 11 scattered the fleet, and one of the biggest peacetime rescue operations ever undertaken was launched.

The waves ran at 40 to 60 feet and virtually every yacht in the race suffered some degree of distress, from extreme discomfort to mortal danger. Six Sea Kings, flying for three days through salt spray which filled the air up to 1,000 feet, rescued 73 people. Another 17 yachtsmen died. The Sea Kings' engines swallowed so much salt that they had to be washed out during refuelling stops on the ground.

During the 1985 Fastnet race, a Sea King made another dramatic rescue when the pop singer Simon Le Bon and members of his crew were trapped in the overturned hull of his yacht *Drum*. Le Bon, lead singer with the group Duran Duran, was asleep when a force 8 gale ripped the keel off his boat and overturned it. Trapped in the hull with five crew members, Le Bon was rescued by Petty Officer Larry Slater, a Royal Navy frogman dropped from a Sea King, who swam through the hatch into the hull and pulled them out one by one.

The Sea King was originally designed by Sikorsky helicopters in the United States as a platform from which to seek and destroy enemy submarines and ships. It made its first flight in 1959, and in 1966 was the subject of a licensing agreement between Sikorsky and Britain's major helicopter manufacturer, Westland. Since then Westland has sold 320 Sea Kings out of a total of 1,400 of the type manufactured. American production of the model has now stopped, but Westland continues to make it at its factory in Yeovil, Somerset.

From the beginning Westland made Sea Kings specifically tailored for the search and rescue role, omitting the sonar equipment used to track submarines and extending the cabin 5 feet farther aft, in order to find room for more survivors. By the mid-1970s Westland was producing the Sea King HAR Mk3, with twin Rolls-Royce Gnome engines, a two-tank fuel system and comprehensive equipment for the search and rescue function.

It is a combination of features that makes the Sea King such an effective life-saver. One of the most important is size: it is small enough to operate from ships at sea, yet big enough to carry 20 survivors and 4 crew. In extreme cases, even more people have been carried. It has huge doors, necessary for the winching operations, and two engines which provide a degree of reassurance when operating over water. It can operate on one, if necessary, as long as the load is not too great.

At a cruising speed of 115 mph, the Sea King can operate for nearly six hours, but it is also extremely effective at low-speed hover just above the sea. There is provision for automatic transition from forward flight to hover, and height hold which will maintain the aircraft at any height between 0 and 140 feet, within a couple of feet. The pilot can set the controls so that the Sea King automatically slows down over a distance of half a mile before settling at a preset hover height over the sea. When departing, the pilot can select autotransmission up, which will fly the aircraft to a preset height and a speed of 103 mph before he has to take over manual control.

The stories of rescues performed by Sea Kings are extraordinary. Often divers must be sent down to help crewmen on sinking ships escape, putting themselves into appalling danger. In 1989, the 18,000-ton Pakistani-registered *Murree*, bound for Egypt from London with building materials, foundered 25 miles off Start Point in

FACT FILE

The definitive search and rescue helicopter

Date built: 1959–

Length: 57 feet 2 inches

Diameter of rotor blades: 62 feet

Range: 870 miles

A German Sea King lifts a survivor from a life raft (above). The West German navy ordered enough Sea King airframes to equip a complete search and rescue squadron. Sea Kings were used during the Falklands War in 1982, most memorably to rescue survivors from the blazing landing ship Sir Galahad (left), at Bluff Cove. Eventually the ship was towed out to sea and sunk as a war grave.

Rescue from the Skies

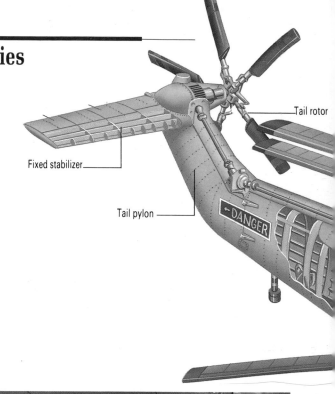

The specification of the most modern Sea Kings (right) maintains the helicopter's reputation as a world leader in air-sea rescue. Its tactical air navigation system (TANS) computes, from a variety of input data, wind velocity, track, groundspeed and present position. It also calculates bearing and distance to a selected point, as well as the time needed to reach it.

Tail rotor

Fixed stabilizer

Tail pylon

DANGER

IGOR SIKORSKY

The hundreds of people rescued by helicopters owe their lives ultimately to Igor Sikorsky, the first man to establish the configuration of the modern helicopter. A pioneer aviator in pre-revolutionary Russia, Sikorsky designed a series of aircraft, culminating in the remarkable Grand, the world's first four-engined aircraft, which he first flew in 1913. In 1918, he departed for the United States, and during the 1920s and '30s he designed a series of aircraft and flying boats.

In 1939, he turned again to a dream—creating an aircraft that would take off and land vertically. His earliest attempts failed for lack of power; but by 1936 the first flights had been made in helicopters with two rotors, and Sikorsky determined to solve the problems of creating a stable aircraft using one main rotor for lift.

His first experiments with the VS-300 involved sitting amidst a box framework with a large rotor above and secondary rotors at the tail to provide stability. Improvements led, by 1942, to the XR-4 variant of the VS-300, with the main rotor providing lift and forward motion, and a single tail rotor to prevent the aircraft whirling around. Manufactured during the war as the R-4, Sikorsky's helicopter made the first aerial rescue under combat conditions in Burma in April 1944.

Sikorsky always believed the helicopter's role would include rescue missions and he experimented using a winch attached to a US Navy version of the R-4. The first air-sea rescue, by a US Army Sikorsky R-5, took place on 29 November 1945 off Long Island Sound.

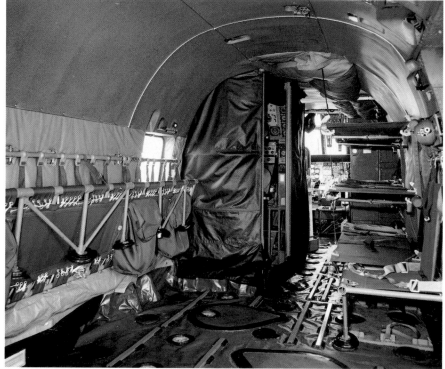

The cabin of a German Sea King (above and left), showing the enlarged space in the search and rescue versions, created by moving the after bulkhead. The cabin is 24 feet 11 inches by 6 feet 6 inches, providing seats for 20 survivors and 4 crew, although as many as 27 people have been carried in extremis.

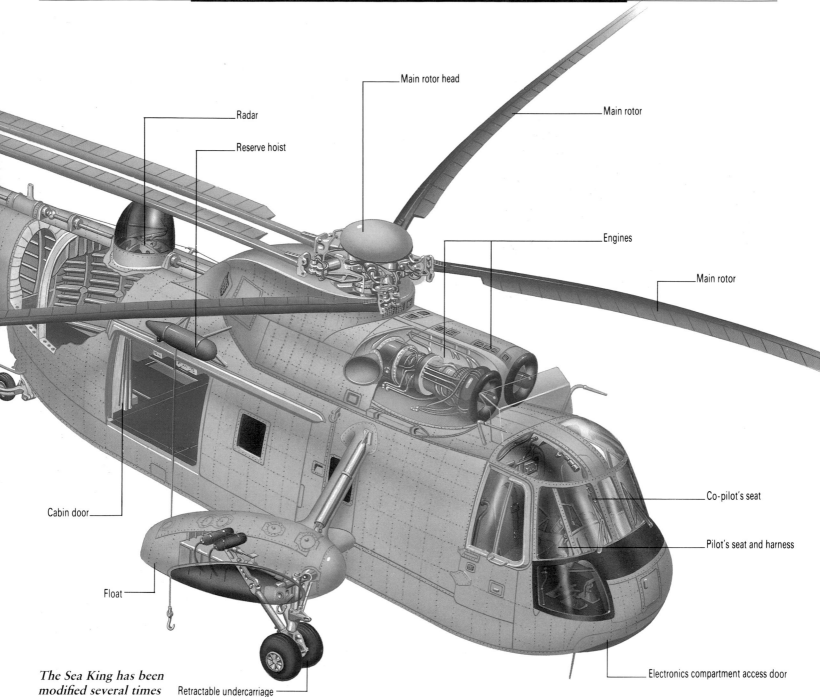

Radar

Reserve hoist

Main rotor head

Main rotor

Engines

Main rotor

Cabin door

Co-pilot's seat

Pilot's seat and harness

Float

Electronics compartment access door

Retractable undercarriage

The Sea King has been modified several times *since the original US navy version was first made. The Sea King built by Westland today (above) is very different from the American standard. Besides its search and rescue role, the Sea King has been adapted for anti-submarine warfare, for anti-surface vessel combat and for logistic support and troop transport. There are over 1,400 Sea Kings in service worldwide.*

Devon. The bows of the ship were already awash when the first Sea King landed diver Steve Wright on board. He helped to winch 30 crew from the ship to safety, but by then the *Murree* was sinking fast. His colleague Dave Wallace was sent down to help. They managed to get the last ten crew off on to the second Sea King just seconds before the ship gave a huge lurch and began to turn over.

"There was an almighty bang," said Wallace later, "and we could see the boys in the aircraft signalling us to jump. We were slipping down the deck and I got my foot caught in a rope. As soon as I got free I jumped and Steve went over the rail at much the same time. I knew it was a long fall, and I went very deep into the water. It felt like an age before I came up again, and when I did I could see the ship's stern towering above us. We both thought we were going to be sucked under so we swam like hell to get away, and then the winchman came down and we got hooked on and taken back up again. It could not have been closer. It was last second stuff and very frightening, there's no doubt about that." Together the two Sea Kings had rescued the entire 40-strong crew of the *Murree* in 100-mph winds.

Aerial Fire-Fighters

The days of barnstorming are long over for most pilots, who today must abide by increasingly restrictive regulations. Some airline captains, bored by long flights when all the work is done by autopilots, complain that they are beginning to lose their edge. It is not a complaint ever heard from the crews of the Canadair CL-215, perhaps the last fliers outside the air forces of the world who have the chance to fly a big aircraft to the limit of their ability. The CL-215 is an amphibious plane designed for one specific purpose: dousing fires, especially forest fires, with 6 tons of water at a time, then skimming across a lake to pick up another load. It requires hair-trigger judgement, great skill and a lot of confidence. It is never boring.

Canada is a land of forests and lakes. In the fire season between April and October, lightning strikes and human carelessness often set the forests ablaze. There is plenty of water in the lakes to fight the fires, but getting it to where it is needed was an impossible task before the development of fire-fighting aircraft—first the Canso and later the much bigger CL-215. For 20 years the CL-215s have been proving their value, not only in Canada but also in France, Spain, Yugoslavia and other countries. There is no other aircraft like it, and flying it is an experience that would soon shake a jaded airline pilot out of the rut.

In many ways, the CL-215 is an anachronism. Years after the jet and the turboprop have taken over, the CL-215 still uses piston engines, 18-cylinder Pratt & Whitney Double Wasps originally chosen for their rapid acceleration and good low-speed performance. Some of the aircraft have now been converted to turbo-prop operation but most of them still have the thunderous 2,100 hp radials.

The CL-215 is a flying boat, a type of aircraft that is now a rarity in the skies. Most important of all, despite its size, it still needs to be flown like a fighter, swooping down on lakes at a steep angle, taking off again fully laden at the very limits of its capability, then flying at treetop height through smoke and ashes to release its water in a one-second burst whose accuracy depends entirely on the judgement of the crew.

The CL-215 emerged from a market research programme by Canadair in the early 1960s. Careful study of how forest fires start and spread showed that substantial amounts of water needed to be delivered in a very short time to have much chance of putting them out. The biggest aircraft that could be operated at reasonable cost turned out to have a payload of 1,200 gallons of water. To be able to lift water from any convenient lake it would need to be an amphibious flying boat. The first aircraft, bearing the registration letters CF-FEU-X, made its maiden flight in October 1967.

To reduce production costs, the CL-215 is a simple slab-sided box, made of aluminium alloy. The water is carried in the lower part of the hull, and picked up by two probes which descend and dip into the water, their openings facing forward. The movement of the aircraft, at speeds of 92 mph, is sufficient to fill the tanks in 10 seconds. The probes are lowered as the aircraft descends toward the water, and non-return valves prevent the water escaping. As soon as the tanks are full the pilot selects full power and takes off again.

Once in the air, a small amount of fire retardant is added to the water, to improve its ability to douse flames. The retardant also creates a foam effect which acts as a target for other aircraft following behind. In a big fire, a team of CL-215s working together make a series of runs. A single load would never be sufficient to douse a fire, but might delay its spread for 15 minutes or so. As long as the aircraft is capable of returning with another load within 8 to 10 minutes, it stands every chance of bringing the fire under control or at least of stopping its spread. A team of aircraft working together, if there is a suitable lake nearby, can deliver a full load every few minutes.

The skill of the pilots is tested at every stage of the operation. Very often, they will be landing on lakes they have never seen before, and there is no way to judge from the air whether the water is deep enough—the CL-215 needs 4 feet 6 inches of water—or whether there are sunken obstacles that will foul the probes.

Once a lake has been selected, the pilot approaches with the probes down. As soon as the probes are in the water, power is increased to compensate for drag and increasing weight. Once the tanks are full, in about 10 to 12 seconds, full power is selected and the CL-215 takes off at just under 92 mph. Often, if the

FACT FILE

The piston-engined planes that water-bomb fires

Date built: 1972–

Wingspan: 93 feet 10 inches

Length: 65 feet

aircraft is carrying a full load of fuel as well, these takeoffs may be made in an overweight condition, so the pilot keeps his finger on the water release button. In an emergency, if it looks as if he is not going to manage to clear the trees at the water's edge, he can release the cargo in a second.

Bombing the fires also requires great skill. The heat can be stifling as the CL-215s come in over the forests at heights of between 100 and 150 feet.

If they flew any higher, their water would be dissipated before it could have any real effect on the flames. The final approach is usually made through choking smoke and always in severe turbulence caused by the hot air rising from the fire. Strong wind shears may be experienced from violent low-level winds.

To help to reduce side slip, the turboprop-fitted CL-215, designated CL-215T, has large endplates at the wing tips. The engine's greater

A CL-215 drops 6 tons of water on a fire. Although the capacity of the CL-215T is the same, the greater power, speed and quick start mean a 119 percent increase in the number of tons of water delivered in the first hour of a mission.

Aerial Fire-Fighters

power helps the rate of climb and acceleration, and the pilot no longer has to endure the heat of fires as air-conditioning is now fitted.

The aircraft fly over the fires at 115 to 126 mph, and can opt either to drop their entire load in a single burst, or to open the two bomb doors successively to produce a narrower but longer spread. As the water drops away, the aircraft surges upward, but there is no danger of losing control because the tanks are placed close to the centre of gravity. Judgement of when to release the water is simply a matter of experience, although care must be taken to avoid any fire-fighters on the ground, who could easily be killed by 6 tons of water falling on them.

One of the greatest dangers is colliding with "cheekos"—tall, dead trees that blend into the background and cannot be seen until the very last moment. Fortunately, the CL-215 is an extremely strong aircraft. Once, a pilot heard a clatter as he flew over a fire, but sustained little damage. He was astonished when a forester brought him a sample of the tree which he had felled, a massive branch that would have brought most other aircraft down.

One of the most dramatic operations undertaken by the CL-215 was the fight against a fire close to the town of Val d'Or in Quebec in 1972. To control this fire took four CL-215s and two Canso aircraft, working together. During the battle one pilot spotted a small but very violent fire in a nearby wood just a few hundred yards from a railway junction and a propane and petrol storage plant.

The fire was "crowning"—sweeping through the very tops of the trees—always an indication of great heat intensity. At virtually the same moment a second fire broke out 1½ miles to the east. Careful control was needed to coordinate the attack on two fires less than 2 miles apart, but soon the aircraft were dropping their loads of water at one-minute intervals. Every few circuits an aircraft would detour and drop its water from a greater height on to the roofs of houses, to protect them from flying embers. The fire was eventually stopped just 20 feet from the propane storage tanks.

In the space of two hours, the six aircraft had made 65 drops, totalling just under 300 tons of water. The single operation saved the propane plant, worth £160,000, and other property, the total value of which was equal to half the cost of operating Quebec's fleet of fire-fighting aircraft for a whole season.

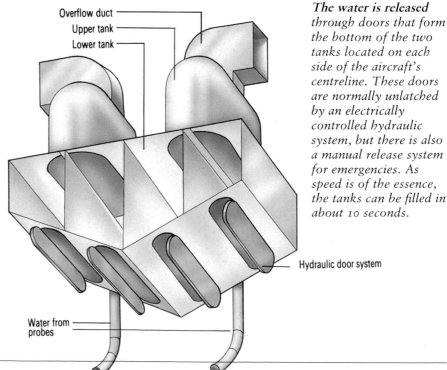

Overflow duct
Upper tank
Lower tank

Hydraulic door system

Water from probes

The water is released through doors that form the bottom of the two tanks located on each side of the aircraft's centreline. These doors are normally unlatched by an electrically controlled hydraulic system, but there is also a manual release system for emergencies. As speed is of the essence, the tanks can be filled in about 10 seconds.

The water tanks are empty in less than a second, once the release button has been pressed (above), causing a pronounced upward pitch. A similar but opposite reaction is felt landing on the water at high speed (left) when a severe nose-low pitch can cause inexperienced pilots to lose control. The record for the number of pick-ups and drops in a day is held by a Yugoslavian CL-215, at 225.

Juggernaut of the Air

FACT FILE

The world's largest aircraft

Built: 1985–88

Wingspan: 290 feet

Length: 276 feet

Power output: 311,700 lb of thrust

Cargo load: 250 tons

The principal difference between the An-124 and An-225 lies in the twin fins at each end of the tailplane of the An-225, the larger aircraft (opposite). This is designed to make it easier to carry loads mounted on top of the fuselage. The droop of the wings can be seen clearly as the An-225 comes in to land (below).

The biggest aircraft in regular service in the world's airlines is the Boeing 747 jumbo jet, able to carry more than 400 passengers over distances of 8,400 miles. Only one American aircraft, the Lockheed C-5 cargo aircraft, is bigger, although its engines are less powerful. The Soviet Union, however, has now produced not one but two aircraft that dwarf even the C-5. When the second of these, the gigantic Antonov An-225, arrived at the 1989 Paris air show with the Soviet space shuttle *Buran* (Snowstorm) riding on its back, there were gasps of amazement. The An-225, or Mriya (Dream), had rewritten almost all the superlatives of the aviation industry.

It was a product of the Antonov design bureau in Kiev, led by chief designer Pyotr Balabuyev. To the already gigantic An-124, which first flew in 1982, the Antonov team had added a longer body, bigger wings, more engines and more wheels. At the back, looking down on the football field of the cargo hold, is an area where 70 passengers can be seated. The An-225 is the first aircraft able to take off with a gross weight of more than a million pounds; fully laden it leaves the ground weighing 1,320,750 lb, or 600 tons. It can lift a cargo load of 250 tons, against the C-5 Galaxy's 132 tons.

The An-225 was designed for a specific purpose: carrying the Soviet space shuttle, its huge rocket launcher, or other heavy pieces of

equipment for the oil, gas or electricity generating industries to wherever they are needed in the Soviet Union. Confidence that this could be done had been gained after experience with the An-124, which itself was a huge aircraft. In the mid-1980s, the An-124 took all the world records for maximum weight lifted and long-distance endurance. On 6/7 May 1987, an An-124 covered 12,521 miles without refuelling, around a circuit that took it from Moscow to Astrakhan, Tashkent, Lake Baikal, Petropavlovsk, Chukot Peninsula, Murmansk, Zhdanov and back to Moscow, arriving with some fuel left.

The An-124 is powered by four Lotarev D-18T turbofans, each producing 51,950 lb of thrust. Its wingspan is 240 feet, while its hold is 118 feet long, 21 feet across and 14 feet 5 inches high. It lands on ten wheels. All these figures are, however, easily exceeded by the An-225, which is an An-124 stretched in every direction. Instead of four engines, it has six; its wingspan is increased to 290 feet by adding an extra section that carries the two additional engines, and the length of the cargo hold is increased to over 141 feet. The total length of the aircraft is nearly 276 feet and when it is parked on the runway a double-decker bus can drive under its wings.

Design of the An-225 began in 1985, and it made its first flight on 21 December 1988. On 22 March 1989 it set a total of 106 world and class records in a single day, taking off at a gross weight of 1,120,370 lb and flying 1,250 miles at a speed of 505 mph and at heights of up to 40,000 feet. According to deputy aviation minister Vladimir Ivanov, who spoke during a visit of the An-225 to the 1990 Farnborough air show, the huge aircraft does not need a special runway.

The total cost of the An-225 programme has been £150 million, but it is not clear how many will be built. In September 1990 a second was almost complete, and six crews had been trained to fly the aircraft. Pyotr Balabuyev said "There will be others, but not very many. And so far as we can see, this is about as big as we can get."

The principal purpose of the An-225 is to fly the shuttle orbiter *Buran* from the factory where it is built to the Baikonour Cosmodrome for launch. *Buran* is believed to weigh 70 tons, too heavy for the modified M-4 bomber which had been used for similar tasks before.

In November 1988, the *Buran* orbiter was

Juggernaut of the Air

The carrying capacity of the An-225 was put to use in the 1990/91 Gulf crisis, carrying Bangladeshi refugees to safety (above). The cargo hold is 141 feet long and loading is facilitated by the fact that the entire nose section swings upward. The aircraft can be made to "kneel" by retracting the nosewheel and settling on to two extendable feet to give the floor an upward slope. The 16 landing wheels (right) are independently sprung to help the aircraft tolerate makeshift runways.

disaster of 1986. Leaving the children in the US for medical treatment, the An-225 flew back to Kiev with 200 tons of medical supplies on board for other Chernobyl victims.

If the Soviet shuttle has hit problems, the An-225 may find that its primary purpose no longer exists, but there are likely to be plenty of other things it can do. Many large machines or structures, such as turbogenerators, boilers or oil industry equipment, are difficult to transport by road or rail. Often they have to be transported in pieces and reassembled on site. The An-225 makes it possible to carry loads never before carried by air, not only in the USSR but in other countries too. In the post–Cold War climate, the Soviet authorities could well create a successful business shifting heavy loads.

The An-225 might also come to the rescue of a British development for launching satellites. Hotol is a space plane which uses a revolutionary engine able to convert from a jet to a rocket high in the atmosphere. As originally conceived, Hotol (standing for horizontal takeoff and landing craft) would take off from a normal runway using its engines as air-burning jets. When it reached the upper limits of the atmosphere, it would start burning rocket fuels in the same engines, making the transition from aircraft to space plane. The difficulty is that the British government has declined to contribute to the £6 billion cost of developing Hotol.

Late in 1990, British Aerospace and the Soviet authorities began discussing whether it would be possible to launch Hotol from the An-225. It would be carried to the aircraft's ceiling and then released, burning rocket fuel to put it into orbit. If this proved feasible, BAC engineers believed it would be possible to reduce the cost of developing Hotol to £2.5 billion, largely because they could eliminate the air-breathing engine. This might then cut the cost of launching satellites to as little as $8 million a shot, against the $70 million a launch of the US shuttle. Hotol would go into space, and then re-enter the atmosphere and land at an ordinary airport like the shuttle.

BAC believes there would be an enormous market for such a system, and if the feasibility studies work out, intends to approach European governments and the European Space Agency for support. Projects like the American space station desperately need a cheap, re-usable launch system if they are ever to work. Perhaps the An-225, the world's biggest aircraft, could help provide it.

launched from Baikonour for the first time, making two unmanned orbits of the Earth before coming in to land under automatic control. Since then there have been no further flights, suggesting problems in the development of *Buran*. As a result, the An-225 has been underemployed, although it has been used to carry bulky engineering equipment to remote sites in Siberia, and during the Gulf crisis it was used to rescue a large number of refugees displaced by the Iraqi invasion of Kuwait.

In March 1991, an An-225 went to the US, carrying two children suffering from radiation injuries as a result of the Chernobyl nuclear

An An-225 performing the task for which it was primarily designed: carrying the space shuttle Buran. Although the estimated 70-ton weight of Buran would be within the capacity of the An-124 with its 125-ton payload, it may be that parts of the huge Energia booster used to put the shuttle into orbit are too heavy for the An-124. Energia was first tested in May 1987 and is one of the biggest rocket boosters ever made, able to put 100 tons into orbit around Earth.

Captain Charles "Chuck" Yeager (right) was a classic test pilot—cool, laconic and determined. On the nose of the P-51 he had flown in Europe at the end of World War II, he had written the name "Glamorous Glennis", after his wife. He had the same legend inscribed on the X-1 (above).

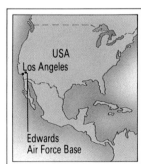

Edwards Air Force Base in California is famous as the landing site used for the space shuttles. When the X-1s used it, the air force base was named Muroc.

Beyond Mach 1

Toward the end of World War II, the air forces of Britain and the United States began experimenting with speeds close to the speed of sound. In 1943, a Mk IX Spitfire, one of the fastest fighters of the day, was used for a series of tests during which it dived from 40,000 feet at speeds which approached Mach 0.9—90 percent of the speed of sound.

The flights produced some curious results because the Spitfire did not really have a structure strong enough for speeds like these. The front edge of the tailplane had a tendency to bend upward, which meant that the elevator was enveloped in the slipstream and ceased to work normally. In fact, under these circumstances it was found that the controls reversed, so that any attempt by the pilot to pull out of the dive merely pitched the aircraft's nose even farther down. In 1946, Geoffrey de Havilland, the son of the founder of the company, was killed when his de Havilland 108 failed to emerge from such a dive.

The strange changes that seemed to set in close to the speed of sound led to the belief that it might be a barrier. One possible origin of this phrase was a remark by Dr W. F. Hilton of Armstrong-Whitworth, who suggested that as aircraft neared the speed of sound, drag would suddenly increase "like a barrier against the future". De Havilland's death lent credibility to the prediction, and the myth of the sound barrier was born.

Why it was ever believed is a mystery, for rifle bullets had long been travelling faster than the speed of sound without coming to grief. The wind tunnels available in the late 1940s could not reproduce supersonic conditions, so it was left to the test pilots to find out for themselves. Physical theory, first enunciated by Ernst Mach in the nineteenth century, indicated that there would be a change in the behaviour of the air at these speeds because the aircraft would overtake its own pressure wave. At normal speeds, these pressure waves spread away ahead of the aircraft; at transonic speeds, the aircraft would catch up with its own waves, compressing the air and causing instability.

In 1944, a research programme was launched in the US to investigate the question. The Army Air Force and the National Advisory Committee on Aeronautics (NACA) agreed to design a rocket-propelled aircraft, and a contract was signed with the Bell Aircraft Company of Buffalo, New York, on 16 March 1945. The design was largely a matter of fumbling about in the dark, but the team sensibly set out by basing the shape of the aircraft on an object that was known to fly straight at supersonic speeds, the .50 calibre bullet.

The result was a short, rather fat fuselage, straight wings and a very clean profile. The absence of propellers or a jet engine intake simplified the design, which was ready by the middle of October. The aircraft was called the Bell XS-1, X standing for experimental and S for supersonic. The S, however, was quickly dropped and it became known as the Bell X-1.

The first flight was made on 25 January 1946, with Bell test pilot Jack Woolams at the controls; the aircraft was taken aloft by a B-29 bomber, which was to be normal practice. On these first flights the rockets were not used, but the X-1 was simply glided down to land to test its flight characteristics. Woolams's report was enthusiastic. He had reached a speed of 275 mph and found the X-1 rock steady and easy to fly. After another nine test flights the decision was made to move the whole operation to Muroc Air Force Base in the Mojave Desert of California, a huge dry lake bed ideal for flying because of its vast flat area and the fact that the weather is perfect 350 days a year.

The first powered flights were made at Muroc by another Bell test pilot, Chalmers "Slick" Goodlin, who took the X-1 up to Mach 0.8, the figure guaranteed by Bell in their original contract. When this had been achieved, the first two X-1s were handed over to the Air Force. The first Air Force test took place with Captain Charles E. "Chuck" Yeager at the controls. According to Tom Wolfe, who chronicled the birth of the US manned space programme in his book *The Right Stuff*, Yeager celebrated this first flight by executing a barrel roll with a full load of rocket fuel, then pointed the aircraft vertically upward and accelerated to Mach 0.85—but this incident is not mentioned in more restrained histories.

Gradually the test flights got faster and faster as Yeager edged toward Mach 1. He experienced the buffeting that had become familiar but was convinced that the closer he came to Mach 1 the smoother it would become. He appears to have been quite genuinely unimpressed by the fears of

Beyond Mach 1

Yeager broke his own record on several occasions. On 26 March 1948, he reached 957 mph (Mach 1.45), the fastest ever reached by the X-1. In subsequent X-craft he reached yet more prodigious speeds, taking the X-1A to Mach 2.44 (1,650 mph) on 12 December 1953. In principle, it was possible for the X-1 to take off from the ground normally, but to make optimum use of the fuel, it was usually carried to high altitude underneath a B-29 bomber (above), before it was released and the rocket engines were ignited.

the engineers that the speed of sound would prove an impenetrable barrier. By his eighth flight Yeager had pushed X-1 to Mach 0.997, the very verge of the sound barrier. The attempt to break through it was set for 14 October 1947.

Two days before takeoff, Yeager took his wife Glennis out to a bar called Pancho's for a drink. About 11 p.m. , he decided it was a good time to take a ride on a couple of the horses that were kept at the bar by its owner, a woman called Pancho Barnes. Galloping back toward the bar, Yeager failed to see that a gate had been closed, ran straight into it and fell off, breaking two ribs. The next day, in some pain, Yeager realized that if he told the Air Force about his injury he would be taken off the flight, so instead he went to see a doctor in nearby Rosamond, who taped up his ribs and told him to keep his right arm still for a fortnight. The next day, at dawn, Glennis drove him over to Muroc for the flight.

By this time, Yeager was in considerable difficulty. His side hurt badly and he could

hardly move his arm. The major problem that faced him was how he was going to close the hatchlike door of the X-1 after he had climbed down into it from the B-29, for that involved pushing a handle forward with his right hand. He confided in the flight engineer, Jack Ridley, who solved the problem by cutting about 9 inches off a broom handle, which Yeager could use as a lever to close the handle with his left hand. Neither Ridley nor Yeager told anybody else of the problem.

At 7,000 feet Yeager climbed down the ladder from the B-29's bomb bay and into the tiny cockpit of the X-1. Ridley slotted the door, which had no hinges, into place, and with the broom handle Yeager managed to close the latch. Then the B-29 climbed to 29,000 feet, went into a shallow dive and then pulled up, releasing the X-1 like a bomb being thrown forward. Yeager ignited the rockets and was immediately thrown backward so hard that he could hardly get his hands to the controls. He shot upward to

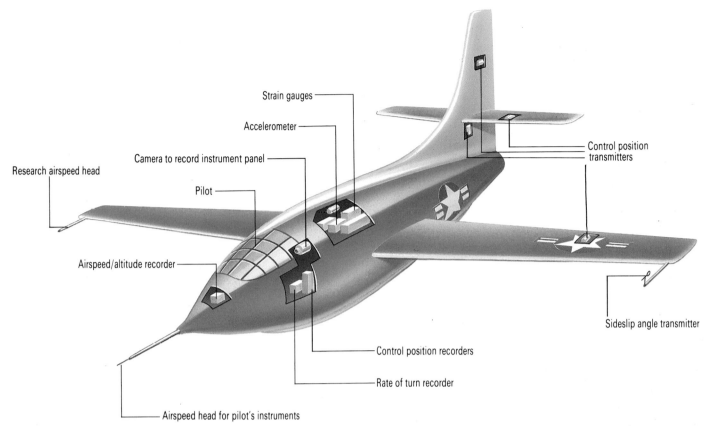

Strain gauges

Accelerometer

Camera to record instrument panel

Research airspeed head

Pilot

Control position transmitters

Airspeed/altitude recorder

Sideslip angle transmitter

Control position recorders

Rate of turn recorder

Airspeed head for pilot's instruments

The X-1 that broke the sound barrier can be seen at the National Air and Space Museum in Washington (above). It was one of only three built. The second is on display at Edwards Air Force Base, the third was destroyed by fire.

***The X-1 was simple** and very strong, made of aluminium and designed to withstand stresses 18 times those of gravity. It was 31 feet long and weighed just over 12,000 lb. Most of the fuselage was filled with two large stainless-steel fuel tanks, one of which contained liquid oxygen, the other ethyl alcohol. The fuel was fed to a single four-chamber rocket motor; each chamber fired separately and was capable of 1,500 lb of thrust.*

40,000 feet and then nosed the X-1 over for the record attempt. At Mach 0.87 he reported a mild buffet, but by Mach 0.96 he was telling Ridley that his elevators were working well again.

Seconds later, without any evidence that anything dramatic had happened, the needle jumped to Mach 1.06. "Say, Ridley, make another note, will you," Yeager said. "There's something wrong with this machometer . . . it's gone kind of screwy on me." This was Yeager's

way of conveying that he had exceeded Mach 1 without allowing outsiders who happened to be tuned to the right frequency to understand. As he did so, those on the ground heard a boom sound across the desert floor—the first sonic boom ever from a manned aircraft. When Yeager landed, the instruments were checked and confirmed that he had indeed gone supersonic.

This was the achievement that everybody interested in flight had been waiting for, but for some unexplained reason the Air Force put a total blackout on the news. Nobody was to be told that an American, in an American aircraft, had broken the sound barrier. It was two months later before the news appeared, as a leak in the magazine *Aviation Week*. The Air Force was furious and even contemplated legal action, but such a step would have been pointless.

In a very short time, the X-1 had shown all the fears about the sound barrier to be imaginary. Its example has since been followed by hundreds of different aircraft.

The Big Bird

Few aircraft have survived a more difficult gestation than Concorde, the world's first commercial airliner to fly scheduled services faster than sound. Assailed by economists, noise campaigners, cost cutters and fainthearts, and built in an unlikely collaboration between two countries traditionally suspicious of each other, Concorde emerged to discomfit its critics. Not only was it strikingly beautiful, but it worked, solving almost all the awkward problems of supersonic passenger travel. Only the bottom line let it down, for it was never built in sufficient numbers to recoup its huge development costs. To that extent, at least, its critics were right: but if every human endeavour were to be judged solely by profit and loss, it would be a dull world.

When aircraft first approached the speed of sound, it was seen as a barrier, a region of instability where the normal rules of aerodynamics no longer applied. Experience with the Bell X-1 in the US and the Fairey Delta 2 in Britain showed, however, that supersonic flight could be achieved by aircraft of the right configuration. The shape chosen for the Fairey Delta 2, which achieved a world air speed record for a jet aircraft of 1,132 mph in March 1956, was a sharply swept delta wing, and no tailplane.

At transonic speeds, several designs with tails had suffered problems as the airflow over the wings caused buffeting at the tail surfaces. Fairey decided, therefore, to dispense with the tail altogether, a bold move because it cast doubt on how controllable the aircraft would be.

The gamble succeeded, but another question then presented itself. The slender delta wing form worked well at supersonic speeds, but could it produce sufficient lift at low speeds during takeoff and landing? A small experimental aircraft, the Handley-Page 115, was built and showed that such a wing could indeed provide low-speed lift, without needing complex flaps or slots. However, the higher drag of such wings could only be overcome by carrying more fuel. Were it not for the greater efficiency of jet engines at supersonic speeds, long-distance supersonic transports (SSTs) would be impossible.

By 1961, it was apparent to aircraft designers in both Britain and France that a supersonic transport aircraft could be built. The French favoured a range of 2,000 miles, while the British insisted that an aircraft that could not cross the Atlantic would be worthless. A deal to build

FACT FILE

The first supersonic airliner

Built: 1965–67

Wingspan: 83 feet 10 inches

Length: 202 feet 4 inches

Power output: 38,050 lb of thrust

Maximum speed: Mach 2.04

A mock-up of the flight deck (left), showing the ram's-horn-shaped control columns and the flight engineer's panel on the right. Concorde has a greater thrust to weight ratio than subsonic aircraft so the feeling of acceleration on takeoff (right) is more pronounced. Fuel has to be moved from one tank to another or "burned off" prior to takeoff to make sure that the centre of gravity is positioned at a specific point. This is particularly important for stability, since Concorde does not have a tailplane. Fuel is redistributed throughout the flight.

The Big Bird

The intricate patterns of airflow over the wings and fuselage of a model of Concorde are revealed by a hydrodynamic tunnel test. The penalty of the slender delta wing necessary for supersonic speeds is its greater drag. The ratio between the lift produced by such a wing and the drag it generates is much less advantageous than conventional wings. To overcome this might have involved carrying so much fuel that there would have been no room for passengers. However, jet engines become more efficient at supersonic speeds because more air is crammed into them.

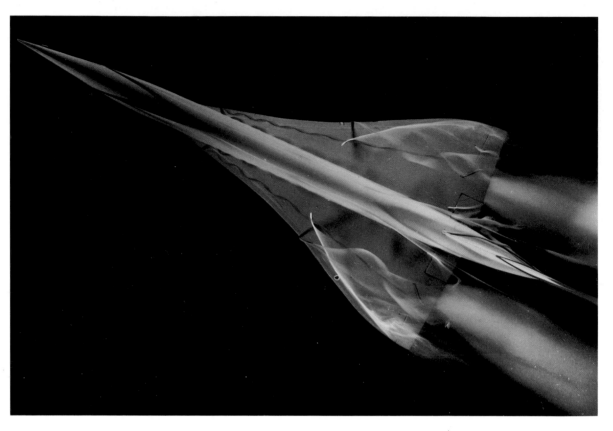

both versions was signed between Britain and France in November 1962, providing for equal distribution of costs and revenues. There was no provision in the treaty for either partner to withdraw. The medium-range version was later dropped, as the British view was adopted.

The designers of Concorde had little room for manoeuvre. When they began, the only people to have flown as fast or as high as Concorde were military pilots wearing pressure suits and provided with oxygen supplies—yet they were planning to carry more than 100 passengers, on regular services, in air-conditioned comfort.

At 60,000 feet, Concorde's cruising altitude, the air pressure is only one-tenth that at ground level, which meant that Concorde's fuselage had to be very strong to withstand the pressure differential. If it were made too strong, however, it would be too heavy. The payload on a long-haul trip was already small, only 5 percent of the all-up weight, compared with 10 percent for subsonic jets, and 20 percent for today's jumbo jets. A small error in engine performance, lift, drag or any other variable could have eliminated it altogether, which would mean that Concorde could cross the Atlantic only if it were not carrying any passengers.

The actual development of Concorde took

place against a background hum of political discord, dismay about the rising costs, and public apathy. The Labour government elected in Britain in 1964 attempted to cancel the project, but found that their Conservative predecessors had provided no get-out clause, for fear that the unreliable French would let them down. In fact, it was the British who proved the more faint-hearted. Reluctantly the teams at British Aerospace and Sud Aviation were allowed to continue their work, as the costs mounted.

On the other side of the Atlantic, attempts to develop a more ambitious SST, bigger and faster than Concorde, were running into the sand. Boeing had been chosen for the job and had submitted a swing-wing design which would have been the longest aircraft ever built, capable of carrying 300 passengers at Mach 2.7 at heights of up to 70,000 feet. Boeing, however, had bitten off more than they could chew. In 1969, they abandoned the swinging wings and went for a delta shape like Concorde's. Speed would still have been Mach 2.7, necessitating a titanium fuselage. In 1971 the project was cancelled.

While officials on both sides of the Atlantic chewed their pencils, Concorde took shape. On 2 March 1969, the first Concorde to fly, 001, lifted off from Toulouse in the hands of test pilot

The Concorde production line at Filton, Bristol, was in the hangars originally built for the manufacture of the Bristol Brabazon. The 16 production Concordes were completed between 1973 and 1979. Further production was made prohibitively expensive by the disposal of the French jigs at Toulouse by December 1977 and those from Filton, after a period of storage, in October 1981.

Mach 2 is the limit that will allow aluminium alloys to be used in aircraft construction. Beyond Mach 2, the flow of air over the fuselage causes excessive heating, requiring the use of more expensive high-temperature materials like titanium or stainless steel. This is part of the complex balancing of options that went into the design of Concorde. From the point of view of the engines, an ideal maximum speed would have been Mach 3, because their efficiency goes on increasing up to that speed. In the case of Concorde, a speed of Mach 2.04 was chosen because that reduced the temperature of the fuselage from 313°F to 261°F, easing problems with the handling of fuel and oil.

The Big Bird

BAC chief test pilot of Concorde, Brian Trubshaw (left) with Roy Radford, another BAC test pilot, aboard the British prototype 002. Concorde was tested for six years before entering commercial service. While the test pilots were putting the pre-production Concordes through their paces, structural tests on a specimen were carried out by the Royal Aircraft Establishment at Toulouse and at Farnborough where a supersonic "flight" was simulated. The airframe was covered in ducts linked to a hot air supply to replicate the heating and cooling of a flight. A specimen was also placed in a thermal duct with full fuel tanks and the cabin pressurized to reproduce the correct load.

André Turcat. Thirty-five minutes later he landed and declared: "The big bird flies". It would have been a serious disappointment if it had not. One month later the first British-assembled Concorde prototype, 002, took off from Filton with BAC's chief test pilot, Brian Trubshaw, at the controls. It had taken more than six years to get Concorde into the air, but it was to be another six before it carried paying passengers for the first time.

Concorde was not, however, the only SST in the air. The Soviet Union produced the TU 144, an aircraft similar in conformation to Concorde and which flew two months earlier. The TU 244 was designed to carry 121 passengers at Mach 2.35 over 4,000 miles, an impressive specification on paper. In reality it was never achieved.

In 1973, the modified TU 244 crashed at the Paris air show, which did little to inspire confidence. Nevertheless, it beat Concorde into service, flying mail and freight between Moscow and Alma-Ata for the first time in December 1975. The chances are that the TU 244 never achieved its design specification, and may have needed to use full afterburners during supersonic cruise, making it totally uneconomic. By 1985, if not sooner, it was out of service. "Concordeski", as it had been christened in the West, was an expensive failure.

No supersonic aircraft had ever been certified for passenger use, so the Concorde test pro-

gramme was exhaustive. Every conceivable mode of failure was explored, from stalls to multiple engine failures. Fatigue testing of a complete fuselage began. On 1 October 1969, 001 achieved Mach 1 for the first time and on 4 November 1970, it reached Mach 2. In 1973, the second pre-production aircraft, 002, broke the Washington–Paris record, setting a time of 3 hours 33 minutes.

By October 1973, 001 had been retired to the French Air Museum at Le Bourget, and in December that year the first production Concorde, 201, flew for the first time. By September 1974, a total of 3,000 hours of flight testing had been completed. During 1975 the first certificates of airworthiness were issued on both sides of the Channel. Finally, in January 1976, both British Airways and Air France were ready to make their maiden flights.

At 11.40 a.m. on 21 January the British Airways Concorde took off from Heathrow for Bahrain. At the same moment, the Air France aircraft took off for Rio de Janeiro via Dakar. Neither was a viable route, but the potentially profitable American destinations were still closed by environmental arguments. Those on board the British Concorde were greatly cheered by the tremendous reception they had from the emir of Bahrain, who gave them a banquet.

While destinations all over the world were sniffily turning their faces against Concorde, Bahrain welcomed it with open arms. Perhaps, after all, it might yet convince others that it was not the threat they believed it to be. Eventually, the US authorities allowed a Concorde service to Washington and New York, although by the time they did, the damage was done; both Pan American and TWA had cancelled their options to buy the aircraft.

A typical flight on the Atlantic route begins for the crew two hours before takeoff, as they go through the flight plan at Heathrow. Knowledge of the winds and temperatures along the proposed flight path is important for calculating the amount of fuel required—typically around 90 tons for a passenger load of 100.

Takeoff, at around 250 mph, is fairly quickly followed by turning off of the afterburners to reduce noise around the airport. At the same moment the rate of climb is reduced to compensate for the diminished thrust. Some 7 miles from Heathrow power is increased and the nose, which is lowered to improve visibility during taxi and takeoff, is raised into its flight position.

Between 6,000 and 32,000 feet Concorde climbs at 400 knots, increasing its Mach number toward 0.93 as the air gets thinner. As the speed rises, the centre of lift of Concorde's wing moves toward the rear and, to keep the aircraft balanced, the centre of gravity must also be moved backward by about 2 feet, accomplished by pumping fuel backward.

As Concorde crosses the coast, it changes gear. The reheaters are lit, first on the inboard and then on the outboard engines. With a perceptible nudge Concorde accelerates and soon exceeds Mach 1. At Mach 1.3 the complex engine inlets begin to rearrange themselves to achieve the best compression of the airflow entering the engines. At Mach 1.7 the after-burners are switched off, for now the increased speed has begun to improve the efficiency of the engines. Mach 2 is reached at about 50,000 feet, 40 minutes after takeoff.

At cruising height, 58,000 to 60,000 feet, the sky above is black, like space, and the temperature of the air is −58°F. But friction heats up the fuselage of the aircraft to more than 212°F, and it expands by 8 inches. Between the bulkhead and the engineer's panel, a gap opens up wide enough for the engineer to put his fingers in.

Two hours out of London, Newfoundland can be seen. Deceleration begins over the ocean before New York is reached, to ensure that Concorde is subsonic at least 35 miles out to sea.

As the aircraft slows, its angle of attack must be increased to maintain lift, which means that the nose must be drooped, first by 5 degrees and on final approach by 12.5, to preserve visibility forward. As speed falls below 253 mph, drag actually increases, a feature unique to Concorde which necessitates a modest increase in power to accommodate it.

Landing is made at 188 mph, which thanks to the paradoxical nature of the drag on Concorde, requires more power than 219 mph. At this speed, Concorde's fuel consumption is ten times greater than at supersonic cruise, for her engines are not optimized for dawdling. In case of delays at New York, an extra 15 tons of fuel are carried, sufficient for 50 minutes in a stacking pattern. As Concorde lands, the tyres produce a brief flurry of smoke which flows outward and around the wing tips, evidence of the vortex lift which enables the delta wings to function at low speeds.

Since those first flights, Concorde has carried millions of passengers to many different destinations, some on scheduled services and some on special charter flights. Speeds and heights that once were the realm of the test pilot have become almost routine, although such is the expense of Concorde flights that they still have a special aura. More than 30 years after it was conceived, Concorde is still the most sensational shape in the air, looking as advanced today as it did when it was first rolled out.

The choice of the four Bristol-Siddeley Olympus turbo jet engines mounted under the wings was crucial: to operate efficiently at all speeds would require very complex inlet arrangements and afterburner nozzles, all under computer control. The Olympus appeared to be the only suitable engine. That this engine existed at all was in defiance of British government policy, for it had decreed that all jet engine development should be concentrated in one company, Rolls-Royce. Against official wishes, the Bristol Aeroplane Company had persisted with the remarkable Olympus, capable of producing over 38,000 lb of thrust with full reheat. This pre-production Concorde has its nose in the flight position.

Ballooning in the Jet Stream

When Richard Branson, entrepreneur and founder of the Virgin group of companies, and balloonist Per Lindstrand came down in the frozen wastes of the North West Territories of Canada on 17 January 1991, they had achieved a unique double—crossing first the Atlantic and then the Pacific oceans in hot-air balloons. Strangely, the feat received little recognition, for the first allied bombing raids in the Gulf war had just been launched.

The challenge of crossing both the great oceans of the world by hot-air balloon had long been considered impossible. Both had been crossed by helium-filled balloons—the Atlantic in 1978, by the American team of Ben Abruzzo, Maxie Anderson and Larry Newman, flying *Double Eagle II*, and the Pacific in 1981, by a four-man crew led by Rocky Aoki of Japan.

To make such a crossing in unpowered balloons, it is necessary to fly at above 20,000 feet to take advantage of the jet stream winds, which blow at up to 200 mph. Nobody had ever flown a hot-air balloon in such winds, and many thought it impossible. To survive so high also requires a pressurized capsule, previously considered too heavy for a hot-air balloon. Thirdly, theory said that no hot-air balloon could carry sufficient propane gas to cross the 3,000 miles of the Atlantic, never mind the more than 6,000 of the Pacific. The task of solving these problems was given to the British firm of Thunder & Colt, of Oswestry, Shropshire, the largest manufacturer of leisure balloons in the world.

Per Lindstrand, an expert balloonist, believed that the answer to the fuel problem lay in using the heat of the Sun to keep the balloon hot, thereby reducing fuel requirements. The final design for the *Virgin Atlantic Flyer* was a vast envelope of laminated fabric, capable of holding more than 2 million cubic feet of hot air, standing 172 feet high and 166 feet broad.

The *Atlantic Flyer* was launched from Sugarloaf, Maine, early in the morning of 2 July 1987. Immediately there was a crisis as one of the propane tanks fell off as the balloon lifted. In addition, the balloon carried up with it one of the sandbags that had been used to hold it down, and when they reached 9,000 feet Branson climbed out of the capsule and cut the rope holding it with a penknife. The ascent of the balloon was so swift that none of the helicopters trying to take pictures could stay with it as it rose at 1,200 feet a minute. Branson and Lindstrand left the coast at around 25,000 feet, travelling at over 100 mph.

About 200 miles off Gander in Newfoundland they met an intense low-pressure front that buffeted them for three hours. On the instructions of their meteorologist, Bob Rice, they resisted the temptation to come down to calmer air below the storm, sticking firmly to their cruising altitude of 27,000 feet. It was snowing, dark, and the balloon kept shaking but eventually they came through into clear air, as Rice had predicted.

Just before dawn on 3 July they passed the midpoint of the Atlantic. By 2.33 p.m. they crossed the coast of Donegal, just 29 hours and 23 minutes after taking off. Now only the problem of landing remained, and that was to prove the stickiest part of the trip.

Because they had travelled so fast, Branson and Lindstrand still had three full fuel cells on the capsule. Not wanting to land with the fuel aboard, Lindstrand brought them down over Limavady, in Northern Ireland, aiming to come close to the ground and release the tanks at a safe height. But he overdid it and crashed heavily on to the ground, breaking off the tanks. Having lost $2\frac{1}{4}$ tons, the balloon took off like a rocket again before Branson and Lindstrand had time to jettison the canopy.

They were now aloft again, without their spare fuel tanks, and wondering where to come down. Reasoning that the landfall in Limavady

Richard Branson and Per Lindstrand were captain and chief pilot. Branson has become a household name for exploits such as the attempt to win the Blue Riband with the Atlantic Challenger. Lindstrand worked on high-altitude aircraft in the Swedish air force before founding Colt Balloons. The company Thunder & Colt designed both the Atlantic balloon and the Pacific one (opposite).

Ballooning in the Jet Stream

had established ground contact and thus completed the crossing, Lindstrand decided to ditch in the Irish Sea as close as he could to the coast of England. As they touched the water, they fired the explosive bolts to separate the capsule from the canopy, but they failed to work—the battery was flat. Now the huge canopy was towing the capsule along like a speedboat.

They both climbed on top of the capsule and prepared to jump. Lindstrand went, but Branson hesitated. Five seconds later the balloon was up to 100 feet, Lindstrand in the water and Branson clinging on. The situation was now desperate. None of the chase helicopters had seen Lindstrand bale out, so were unaware that he was in the water; and Branson was soaring up with the burners at full tilt, turned on to try to provide a soft landing. He turned them off and came down through cloud, seeing to his intense relief a Royal Navy frigate, the HMS *Argonaut*, just below.

This time there was no mistake; Branson bailed out a few seconds before the capsule hit the sea. He was rescued by a Royal Navy helicopter, and provided instructions on where to find Lindstrand. Happily he too was fished out of the sea alive. Both men were cold, shocked and shaking. The entire flight, to "landing" in Limavady, had taken 31 hours 41 minutes.

Having beaten the Atlantic, it was inevitable that Branson and Lindstrand would attempt the Pacific. An even bigger balloon with a capacity of 2.6 million cubic feet was designed for this purpose, standing as high as the Statue of Liberty. The takeoff point this time was Miyakonojo, nearly 600 miles southwest of Tokyo, chosen because it lies under the course of the jet stream and is safely out of Tokyo airport.

After a smooth takeoff at 3 a.m. on 15 January, all went well until after seven hours of flight the first fuel tank was empty, the balloon cruising easily at 30,000 feet. They decided to dump the empty fuel tank but, to their horror, when Branson pulled the switch on the tank release panel, the balloon tilted and soared upward to 36,000 feet. Not only had the empty tank gone, but it had taken with it two full ones.

This might have spelled disaster, but a quick calculation showed that they still had perhaps 35 hours' worth of fuel left, enough to reach the coast of North America. Landfall was made at Juneau, Alaska, at 2.30 a.m., but it was impossible to land at night so the balloon swept on, crossing the Rockies before dawn enabled a descent to be attempted.

The eight propane burners needed to produce the initial lift were arranged in banks of two. All eight Thunder & Colt B3 units were used during takeoff. During the flight, only one bank was used at any one time. The mouth of the envelope, where the burners fed the hot air in, was protected by black fire-resistant fabric.

The frozen tundra of the North West Territories was ideal for landing because of its flat, wide-open spaces. Unfortunately there was a blizzard blowing, with winds of 35 knots. The cloud ceiling was only 1,000 feet but when the balloon finally emerged their ground speed was more than 30 mph, which made a landing on a frozen lake the preferred option. They hit the ice, jettisoned the canopy immediately, and slid to a stop. The temperature was −20°F and the nearest road was 153 miles away. It was four hours before a helicopter picked them up.

Having conquered both Atlantic and Pacific, all that remains is a flight right around the world. Knowing Branson's appetite for adventures, many expect him to try that one day.

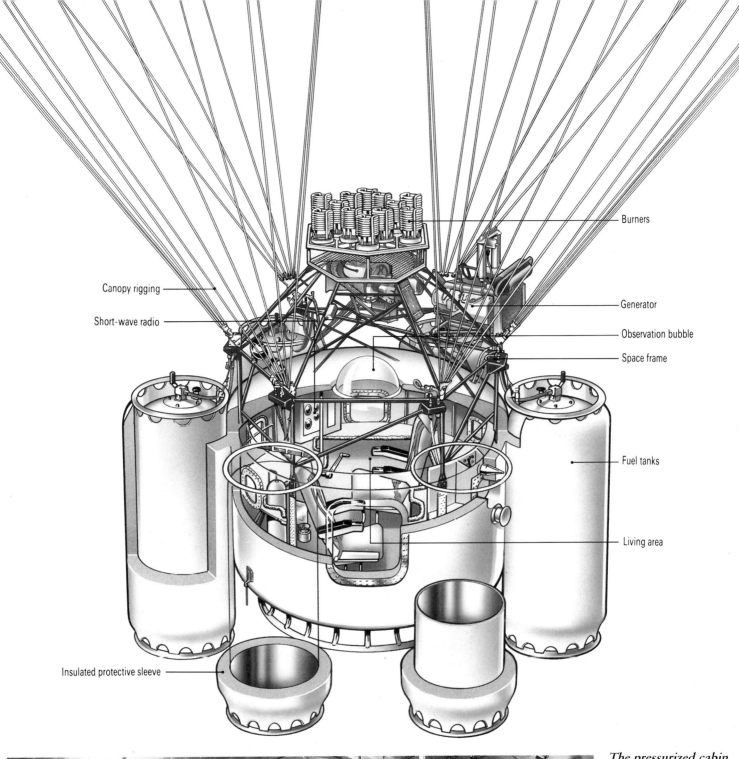

Burners

Canopy rigging

Short-wave radio

Generator

Observation bubble

Space frame

Fuel tanks

Living area

Insulated protective sleeve

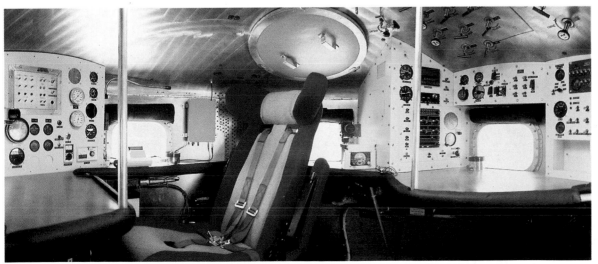

The pressurized cabin of Virgin Atlantic Flyer *was made of aluminium rolled into a cylinder almost 8 feet in diameter and 8 feet high. Aluminium domes were fitted at each end, the upper one having a window so that an eye could be kept on the burners. Ports in the side provided views of the surroundings from the airline-style seats.*

CHAPTER FIVE

INTO SPACE

I n 1961, humankind for the first time left its own environment. After thousands of years of gazing at the stars, we now have the technology to explore them. So far we have done no more than dip a toe into the immensity of space; but if past history is any guide these first steps will lead eventually to expeditions that will leave our own solar system, just as the medieval mariners first set sail across the oceans.

The history of space travel may be short, but it is full of incident. To begin with, few believed in it except for the pioneers of rocketry in Russia, Germany and the United States. As late as the 1950s a British Astronomer Royal declared that space travel was "bunk", but by the dawn of the 1960s Yuri Gagarin had proved him wrong, riding into space in a small and primitive Vostok spacecraft and returning alive after a single orbit.

Soviet successes stimulated a response from the United States, shocked that they should have been overtaken. This response was the Apollo programme, the brilliantly successful attempt to put a man on the Moon. In later Apollo missions, the astronauts were provided with their own vehicles to make the process of exploration easier.

After the success of the Moon landings, space travel has entered a quieter phase. The American and Soviet space shuttles, originally intended to make the orbiting of satellites easy and cheap, have failed to do so. The US programme was set back by the *Challenger* disaster and a series of more minor technical problems, while the Soviet programme remains a mystery—a single unmanned launch in 1988 being followed by a long silence. The Russians have, however, developed the ability to remain in space for very long periods in the Mir space station, building up the experience which will be necessary for establishing colonies in space or on the Moon.

In the following pages we look at a few highlights in the history of space travel. If, as most people expect, the future involves manned missions to the planets, their success will depend on the data gathered in the few years since the world was stunned to hear that a man had gone into space for the first time.

Gagarin's Momentous Orbit

The night before he was launched into space, Yuri Gagarin slept soundly. We know this because under his bed, close to the launch pad at Baikonour Cosmodrome, officials of the Soviet space programme had fitted special sensors. They wanted to be sure that the first man in space was thoroughly rested before he took his chances strapped into a cramped capsule on top of the Soviet Union's SS-6 intercontinental ballistic missile.

The space programme that culminated in Gagarin's flight on 12 April 1961 had its origins in pre-revolutionary Russia. Konstantin Tsiolkowski, born near Moscow in 1857, was a brilliant engineer who believed that the only form of propulsion possible in space would be the rocket. In 1903 he wrote an article that first suggested the use of liquid fuels in rockets and anticipated the need for a multistage rocket, with each stage dropping away as its fuel was exhausted. Tsiolkowski was a theoretician—he did not put any of these ideas into practice—but his judgement proved to be uncannily accurate.

After the revolution in 1917, Soviet interest in space travel was stimulated by a society called the Group for the Study of Jet Propulsion. In 1932, the Moscow and Leningrad branches were amalgamated by the government to form the State Reaction Scientific Research Institute, with Sergei Korolyev at its head. It was a brilliant appointment, for Korolyev was later responsible for all the Soviet Union's early success in space exploration. Without him it is likely that the first man in space would have been an American.

World War II, and the success of Germany's V-2 missiles, showed that orbital flight was not beyond imagination. In their attacks against London and Antwerp, the V-2s reached heights of 50 miles, taking them to the very edge of the Earth's atmosphere. Encouraged by this, and armed with information obtained from captured German specialists, Joseph Stalin ordered a serious study of ballistic missiles soon after the war. The Soviet Union started producing its own V-2s from German plans, using them to carry dogs in high-altitude biological research flights. By 1953, Korolyev had designed a multistage missile as powerful as 20 V-2s. Known in the West as the SS-6, it was the first intercontinental ballistic missile, able in theory to reach America from its launch sites in the USSR.

Nikita Khrushchev, who had succeeded Stalin, gave approval for the SS-6 programme, and the first successful launch was on 3 August 1957, four months before the first US ICBM, *Atlas*. Korolyev had always wanted to use his launcher to put up a satellite, and Khrushchev now saw the opportunity to steal a march on the Americans. Korolyev was told to put a satellite into orbit as quickly as he could.

In just six weeks an SS-6 launcher was united with a simple satellite consisting of a globe 22 inches in diameter, with four aerials and a radio transmitter. The whole satellite, called *Sputnik*, weighed 184 lb and was launched successfully on 4 October 1957. As it circled the Earth, its beeping sound provided powerful evidence of the Soviet lead in space flight, causing something of a panic in the US. The national gloom deepened when on 6 December the US Vanguard rocket, attempting to put a tiny $3\frac{1}{2}$-lb satellite into orbit, rose a few feet from its pad and crashed.

By then, the Soviet Union had launched its second Sputnik, a much more significant satellite, for it weighed half a ton and carried a live creature, a dog called Laika, together with the systems needed to keep the creature alive in the vacuum of space. Now the Soviet intentions were clear. It had the ability to lift very large payloads into orbit, and it was interested in testing how living systems would fare in space. Poor Laika was not, however, provided with any means of coming down again, so she died of asphyxiation when her air supply ran out, and was cremated when *Sputnik 2* re-entered the Earth's atmosphere after three months in orbit.

The Soviet Union and the United States now began a race to be first to send a man into space. The Russians had the advantage of a powerful rocket, but the Americans, after their slow start, were focusing their resources on the problem. It took the Russians two years to design their first manned spacecraft, *Vostok* ("East"), and it set a pattern that has been followed ever since. Designed for automatic operation, *Vostok* could be launched manned or unmanned. This made it possible to carry out a series of unmanned tests without risk to life before the first cosmonaut took his chances.

The spacecraft itself required more work because, unlike the Sputniks, it had to be designed to re-enter the atmosphere safely and

FACT FILE

The first journey by a person in space

Date: 12 April 1961

Distance: Single orbit of Earth, about 25,000 miles

Duration: 1 hour 48 minutes

make a soft landing on the ground. That meant it needed retrorockets to slow it down, a heat shield to resist the blistering temperatures on re-entry, and some sort of parachute—although it was always the intention that the cosmonauts should eject and come down independently. The spacecraft was ready for testing early in 1960.

Things did not go as smoothly as Korolyev would have liked: in testing the ejection system, a pilot was killed; the first orbital tests of the system, on 15 May 1960, in which a dummy took the place of the cosmonaut, failed. The launch was successful and the spacecraft entered a stable orbit, but when the order was given to fire the re-entry rockets, the spacecraft was facing in

The launch of Vostok 1 *(above) was celebrated with commemorative posters (right). The spacecraft was propelled by an SS-6 rocket with an extra stage; this was powered by a single rocket engine, burning alcohol and liquid oxygen. The SS-6's core was made up of thick-walled, heavy steel tanks to contain its fuel—liquid oxygen and kerosene.*

12·IV·1961

Gagarin's Momentous Orbit

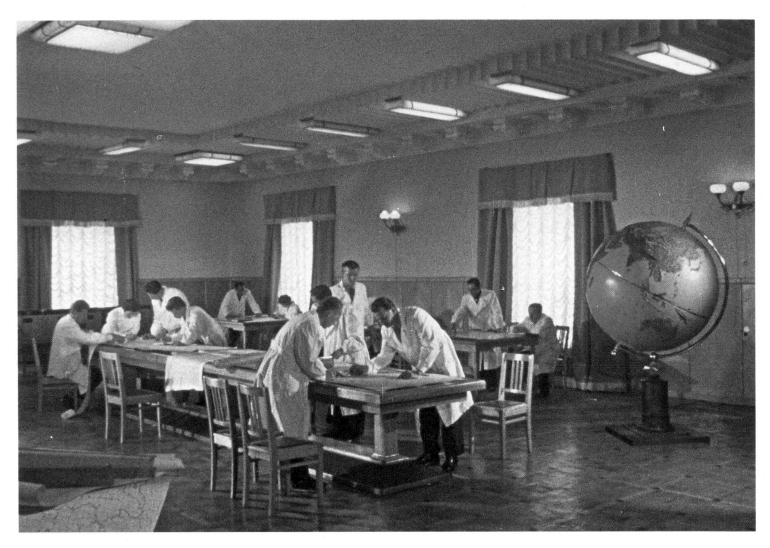

the wrong direction because a sensor had failed. Instead of re-entering it went into a useless orbit from which it eventually re-entered and burned up in October. In July, a launch failed when the rocket refused to ignite on the pad.

Further failures preceded two completely successful tests in March 1961, when officials at last decided the spacecraft was proven enough to carry a man. The risks were emphasized when on 23 March a cosmonaut was killed in a fire while testing the spacecraft on the ground.

In view of the chequered history of the test programme, Gagarin's flight had been reduced from the planned 6 to 18 orbits to a single orbit. Gagarin went aboard at about 7.30 a.m. on the morning of 12 April and while the countdown proceeded, music was played to him through his headphones—a practice which continued for Soviet manned launches for many years. Whether this helped relax Gagarin is not clear, for during the launch his pulse rate rose to 158.

The engines fired at 9.07 a.m. and with a roar *Vostok* was launched into space.

Throughout the short flight all systems worked well, and Gagarin's main job was to observe them. The engineers in charge do not seem to have had much confidence in the ability of cosmonauts to control their spacecraft and preferred to rely on the automatic systems. *Vostok* did possess a manual system for orienting itself for retrofire, but there was no need to use it; the retrorockets fired as the spacecraft came around the world over Africa, and the capsule separated successfully.

At a height of 22,750 feet the capsule hatch was blown off and Gagarin was ejected, landing by parachute. The capsule also landed by parachute but it was feared that the shock of impact might be too violent. The two came down southwest of Engels in the Saratov region, where a titanium monument, 130 feet high, now marks the spot. Many subsequent reports

Control of Vostok 1 *was firmly in the hands of ground control (left), since Soviet doctors feared that a cosmonaut might become mentally disturbed in flight. The descent module (above) was known as Charik, or "little ball", and measured only 7 feet 6 inches across.*

Major Yuri Gagarin (below left) with Nikita Khrushchev at Vnukovo airport on his return to Moscow on 14 April 1961. Tragically, Gagarin did not live long to enjoy his fame: he died on a routine training flight in a Mig-15 trainer on 27 March 1968.

suggested that Gagarin had landed inside the capsule, but they were not true.

The Russians deliberately obscured the issue because the rules of aerospace records demand that the pilot be in charge of the vehicle, or at least in it, throughout the voyage. If they had admitted that Gagarin had bailed out at 22,000 feet the flight might not have been acknowledged as a first by the Fédération Aéronautique International-nationale. The FAI did ask a lot of questions, but eventually admitted the flight as a first; it would have been pedantic to do otherwise. In fact, all the Vostok cosmonauts ejected as Gagarin did, so the legally minded could argue that the first manned flight, takeoff to landing, was made by American John Glenn in February 1962.

That is not, of course, the way the world saw it. The handsome, cheerful Gagarin became a celebrity overnight. For the first time man had set foot outside his own planet, an event as historic as the voyages of Magellan and Columbus.

Man on the Moon

FACT FILE

The first Moon landing

Date: July 1969

Distance: 952,702 miles

Duration: 195 hours

The Apollo 11 *command and services modules (opposite) photographed from the lunar module in orbit around the Moon. On the surface below them is the Sea of Fertility. Six hours after landing on the Moon, Neil Armstrong was the first human being to set foot on an extraterrestrial surface (below).*

The night of Monday 21 July 1969 was unique in human history. While four billion or so people slept on Earth, two of their kind were spending the night on the Moon, the first creatures ever to set foot there. It was the culmination of an ambitious programme launched eight years earlier by President John F. Kennedy and carried out with exemplary efficiency by the US National Aeronautics and Space Administration (NASA). By the success of the Apollo programme, as it was called, the US was able to vault ahead of the early lead in space exploration established by the Soviet Union.

The mission to the Moon was born of pride and frustration. America's leaders could not believe that they had been left behind by their Soviet rivals, and Kennedy resolved to find a dramatic way of catching up. In his address to Congress on 25 May 1961, Kennedy declared: "I believe that this nation should commit itself to achieving the goal, before the decade is out, of landing a man on the Moon and returning him safely to Earth."

Many questioned whether it was wise to declare both an objective and a timetable before it was certain that the job could be done. At the time of the president's speech, the US had yet to achieve even a full Earth orbital flight.

NASA had, however, already been working on a proposal for a three-man spacecraft able to go into orbit around the Earth or the Moon. That would be launched by the *Saturn 1* rocket, with its 665 tons of thrust. Actually landing on the Moon would require a much bigger launcher, with five times the power, larger than anything so far developed anywhere. It would also need a spacecraft capable of navigating across space, landing on the Moon, taking off again, and making it back to the Earth. Nobody had yet worked out quite how to do this, but proposals were soon being discussed.

The best, it was decided, involved making the assault on the Moon in a series of steps. First a spacecraft would be put into Earth orbit. Once there, it would fire rockets to take it out of Earth orbit and toward the Moon. When it reached the Moon it would not land directly, but again go into orbit. If all went well up to that point, a special landing craft would separate from the lunar orbiter, descend to the surface and land. When the mission was complete, part of it—the ascent module—would take off again, rendezvous with the orbiter which was still circling the Moon, and transfer the crew. The orbiter would then escape from Moon orbit and return to Earth, re-entering the atmosphere and landing in the sea.

To make it work, however, NASA would have to learn a lot of new tricks. One was finding, tracking and locking on to another spacecraft in space. Another was to design controllable rocket engines for the lunar lander so that the pilot could use them as delicately as a helicopter's rotors to land on the Moon. Yet a third was to devise an absolutely reliable rocket to get the lander off the Moon again, for if that failed the crew would be stuck there with no hope of rescue. And before a landing could be risked, more would have to be learned about the surface of the Moon itself.

NASA set about answering those questions in a systematic way. The problems of rendezvous and docking were solved during the Gemini missions, while work on the huge *Saturn 5* went on in parallel. Unmanned missions were sent to land on the Moon, sending back pictures and data more detailed than any that could be obtained from Earth. It was clear that the Moon's surface was firm, if not exactly flat. There were thousands of craters, but it looked as if there were sufficient flat places to land safely. Precisely where the astronauts landed would be left to their judgement.

When complete, *Saturn 5* was a prodigious piece of engineering. The noise it made—190 decibels—is the loudest sound that man has ever produced. Firing it was the equivalent to setting off an explosive under a naval destroyer balanced upright and blowing it 30 miles into the air, without breaking a single thing on board. *Saturn 5* was tested for the first time in November 1967, with an unmanned spacecraft, and worked perfectly.

The success had come at a good moment, for earlier in 1967 the programme had suffered a terrible blow, when a fire aboard an Apollo spacecraft being checked out on the ground killed three astronauts. They were breathing pure oxygen, and a spark set plastic in the spacecraft alight. The fire revealed many design failings, which were corrected, but it delayed the first manned launch for 18 months.

Man on the Moon

That mission, *Apollo 7*, was launched into Earth orbit in October 1968. It worked well, paving the way for the first trip around the Moon in *Apollo 8*, launched in December 1968. Frank Borman, James Lovell and William Anders spent 20 hours circling the Moon, taking photographs, including Borman's famous shot of the Earth rising above the lunar horizon.

Apollo 9 was an Earth orbit mission in which the astronauts practised removing the lunar module from the third-stage rocket casing in which it was stored during launch, docking with it, and test-firing its engines. *Apollo 10*, in May 1969, was a full dress rehearsal for the actual landing, except that the astronauts stopped short 10 miles from the lunar surface before returning and docking with the lunar orbiter. So finally, with just six months to go before the deadline set by President Kennedy, all was ready.

Three astronauts had been selected for the crucial *Apollo 11* mission: Neil Armstrong, Edward (Buzz) Aldrin and Michael Collins. Launch from Cape Canaveral on 16 July went perfectly and the voyage to the Moon was routine. On 19 July they reached the Moon, fired the service module rockets and went into lunar orbit. On Sunday 20 July, while Collins stayed in the command module (codenamed *Columbia*), Armstrong and Aldrin got into the lunar module (*Eagle*) and separated on the 13th orbit.

While *Eagle* was around the far side of the Moon, Armstrong fired the descent engine and started toward the surface. As he approached he saw that they were heading for an area strewn with boulders, so took over manual control. At 9.17 p.m., as the descent engine came close to running out of fuel (it had only 2 percent left), the module made contact with the surface. The 500 million people watching television on Earth heard Armstrong say: "Contact light. OK, engine stop . . . Houston, Tranquillity Base here, the *Eagle* has landed."

At this point of maximum excitement, Armstrong and Aldrin were supposed to sleep for four hours, a plan now recognized as absurd. Instead, the two men had a meal, and then prepared to take the first walk on the Moon. It took them nearly six hours to eat, set up the spacecraft for a quick getaway if that should be needed, and put on their bulky spacesuits. Finally, Armstrong moved with deliberation down the stairs, put his foot on the ground, and uttered a sentence carefully composed and committed to memory in advance: "One small

Aldrin descends the ladder from Eagle *to join Armstrong on the Moon. They set up a TV camera, placed a US flag on a pole, gathered rock samples, took a call from President Nixon, and set up various experiments. These included a laser reflector that enabled scientists to measure the distance of the Moon from Earth to within 6 inches. Finally, and controversially, they left their rubbish on the Moon before re-entering the lunar module.*

step for man. One giant leap for mankind."

Aldrin soon joined Armstrong on the Moon for 2½ hours before they got back into the lunar module to sleep. After 22 hours on the Moon, they fired the engine to put them back into lunar orbit, aboard *Eagle*'s ascent stage. It simply had to work, and it did. There was a wobble as *Eagle* docked, but all was well. Armstrong and Aldrin then joined Collins in the command module, jettisoning the ascent module, and fired their propulsion rockets behind the Moon to bring them out of orbit and back on course to Earth.

They arrived home to a splashdown on 24 July at 17.50 BST, just 30 seconds later than had been predicted at the start of the 195-hour mission. In eight days, they had travelled almost a million miles and set foot on a planet no living thing had ever visited before. A mission designed with the precision of a clock had run like clockwork.

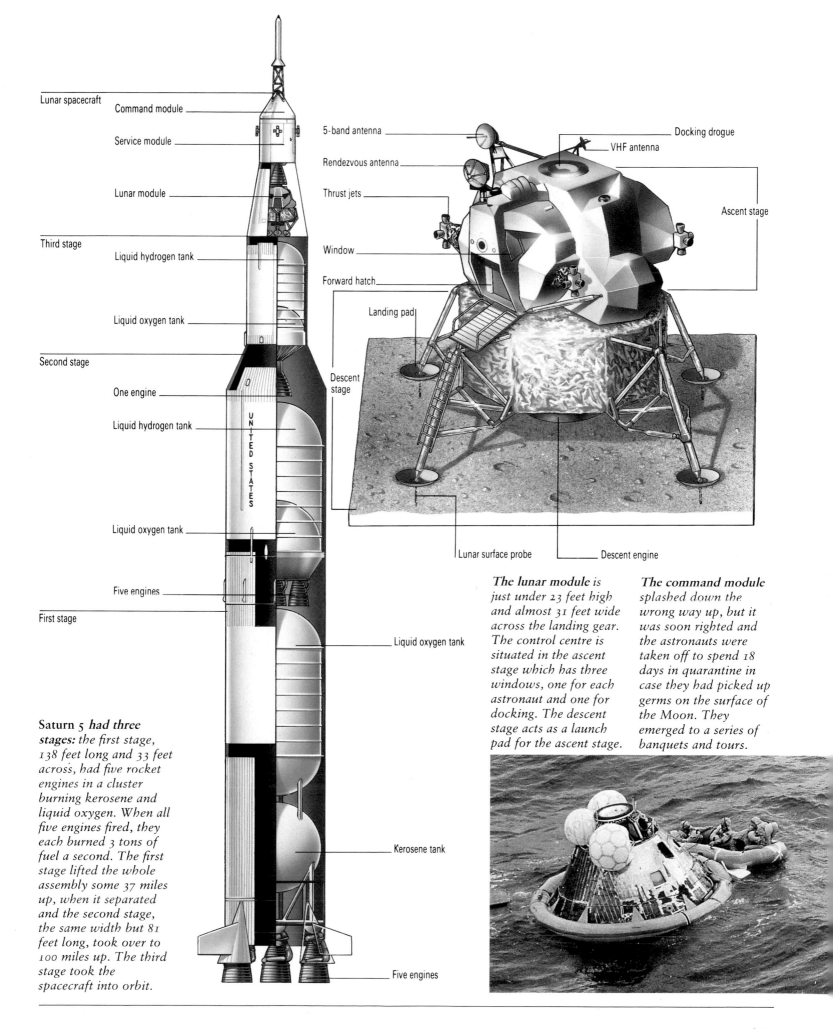

Lunar spacecraft

Command module

Service module

Lunar module

Third stage

Liquid hydrogen tank

Liquid oxygen tank

Second stage

One engine

Liquid hydrogen tank

Liquid oxygen tank

Five engines

First stage

Saturn 5 *had three stages:* *the first stage, 138 feet long and 33 feet across, had five rocket engines in a cluster burning kerosene and liquid oxygen. When all five engines fired, they each burned 3 tons of fuel a second. The first stage lifted the whole assembly some 37 miles up, when it separated and the second stage, the same width but 81 feet long, took over to 100 miles up. The third stage took the spacecraft into orbit.*

UNITED STATES

Liquid oxygen tank

Kerosene tank

Five engines

5-band antenna

Rendezvous antenna

Thrust jets

Window

Forward hatch

Landing pad

Descent stage

Docking drogue

VHF antenna

Ascent stage

Lunar surface probe

Descent engine

The lunar module *is just under 23 feet high and almost 31 feet wide across the landing gear. The control centre is situated in the ascent stage which has three windows, one for each astronaut and one for docking. The descent stage acts as a launch pad for the ascent stage.*

The command module *splashed down the wrong way up, but it was soon righted and the astronauts were taken off to spend 18 days in quarantine in case they had picked up germs on the surface of the Moon. They emerged to a series of banquets and tours.*

Lunar Explorer

Three vehicles that are never likely to be given a parking ticket have been sitting stationary and unattended for the past 20 years. It could be half a century or longer before anybody sees them again, although each cost millions of dollars to make and has no more than delivery mileage on the clock. The lunar rovers carried to the surface of the Moon by the last three Apollo missions in the early 1970s are among the oddest wheeled vehicles ever built. Their existence is evidence, if any were needed, that Americans cannot imagine life, anywhere, without the automobile. To ensure that the Moon had been truly claimed for humankind, it had to be driven over as well as trodden on.

More seriously, the rovers enabled the astronauts on the *Apollo 15*, *16* and *17* missions to travel more widely and with much less risk than they could have done on foot.

Designing a vehicle to be carried to the Moon presented special difficulties. The payload of the Apollo spacecraft was limited, so the rovers had to be made extremely light, and the cargo space was small so that they had to be able to fold up like a portable bicycle. In the one-sixth gravity experienced on the lunar surface, supporting the weight of the astronauts was less demanding than it would have been on Earth, but this meant that the rovers could not be test-driven before they reached their destination. If an Earth-

FACT FILE

The first wheeled vehicle used extraterrestrially

Built: 1969/70

Length: 10 feet 2 inches

Maximum speed: 10 mph

Range: 57 miles

weight astronaut had sat in the rover it would have collapsed. Special normal-gravity models had to be made to teach the astronauts how to drive them.

The job of designing and building the lunar rovers was awarded to the Boeing aircraft company. The purpose of the vehicles was to transport the astronauts around the lunar surface while using far less energy, and so consuming less oxygen and cooling water. In this way it would be possible to double the time the astronauts could remain on the surface. They could travel much farther from their landing point, and also do more useful work.

The need for the rovers had been realized from the start, but was brought home during *Apollo 14* when Alan Shepard and Edgar Mitchell had to tow some scientific equipment a mile across the Moon's surface, climbing almost 400 feet to the rim of Cone Crater. After two hours and ten minutes they were still not there, and visibly tiring. Shepard's heart rate rose to 150, and Mitchell's to 128 before they turned back short of their destination. Getting about on the Moon was clearly an exhausting job in the cumbersome space suits.

The lunar rover, designed and built by Boeing in only 17 months, was a light-alloy vehicle which weighed only 460 lb but was capable of carrying 1,080 lb, more than twice its own

The **Apollo 15** *mission in July 1971 (above left) was the first to use the rover, travelling 2½ miles from the lunar module* Falcon. *During the* Apollo 17 *mission in December 1972, the rover went on two drives. The second lasted for an hour and took Dr Jack Schmitt and Eugene Cernan 4 miles from the module (above).*

Lunar Explorer

weight. This payload consisted of two astronauts plus equipment, reckoned at 400 lb each, together with another 280 lb of tools, equipment, television and communications gear and lunar samples. By comparison, the average family car can carry only half its own weight.

Power was provided by a quarter-hp electric motor in each wheel, fed from two independent 36-volt battery systems. If either of these broke down, the other was capable of getting the vehicle back to base. Both front and rear wheels could be steered, using a T-shaped hand controller in the middle of the console between the two astronauts. Pushing the controller forward made the rover move forward, while moving it sideways steered to right or left. Pulling it backward applied the brakes. The rover's maximum speed was 10 mph, and its batteries gave it an operational lifetime of 78 hours. In practice, however, its range on the Moon was limited to a radius of 6 miles from base, so that if it broke down the astronauts would be able to walk back.

The rover was designed to be able to climb hills of up to 20 degrees, and to clamber over obstacles and small crevasses. The astronauts found that the ride on the lunar surface was so bumpy that in one-sixth gravity they would have been thrown out of the vehicle if they had not used the seat belts provided. The rovers were also fitted with a sophisticated navigation system, set before they drove off, which used the Sun-angle as a bearing to tell them the precise distance and direction back to the lunar module at any time.

Unpacking the rover after landing on the Moon was designed to be simple. It was fitted into a pie-shaped quadrant of the descent stage of the lunar module during flight, and unfolded itself after the astronauts had pulled on two nylon operating tapes in turn before removing a series of release pins. The rover was fitted with a radio for continuous communication with mission control and a TV camera which could be turned on when it was stationary.

The first time the rover was used was during the *Apollo 15* mission, launched in July 1971. David Scott and James Irwin landed in a basin near Hadley Rille on 30 July. They had some problems deploying the rover, and on their first outing could not make the front wheels steer. It functioned satisfactorily with rear steering only, however, so they drove 2½ miles to the edge of Hadley Rille and turned on the TV cameras for the first time. Scott then collected some geologi-

cal samples, using a drill to produce cores of moon rock 3 feet long which were found to contain 57 separate layers of soil, dating back 2,400 million years.

They made two further trips out of the lunar module, covering a total of more than 17 miles. During the final outing they collected 170 lb of rock samples, including one piece of rock 4,150 million years old. Finally they left the rover with the TV camera running as they took off from the Moon, providing a dramatic two seconds as the screen briefly showed the red and green flame as the ascent stage rocket fired.

Apollo 16, in April 1972, also made good use of the lunar rover. At the end of the first trip out of the lunar module, which had landed at Cayley

Commander Eugene Cernan preparing to board the lunar rover during the Apollo 17 *mission. In the background is the south massif of the Taurus Mountains, which reach 6,986 feet. Mission control was anxious that Cernan and Schmitt had driven as far as 4 miles from the module, since it would have taken 2¾ hours to walk back.*

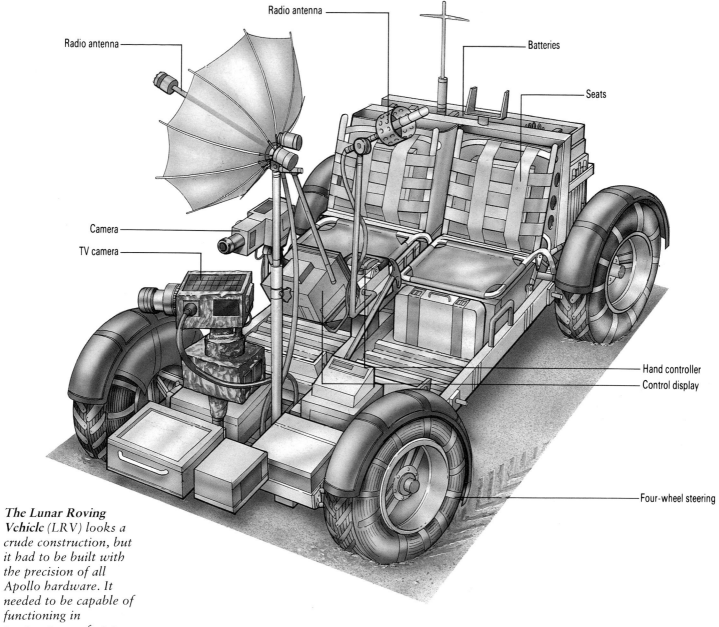

Radio antenna

Radio antenna

Batteries

Seats

Camera

TV camera

Hand controller

Control display

Four-wheel steering

The Lunar Roving Vehicle (LRV) looks a crude construction, but it had to be built with the precision of all Apollo hardware. It needed to be capable of functioning in temperatures of up to 250°F, and in a vacuum which meant that air cooling could not be employed. The rover has enabled astronauts to visit and send back pictures of parts of the Moon that could not have been reached on foot. Unfortunately, it was impossible to send back pictures from the vehicle while it was on the move as the antenna can be unfurled for transmission only when it is stationary.

Plains, John Young drove the rover around and around in tight circles as fast as he could to test wheel grip. Later a rear mudguard fell off the rover, exposing the astronauts to a constant cloud of dust. Exactly the same happened during the *Apollo 17* mission, in December 1972, after Eugene Cernan, the mission commander, had accidentally knocked off a rear mudguard. So much dust was being scattered over them and their equipment that the astronauts were advised to make a temporary mudguard by taping together four lunar maps and clipping them to the vehicle.

Cernan and his colleague, geologist Dr Harrison (Jack) Schmitt, used the rover to make the longest trips yet across the lunar surface. During

their three trips they covered a total of 22 miles, loading up the rover with a massive 250 lb of moon rock. During the final trip the rover was taken up mountain sides so steep that its wheels, made of wire mesh, were dented, fortunately without affecting its performance.

Apollo 17 was the last mission to the Moon, and humans have not set foot on it since. The three rovers left behind are unlikely to be much use to any future explorer—their batteries will be flat, and they were not designed to withstand the bitterly cold temperatures of the Moon indefinitely. As things stand, there are no further plans for exploring the Moon, so it may be a long time before anybody sets eyes on the three vehicles which proved so useful.

The Retrievable Spacecraft

In the history of space exploration sketched out by NASA, the space shuttle was supposed to occupy the same role as the Douglas DC-3 does in aviation: a cheap, utterly reliable workhorse that would transform space flight into a mundane affair. Reality has been crueller. While it has flown well and carried out many space "firsts", including the rescue of a broken-down satellite for repair, the shuttle has failed to make space travel either cheap or safe. Its launches cost just as much as conventional rockets, and nobody who saw it either live or on television can forget the *Challenger* disaster of 28 January 1986, when a shuttle blew up with its crew of seven just after launch from Cape Canaveral.

Designed as a space plane that could take off from and land in ordinary airfields, the space shuttle has been the victim of too many compromises, most of them forced on it by tight budgets. Nor has the copy of the shuttle produced by the Soviet Union performed any better: *Buran* ("Snowstorm"), uncannily similar in appearance to the shuttle, made one unmanned flight in 1988 but then disappeared from sight. The manned flight promised for 1989 was postponed, apparently indefinitely.

Conventional rockets, used only once, will never be an inexpensive form of travel. So when NASA started work on the shuttle in 1972, it made sense to envisage a re-usable spacecraft that could make many flights. Original plans suggested that by 1991 the shuttle fleet would have completed 725 flights, at a rate of 60 a year, each one costing as little as $20 million. All these figures now look absurdly optimistic.

The designers of the shuttle had to produce a vehicle that could function in two quite different environments. In orbit, it is a spaceship, controlled by small rocket motors. In the atmosphere it is a 200-ton glider, which can be controlled aerodynamically and brought in to land, in theory at least, on any runway long enough to accommodate it. Because it has no engines for use in the atmosphere, it has only one chance to land, using gravity to generate enough speed to fly. Its small wings produce little lift, so the shuttle lands fast, at more than 200 mph. So far, thanks to the skill of the pilots, landing has proved no problem.

Liftoff, however, is another matter. In an ideal world, the shuttle would take off like a regular aircraft, using jet engines that would convert themselves high in the atmosphere into rockets to propel it into space. Such "space planes" have been designed, but none has yet been built. The shuttle, by contrast, blasts off like a conventional rocket, with all the same complexities.

Its main engines use liquid hydrogen and oxygen fuel, which are difficult to handle and need a huge external fuel tank. On their own, the main engines provide insufficient lift, so they are supplemented by two solid-fuel boosters strapped on to the tank and discarded before the shuttle goes into orbit. The empty boosters parachute into the sea for recovery and re-use, but the big external tank is discarded after a single launch. Many of these design features were introduced to save development costs, but they added to operational costs, thereby undermining the rationale of the shuttle.

Two of the most difficult features to get right were the main rocket engines and the insulation of the shuttle orbiter to prevent it burning up during re-entry. The shuttle has three main engines, each with enough thrust to power two

FACT FILE

The world's only operational spacecraft to land like a plane

Columbia (OV-101)

Date built: 1974–76

Wing span: 78 feet

Length: 122 feet

The shuttle project was given the green light by President Nixon on 5 January 1972. In July a $2,600-million contract was awarded to North American Rockwell Corporation as the principal contractor, and by May 1973 the design was almost complete. Work began in June the following year on the first shuttle, which was to be used for gliding tests. Two launch pads are available at Cape Canaveral where Atlantis *is prepared for takeoff (left).* Discovery *was launched (right) on 13 March 1969 to deploy the final Tracking and Data Relay Satellite to complete the TDRS network.*

The Retrievable Spacecraft

and a half jumbo jets. The engines work by mixing and igniting liquid oxygen and liquid hydrogen, which are stored in the external tank. The two liquids, at extremely low temperatures, have to be pumped at huge pressures into the combustion chamber where they react, creating pressures 220 times that of the atmosphere.

It was hardly surprising that developing these engines caused a lot of headaches. In tests between March 1977 and November 1979 there was a run of 14 failures, but eventually the engines were made to work. They have not failed in use, even if servicing them between missions has proved more difficult than hoped.

A second major difficulty was with the ceramic tiles that are used to insulate the shuttle against the temperature of re-entry. Earlier spacecraft had used ablative heat shields which protected their occupants by gradually burning off as they re-entered. For a re-usable spacecraft something more permanent was needed, so it was decided to cover the surfaces of the shuttle with silica-based tiles about the size of the tiles on a bathroom wall. These materials are such astonishingly good insulators that it would be quite possible to touch one side of a tile with your finger while the other side was red-hot.

To cover the surface of the orbiter requires 31,000 tiles, each of which has to be stuck on individually, with a small gap between them to allow for expansion and contraction. Sticking these tiles on proved a long and tiresome job, for it was found to the horror of the engineers that they could easily be pulled off. Curing the problem on the first shuttle, *Columbia*, took more than a year from September 1979 and involved a work force of 1,400 people.

The solid fuel boosters, by contrast, seemed to offer few problems, although it was eventually the failure of one of them that caused the *Challenger* disaster. Solid boosters had never before been used for manned missions. Although they are reliable, they have the drawback that once ignited they cannot be turned off again, nor can the power they deliver be controlled as a liquid rocket's can. Without them, however, the shuttle would not get far off the pad; the two boosters provide 5.8 million lb of thrust, against the 1.4 million lb of the main engines.

Eventually, some years after the scheduled date, the first shuttle was ready for launch. A final test of the engines was carried out on the pad at Cape Canaveral on 20 February 1981, running them for 20 seconds to make sure they

The solid fuel boosters (left) *are placed either side of the tank; each is 150 feet long and 12 feet in diameter and is filled with 1.1 million lb of propellants that burn within two minutes. The propellant consists of aluminium powder, aluminium perchlorate, a small amount of iron oxide catalyst and a binding agent that sets the mixture to the consistency of hard rubber. The shuttle's three main engines* (above) *have the greatest thrust-to-weight ratio of any engine ever developed, and they are designed to burn for 7½ hours, or for 55 missions.*

were really working. They were, and launch was set for 10 April. The commander was John Young, a veteran of two trips to the Moon, who was 50 and wore spectacles, the first astronaut ever to do so in space. His pilot was Robert Crippen, who had never been in space before.

The first attempt to launch *Columbia* failed when a tiny computer malfunction was detected 16 minutes before liftoff. It took five hours to sort out the fault, which meant that the external tank had to be emptied, so the launch was put off until Sunday 12 April, 20 years to the day since Yuri Gagarin made the first manned space flight. This time the count went smoothly. A few seconds before liftoff the main engines were ignited, and their performance was instantly scrutinized by a mass of instruments and analysed by computers. If there had been anything wrong, it would have been possible even in those few seconds to abort the launch before the solid boosters ignited. All was well, the boosters were lit and with a tremendous roar and a huge cloud of white exhaust *Columbia* leaped from the pad at just after 7 a.m. local time.

After 2 minutes and 12 seconds the boosters burned out and were jettisoned to splash down in the Atlantic 5 minutes later for recovery. By now *Columbia* was 31 miles up and travelling at 2,900 mph. The main engines ran for a further 6 minutes, cutting out 8 minutes and 34 seconds after launch, when *Columbia* was travelling at 17,502 mph and had reached a low Earth orbit. The final orbit was achieved by firing the orbital manoeuvring system engines four times, putting

Columbia into a stable 170 by 172 mile orbit.

As soon as Crippen opened the payload bay doors it was apparent that *Columbia* had lost some tiles during launch. They were, however, in areas where the temperature was not expected to get dangerously high. From the cabin it was, of course, impossible to see the critical underside of the orbiter, and there was concern that tiles might have fallen off from there too, imperilling the return to Earth.

After two days in orbit, the astronauts

The shuttle's pilots sit in front of large windows and control the orbiter like an aircraft, with columns and foot pedals, while in Earth's atmosphere. In space the craft's attitude is controlled by 44 small rocket thrusters around the nose and rear.

THE FATED MISSION

Shuttle mission 51L had been dogged by frustrating minor technical hitches which delayed the eventual takeoff, on 28 January 1986. The seven astronauts boarded the *Challenger*; the main engines were fired at 11.38 a.m. local time, and the computers verified that all was well with them and the boosters were ignited. Once the level of thrust constantly exceeded the weight of the assembly, the explosive restraining bolts were detonated and the shuttle left the launch pad. In the 74th second of the mission, at an altitude of 10 miles, flames appeared around the base of the tank. It exploded and engulfed *Challenger* in flames. The steel casing of the right booster had ruptured, playing flames on to the tank. The disaster shocked the world, and set back the US space programme by years.

The Retrievable Spacecraft

The Remote Manipulator System (above and right) is the key to manoeuvring satellites out of and into the shuttle's payload bay. The 50-foot-long jointed robot arm, built by the Canadians, is stowed along the payload bay. Electrically operated from one of the flight deck windows that overlooks the payload bay, the arm has flexible joints and a rotating wrist. Manoeuvring the large satellites that shuttles have carried and placing them in a precise orbit is a highly skilled operation. A close-up TV camera on the "forearm" assists the operator.

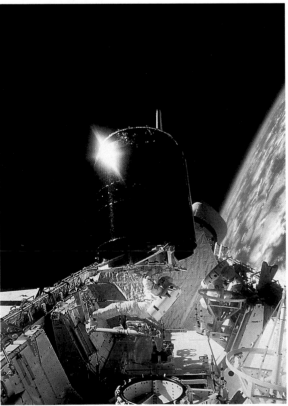

prepared to return. First, Young rotated *Columbia* so that it was going backward, then fired the manoeuvring engines to slow it down by 200 mph and bring it back into the fringes of the atmosphere. After another orbit *Columbia* began to dig into the atmosphere with its nose angled up by 40 degrees and the thermal tiles glowing red. Radio contact with Earth was lost for 16 minutes when the temperature rose high enough to ionize the air around *Columbia*, obliterating radio signals, but this had been expected and caused no anxiety.

When *Columbia* emerged from radio silence it was 35.6 miles above the Earth and travelling at ten times the speed of sound. It was landing not at Canaveral but on the wide-open expanses of Edwards Air Force Base high in the Mojave Desert of California. To lose speed *Columbia* went through a series of S-curves, lining up for final approach to the runway. With no power available, Young had to get it right; the shuttle cannot go around again if it misjudges its approach. There was no mistake. The wheels came down seconds before *Columbia* hit the runway at 215 mph in a copybook landing.

The cargo bay of shuttles (left) was designed with satellites in mind. Placing satellites in orbit or repairing them for communications companies can be lucrative work. This often requires a space walk by astronauts wearing suits (above) that provide water, heat, oxygen, radio contact and waste disposal for up to seven hours. The bay is 60 feet long and 15 feet wide, big enough for four satellites. Once in orbit, the two pairs of payload bay doors swing open to expose heat exchangers for the shuttle's electrical systems.

Satellites are sent into their geostationary orbit at a height of 22,000 miles by rocket motors, since the shuttle cannot climb above 690 miles.

Most often, an electric turntable spins the satellite like a top before a spring is released to send it on its way. The rocket motors are fired once it is a safe distance from the shuttle.

Life in Space

From the first unfortunate animals sent into space to the more recent tests on humans, much of the United States and Soviet space programmes has been directed at understanding more about the effects of weightlessness. This is vital if a space station is to be built. The Soviets lead the field in long-term exposure to weightlessness: Valery Ryumin has spent a cumulative total of 361 days in orbit, while Anatoly Berezovoy was on board the space station *Salyut 7* for 211 days in all. Predictably, psychological pressures have proved more taxing than the physical problems, although a constant diet of largely dehydrated food also becomes a trial.

A major incentive behind this work is the prospect of harvesting both energy and minerals in space. A giant solar collector and satellite could convert the Sun's energy into electricity which would be transmitted to Earth as microwaves. A collector built on a flimsy scale to take advantage of weightlessness would have to be built in space, working from a space port.

The cabin of Voskhod 1, the first three-man rocket, which took Soviet cosmonauts Vladimir Komarov, Konstantin Feoktistov and Dr Boris Yegorov on 16 orbits on 12/13 October 1964. It was the first time a medical man had flown in space and the first time light sports suits rather than space suits were worn.

Space shuttle astronauts (right above) queue up to select their space food in the galley on the orbiter Columbia *on flight 611, launched on 12 January 1986. Daniel Brandenstein, commander of the space shuttle* Columbia *on its STS-32 mission of 19/20 January 1990, celebrated his 47th birthday in space with an inflatable cake (right).*

The 51-D shuttle mission aboard Discovery broke new ground in the United States space programme when Jeffrey Hoffman (left) and David Griggs (right) carried out the first unplanned space walk. It was supposed to be a routine mission, launched on 13 April 1985, to place two comsats, communication satellites, in orbit. On the first day, the $65 million Anik C1 comsat was successfully ejected, but when an attempt was made to release the $85 million Syncom 4-3 comsat, there was no sign of life.

It was decided that the fault probably lay with an arming lever on the side of the comsat, so Hoffman and Griggs donned space suits to try to fix it. A makeshift device was used to try to trip the lever. Although the method worked, nothing happened and later examination of photographs indicated that the lever was already fully extended, so the problem with the comsat was internal.

On 27 August 1985 Discovery was launched to try to repair the satellite and save the huge investment. The mission was a complete success. Its commander, Joe Engle, commented: "It was one of the most fantastic things I've ever been involved with. Five months ago we had no idea we'd be doing this . . ."

Milestones

ACROSS THE OCEANS

Gokstad and Oseberg Viking Longships *c.* ninth century Norway

Two Viking longships uncovered by archaeologists in Norway have been rebuilt and put on display in the Viking Ship Museum in Oslo. Both ships were well preserved by the blue clay in which they were buried. The Gokstad ship was discovered in a burial mound at Sandefjord in 1881, while the Oseberg ship was found in a mound near Tönsberg.

Respectively 76 feet and 70 feet long and each with a beam of 17 feet, the longships would have been used for raiding, often far from the Norse homelands. Despite having neither keel nor deck, longships made remarkable journeys, reaching Iceland, Greenland and the Mediterranean. During the winter, longships were generally hauled ashore until the spring.

Built almost entirely of oak, the Gokstad longship was designed to undertake longer journeys. Her hull was clinker-built with 16 planks contoured to form an identical bow and stern.

Henry Grâce à Dieu 1514 England

When launched at Erith in Kent in June 1514, *Henry Grâce à Dieu* was the largest warship in the world. Built on the orders of Henry VIII, *Great Harry*, as she was better known, had four pole masts, three of which had two circular tops—platforms from which soldiers could fire muskets on to the enemy below.

In common with many ships of her day, *Great Harry* had a large forecastle and sterncastle. She is thought to have weighed 1,000 tons and had a complement of 700 men. Although armed with 21 heavy bronze guns and 231 lighter weapons, *Great Harry* took no part in an engagement, since she was destroyed by an accidental fire at Woolwich, London, in 1553.

HMS *Victory* 1765 Britain

Nelson's flagship at the Battle of Trafalgar in 1805 is one of the best-known warships from the days of sail. *Victory*'s elm keel was laid down in 1759 at Chatham, but it was six years and 2,000 oak trees later before she was launched. Weighing 2,162 tons and mounting 100 guns, *Victory* was one of only five first-rates in the Royal Navy which then comprised 300 ships.

Her first action came in 1778 against the French, and thereafter *Victory* was the flagship of a succession of admirals in campaigns against France. By the end of the eighteenth century, *Victory* was old, but a shortage of good timber prevented her replacement and she was extensively refitted between 1800 and 1803. After the victory at Trafalgar and the death of Nelson in the battle, she was rebuilt and became the flagship of the commander-in-chief at Portsmouth, where the ship is now open to the public.

Charlotte Dundas 1801 Scotland
Clermont *c.*1805 US

These two vessels may be said to have inaugurated the age of steam afloat. *Charlotte Dundas* was the creation of William Symington who built for the governor of the Forth & Clyde Canal, Lord Dundas, a steamboat that could reliably haul two other craft on the canal.

The canal's proprietors thought the wash would erode the canal's banks so *Charlotte Dundas* was laid up; her remains were photographed in 1856 just before they were broken up. A model based on the remains indicates that the boat had a paddlewheel inset into the hull toward the stern, driven by a crank powered by a single double-acting cyclinder.

Robert Fulton studied Symington's boat before building the world's first commercially successful steamboat, *Clermont*, which plied the Hudson River between Albany and New York from 1807. The single vertical-cylinder engine, built by Boulton & Watt of Birmingham, England, drove a pair of 15-foot paddlewheels mounted on each side of the hull.

SS *Great Eastern* 1858 Britain

The third and last steamship built to the designs of the remarkable engineer Isambard Kingdom Brunel was one of the most extraordinary vessels ever built. The *Great Eastern* was more than twice as long and three times as heavy as any other ship afloat, and the enormous difficulties that were encountered during her construction and launch served to undermine the health of her creator.

The ship was intended to carry 4,000 passengers and 6,000 tons of cargo to India or Australia without recoaling. With a gross tonnage of 18,914 tons and a length of 680 feet, the *Great Eastern* had a pair of paddlewheels and a propeller, driven by different engines, as well as sails. She was the first ship to have a cellular, double-skin hull. Her career was a failure. She was too large to be viable and spent more time as an exhibit in United States ports than carrying passengers across the oceans; her one triumph was the laying of the first transatlantic telegraph cable, in 1866. The ship was broken up in the River Mersey in 1889.

Gloire 1859 France
HMS *Warrior* 1860 Britain

It is a matter for debate whether the French *Gloire* or the English *Warrior* was the first true battleship, taking the term to mean a capital ship of a navy built of iron or steel. *Gloire* was a frigate with a displacement of 5,600 tons, clad in armour plate almost $4\frac{3}{4}$ inches thick. However, beneath the iron was a ship of oak.

HMS *Warrior* had three skins to her hull: an inner 1 inch of wrought iron sandwiched 18 inches of teak between the outer skin of 4 inches of wrought iron. Her iron construction and watertight bulkheads returned naval supremacy to the Royal Navy; Napoleon III called the ship "the black snake amongst the rabbits".

USS *Monitor* 1862 US

John Ericsson's shallow-draught ironclad gave its name to a whole class of naval vessels, although his ship for the Union navy was only a limited success. Born in Sweden, Ericsson had emigrated to the United States after a period in England, during which he had entered a locomotive in the Rainhill Trials of 1829, won by the Stephensons' *Rocket*.

When the Union learned that the Confederate navy was converting a wooden ship, *Merrimak*, into an ironclad, plans were made for a response. Ericsson's design was accepted, and *Monitor* was launched in 1862. Two guns were mounted in a revolving turret which was to revolutionize naval design. The encounter with *Virginia*, as *Merrimak* was renamed, was indecisive, and *Monitor* foundered off Cape Hatteras on the last day of 1862.

Turbinia 1894 Britain

Built by Brown & Hood at Wallsend-on-Tyne in 1894 to a design by Charles Parsons, *Turbinia* was the world's first turbine vessel. Although *Turbinia* was only an experimental 100-foot launch, her influence was immense. It was at Queen Victoria's Diamond Jubilee Review at Spithead in 1897 that *Turbinia* made her mark, achieving 34 knots and outstripping the vessels that attempted to intercept her. It encouraged Cunard to adopt turbines for the *Lusitania* and *Mauretania* and the Royal Navy to order two turbine submarines, *Viper* and *Cobra*.

Turbinia is preserved at Exhibition Park, Newcastle-upon-Tyne.

HMS Dreadnought 1906 Britain

Like the USS *Monitor*, HMS *Dreadnought* gave her name to a whole line of battleships. The first "all big gun" battleship, *Dreadnought* was launched at Portsmouth in February 1906 after being under construction for just eight months. Rather than carry a range of guns, she carried ten 12-inch guns, which enabled her to outgun anything else afloat. Her steam turbines also gave her a speed that would eclipse any other battleship in the world, her top speed being 21½ knots. Her superiority prompted the start of the "Dreadnought race" with Germany and Japan. During World War I there was only one engagement between Dreadnoughts, an inconclusive affair at Jutland in 1916. The Dreadnought formula of high speed, heavy protection and big guns continued until after World War II.

USS North Carolina 1940 US

Launched before the United States entered World War II following Pearl Harbor, USS *North Carolina* represents the final stage in the development of the battleship. By the time her keel was laid in 1937, it was evident that the principal threat to capital ships came from aircraft. Her antiaircraft armament was increased with each refit, and by the end of World War II, she had 96 AA guns, supplemented by twenty 5-inch guns; these could fire shells with proximity fuses, fitted with miniature radios that detected the presence of an aircraft within effective range and exploded to shower the plane with shrapnel fragments.

But *North Carolina*'s prime purpose was as a mobile gun platform; she had nine 16-inch guns which were never fired against another battleship, but were used to bombard land and lesser sea targets throughout the war. Her 121,000-hp engines could propel her loaded displacement weight of 44,800 tons at a maximum speed of 25 knots. She was a lucky ship, losing only 6 men in her company of 2,000 during 300,000 miles of war at sea.

North Carolina is preserved at Wilmington, North Carolina.

OVERLAND BY ROAD

Bicycle 1860s US, France and Britain

Extraordinary as it may seem, none of the sophisticated civilizations of the ancient world appear to have had any concept of the bicycle. The first evidence that anyone had considered this means of transport appears in the sketches of a student of Leonardo da Vinci, but as it is included among caricatures and pornographic drawings, it is unlikely that even then—the late fifteenth century—the idea was being taken seriously.

In 1817 Baron Karl von Drais produced the hobby-horse—a body set on two wheels with a handlebar for steering. Although it had no pedals and was powered by the rider pushing his feet along the ground, it attained such speeds that a hobby-horse is reported to have beaten a coach and four in a race from London to Brighton. The bicycle with pedals emerged more or less simultaneously in the US, France and Britain in the 1860s, inspired by the work of Pierre Michaux of Paris who is credited with the first "velocipede".

Two inventions of the 1880s increased the bicycle's practicality and popularity. The Rover Safety Bicycle, designed by John Kemp Starley, was the first to feature a chain-driven rear wheel. This meant that speed was no longer dependent on the size of the wheel, an engineering achievement which led to the fall from favour of the unstable penny-farthing. The second invention was that of the pneumatic tyre by John Boyd Dunlop—what had until then been popularly known as the "bone-shaker" now became a reasonably comfortable means of transport.

Model T Ford 1908 US

Although Karl Benz is credited with the production of the world's first practical automobile with an internal combustion engine, the massive growth in the popularity of the motor car must be attributed to Henry Ford (1863–1947). The Ford Motor Company was founded in 1903 and by 1915 was the largest automobile producer in the world, with over 500,000 Model Ts on the road. Ford pioneered mass production: parts or subassemblies were delivered to the production line with precision timing, so that by 1913 a complete chassis for the Model T could be produced in 93 minutes.

The Model T Ford was the first ever popular car. At its launch in 1908, Ford said, "I will build a motor car for the great multitude"—and he did. Before this time, cars had been the preserve of the rich. The Model T cost $500 in 1913 and $290 by the time it was withdrawn from production in 1927. Ford produced 15.5 million Model Ts—and changed people's lives as radically as any other modern development.

Harley-Davidson c.1910 US

In the early days, motorcycles were not as popular in the US as in Britain and Europe. This may be because the motor car was much cheaper and more readily available in the US; or because the distances a traveller was likely to cover in Europe were small enough to make the comparative discomfort of a motorcycle more tolerable. In any event, it is surprising that what became known as "the motorcycle magnificent" should have developed in a Milwaukee basement around the turn of the century.

The first Harley-Davidson product was a 3-hp, single-cylinder vehicle. Before World War I their motorcycles were widely used by policemen, telephone companies and postal services. During World War I they consolidated their reputation for power, reliability and speed—one model averaged an incredible 89 mph over a 100-mile test.

Expansion in the 1920s added the characteristic bomb-shaped tank, hooded mudguards and wide wheels to the already familiar low saddle position. And throughout this century, with the rise and fall of British, European and Japanese manufacturers, the Harley-Davidson has remained the ultimate "bikers' bike".

Milestones

Bugatti c.1920 France

It is difficult to define a "classic car"—it must simply have something about it that makes it unforgettable. Anything from the unpretentious Austin Seven to the incomparable Rolls-Royce can be included in a list of classics.

Bugattis deserve a place in such a list because they can be likened to thoroughbred racehorses—beautifully designed, impeccably produced and a joy to handle. The Bugatti company, which flourished and produced beautiful cars throughout the 1920s, was founded in France by an Italian, Ettore Bugatti, son of a furniture designer and brother of a sculptor.

Bugattis were nothing if not stylish. As early as 1919, Ettore was criticized for producing a very fast car with poor brakes. "I build my cars to go, not to stop," he is said to have replied.

Volkswagen Beetle 1937 Germany

The Volkswagen company was founded in Wolfsburg in 1937 by the German government. Its brief, as its name suggests, was to mass produce an inexpensive "people's car". The man brought in to design the car was Ferdinand Porsche, whose name is usually associated with sportier vehicles.

The VW factory was destroyed during World War II, along with most of Wolfsburg, but as German industry was rebuilt after the war, automobile manufacture concentrated largely on the people's car. By the mid-1950s, Volkswagen produced over 50 percent of the motor vehicles in West Germany.

Although it was soon one of the most popular cars in Europe, the Volkswagen was not at first a great success in the US. One of the reasons was certainly its Nazi connections, but the American public had not yet recognized the disadvantages of their larger, "gas-guzzling" cars. A brilliant advertising campaign run in 1959 changed all this: it not only emphasized the appeal of the small car, it gave the Volkswagen its popular name—the Beetle. In the early 1960s the Beetle was the most successful imported car in the US.

For 40 years Volkswagen traded on the success of its original model, hardly refining it at all. But by the early 1970s other small car manufacturers were producing more advanced and more attractive rivals.

Volkswagen was forced out of its complacency and began to produce other, sportier models like the Golf/Rabbit. But the Beetle, like the Morris Minor and the Citroën 2CV, retains its place in the hearts of lovers of unpretentious cars.

Mini 1959 Britain

The Suez Crisis of 1956 caused the first international oil shortage of the automobile era and led directly to a demand for smaller, more economical cars. The greatest of these was the Mini, created by the British Motor Corporation's chief designer, Alex Issigonis, who had already shown his genius with the development of the much-loved Morris Minor.

Issigonis's masterstroke lay in giving the Mini a transverse engine—simply turning the Morris Minor's engine through 90 degrees, so that it could be mounted on top of the transmission. The bonnet which covered it was shorter than anything ever seen on a saloon car. But although the Mini itself was tiny, 85 percent of its volume was passenger space: it was remarkably uncramped for such a compact car.

The Mini was cheap, reliable, safe and easy to park—but somehow it was more than that. It rapidly became a British national institution and a symbol of the 1960s, often seen painted with Union Jacks or psychedelic, flower power patterns. Indeed, it attained such cult status that a facsimile edition was launched to celebrate its thirtieth birthday in 1989.

E-Type Jaguar 1961 Britain

The E-Type Jaguar was the attainable sports car of the 1960s. The fact that it had an enormous potential market in the US (in the years before the imposition of a speed limit that curtailed the pleasures of sports-car driving) meant that the manufacturers could keep the price to a realistic level. Owning an E-type need not be a fantasy or a privilege reserved for pop stars—without losing any of its glamour, the E-type became a car the man in the street could just about afford.

The charisma of the E-type lay in its glorious, streamlined shape, but it also boasted a mighty 3.8-litre engine and was the first Jaguar with independent rear suspension, an innovation which made it sturdy, reliable and a joy to handle.

Formula 1 Racing Cars—the Cosworth Engine 1967 Britain

Racing cars are divided into "formulas" or categories defining the size and power of the car—and the most powerful and theoretically the most exciting are classed as Formula 1. In the early 1960s, motor racing was still based on 1500 cc unsupercharged engines, which meant that many sporting models of private cars were faster and more challenging than anything on the Grand Prix circuit. The sport was losing its thrill for drivers and spectators alike.

In 1966, the definition of a Formula 1 car was increased to 3000 cc and motor racing was revolutionized by the invention of the Ford-Cosworth DFV engine. A compact and supremely efficient four-overhead-camshaft unit, the 405-hp Cosworth swiftly became the standard engine for Formula 1 cars and dominated the Grand Prix circuit. The engine had been produced specifically for Lotus, although they had exclusive use of it for only one year, and a Lotus 49 with a Cosworth engine, driven by Jim Clark, won the Dutch Grand Prix in 1967 on its first outing—itself a remarkable achievement.

Clark and his Lotus teammate, Graham Hill, won four more Grand Prix in the course of the year. The engine was subsequently adopted by almost all other major manufacturers and by the time the 3000 cc unsupercharged engine was banned in 1985, cars powered by the Ford-Cosworth DFV had won 155 Grand Prix.

Sunraycer—the Solar Car 1987 US

Sunraycer was produced by General Motors as their entry for the 1987 World Solar Challenge—a 2,000-mile race across Australia intended to encourage the development of solar power for automobiles. Not only did it win, it beat the second placed car by 20 hours.

In some ways, Sunraycer is one of the most successful cars ever produced. Its coefficient of drag—the means by which a car's aerodynamic efficiency is tested—is comparable to that of an aeroplane wing. Its body is exceptionally sleek, with only two small fins to improve stability in cross winds interrupting its smooth lines. It is made largely of lightweight aluminium and powered by solar cells covering all the body except the nose.

However, the cost of production was over $1 million, and it remains to be seen whether it will ever be practical to manufacture such a vehicle on a commercial scale. Drawbacks yet to be overcome include the fact that Sunraycer seats only one person, that it has no headlights, and that it is impossible to put the top in place from the driving seat.

OVERLAND BY RAIL

Lafayette 4-2-0 1837 US

In 1837 William Norris of Philadelphia delivered the first of eight locomotives to the Baltimore & Ohio Railroad. They incorporated several important developments from the Stephensons' *Rocket* of 1829. It had a leading bogie underneath the smokebox, which both improved weight distribution and helped to guide the locomotive smoothly through curves. The cylinders were placed beside the smokebox outside the frames, with the valves placed in a chest on top of the cylinders. The axle of the driving wheels was located in front of the firebox rather than behind, which served to increase the weight placed upon them and so improved adhesion.

The locomotives, the first of which was named *Lafayette*, were a great improvement on the B & O's vertical-boilered locomotives which were all the company owned before the Norris 4-2-0s. Their success led to export orders for railways in Austria, Germany and even Britain, which was at the time the leading producer of railway locomotives.

Merddin Emrys 0-4-4-0 1879 Wales

The Festiniog Railway double Fairlies represent a major development in the history of the steam locomotive. Built to take slate from the quarries of North Wales to the harbour at Porthmadog for shipment, the railway was built to a gauge of 1 foot 11½ inches. Its steep gradients and lack of power in the railway's early engines caused congestion. In 1864, Robert Fairlie, a consulting engineer in London, patented a double bogie locomotive, and received an order from the FR; the first locomotive, *Little Wonder*, was built in 1869. Two more Fairlies followed, and in the third, *Merddin Emrys*, the Fairlie reached its final form. The locomotives immediately proved their worth by hauling twice the load of the railway's previous engines.

A Fairlie double boiler is built as a single unit, with continuous space for water and steam, although there are two fireboxes with separate firedoors. The engine has two sets of wheels, cylinders and valve gear. By the time of Fairlie's death in 1885, 52 railways worldwide were using locomotives based on his patent. Three double Fairlies are still at work on the Festiniog Railway, now a tourist railway.

Jones Goods 4-6-0 1894 Scotland

The remote Highland Railway of Scotland was responsible for introducing the 4-6-0 locomotive to the British Isles. Designed by the railway's brilliant locomotive superintendent, David Jones, the Jones Goods were influenced by some 4-6-0s built in Glasgow for service in India. The 4-6-0 was to become one of the most successful of wheel arrangements for express locomotives, found all over the world, so it is surprising that it took 34 years from the construction of a 4-6-0 in Britain, built for an overseas railway, until an engine of this type was ordered by a British company.

The Jones Goods performed sterling work over the long and steep gradients of the Highland Railway north of Perth, hauling passenger trains as well as goods. With driving wheels of 5 feet 3 inches diameter, they were well suited to hill climbing. Few locomotives have required such little modification to their basic design over a 40-year life. Most were withdrawn from service during the 1930s, but one survives in the Museum of Transport, Glasgow.

Class P8 4-6-0 1906 Prussia

Few 4-6-0s were built in such numbers or found their way on to the railways of so many countries as the P8 class 4-6-0s, first built in 1906 for the Royal Prussian Union Railway (KPEV). They were intended for express passenger work on hilly routes, having driving wheels of 5 feet 9 inches diameter. However, it was found that they were better suited to secondary passenger and mixed traffic use, although they continued to work some expresses. Fitted with superheaters, long-travel piston valves and Walschaert's valve gear, the P8s proved exceptionally efficient locomotives.

By 1918, 2,350 had been built for KPEV. Because many P8s were handed over as part of war reparations after both world wars, or remained in formerly occupied countries where they had been used by the Germans, P8s could be seen on passenger trains in Belgium, Czechoslovakia, Greece, Yugoslavia, Poland, Romania and the USSR. The last was withdrawn from service in West Germany in 1975, although at least eight have been preserved.

K4 Class 4-6-2 1914 US

The 425 K4 Pacifics built between 1914 and 1927 handled all the express trains of the Pennsylvania Railroad until after World War II. A development of the earlier Pacific classes which the railway had operated since 1907, the K4s had driving wheels of 6 feet 8 inches diameter and proved remarkably economical. During the 1930s most of the class were fitted with a mechanical stoker to relieve the fireman of the arduous task of feeding the 70-square-foot grate. The famous designer Raymond Loewy devised a streamlined casing for one engine which regularly operated the Broadway Limited that ran between New York and Chicago. Over the steepest part of the route, on which the gradient was sometimes 1 in 58 (1.72 percent), three K4s were sometimes needed to haul the train.

Two K4s survive, one at Horseshoe Curve, near Altoona, Pennsylvania, where most of the class were built, and one at Strasburg, Pennsylvania.

Castle Class 4-6-0 1923 Britain

The first Castle class 4-6-0, No. 4073 *Caerphilly Castle*, was the most powerful locomotive in Britain when it was built at the Great Western Railway's workshops in Swindon. This power was achieved with an economy that was the envy of the other three main line railway companies in Britain, since the Castles used just 2.83 lb of coal per drawbar-horsepower-hour, when other locomotive engineers thought that they were doing well to produce a figure of around 4 lb.

The four cylinders and inside valve gear made access for maintenance difficult but helped to produce a wonderfully balanced locomotive. The driving wheel diameter of 6 feet 8½ inches helped the Castles to run at high speed, and for some years No. 5006

Tregenna Castle held the world record for an average start-to-stop speed of 81.7 mph over the $77\frac{1}{4}$ miles between Swindon and London Paddington.

Caerphilly Castle is preserved in London's Science Museum, No. 4079 *Pendennis Castle* operates on a private railway in Australia, and several are able to work special trains over main line and preserved railways in Britain.

Pioneer Zephyr 1934 US

The first self-propelled diesel train built by General Motors was put into service after four years' development work, on 26 May 1934. The three-car train ran between Denver and Chicago on the Chicago, Burlington & Quincy Railroad, cutting the usual journey time of 27 hours 45 minutes to just over 13 hours, an increase in average speed from 37 mph to 78 mph. General Motors presented this as a triumph of the diesel engine, when in fact it was a new approach to train operation. The lightweight, stainless-steel train had a limited carrying capacity, and other railroads soon showed that similar improvements in speed could be effected with steam.

Nonetheless, the concept caught on, although self-propulsion soon gave way to locomotive-hauled trains. The Pioneer Zephyr can be seen at Chicago's Museum of Science & Industry.

Class 05 4-6-4 1935 Germany

Although only three locomotives of this class were built for the German State Railway, they had a major impact when new. They were intended to be the steam engineers' answer to the German high-speed diesel railcars that had reached 100 mph in 1931. The limited capacity of the railcars made them unsuitable for many routes, and they were expensive to build. The Class 05 was a streamlined, three-cylinder locomotive with unusually large driving wheels, of 7 feet $6\frac{1}{2}$ inches diameter, and exceptionally high boiler pressure at 284 lb/sq in. The streamlined casing went almost down to the rails and was painted red. The intended high speeds made good brakes vital, so a pair of blocks was fitted to all wheels, including bogie wheels, except those on the leading axle which had a single block.

Expectations were fulfilled when the Class 05 achieved an authenticated world speed record of 124.5 mph on 11 May 1936. This was eclipsed two years later by the London & North Eastern Railway's *Mallard* in Britain. After being stored during World War II, they were rebuilt with new boilers and without their streamlined casing. One has been preserved, at the German National Railway Museum in Nurnberg, in its original condition.

Class 59 4-8-2 +2-8-4 1955 Kenya

For 25 years the metre-gauge Class 59 Garratts held the distinction of being the largest and most powerful steam locomotives in the world, once the "Big Boys" on the Union Pacific in the US had been withdrawn. The Class 59s were the last of a line of Garratt classes built for the Kenya & Uganda Railway, later East African Railways, and were designed to haul freight trains over the 350 miles between Mombasa and Nairobi. The line has a ruling gradient of 1 in 65 (1.5 percent) and the earlier Garratts could not cope with the demands of traffic. The 59 class had driving wheels of 4 feet 6 inches diameter and produced a tractive effort of 83,350 lb, twice that of the most powerful passenger locomotive operated in Britain.

The Garratt was conceived by an English engineer, Herbert Garratt, who interested locomotive builders Beyer, Peacock of Manchester in an articulated locomotive with high-pressure cylinders at each end of two sets of wheels. Between them is the boiler unit, and water tanks over the two sets of motion help to provide weight for adhesion. The first Garratt was built for Tasmania in 1907, but it was in Africa that the type had the greatest impact, especially in South Africa.

No. 18000 A1A-A1A 1950 Britain
No. 18100 A1A-A1A 1950 Britain

At the end of World War II, the increasing use of diesel traction in the United States and the work done on aircraft gas turbines during the war encouraged British railway companies to look to these forms of motive power as possible successors to steam. The simplicity of gas turbines over diesels appealed to the Great Western Railway, which ordered two such locomotives, one from Brown Boveri in Switzerland and one from Metropolitan Vickers in England.

The Swiss gas turbine, No. 18000, was delivered in 1950, by which time the GWR had been nationalized to become part of British Railways. The unit produced 2,500 hp to drive a generator that supplied current to four traction motors, driving the outer axles of each six-wheeled bogie.

The Metro-Vick locomotive, No. 18100, was delivered a year later and produced 3,500 hp, enabling it to start trains on the Devon banks that were twice as heavy as those the Swiss engine could get under way. However, the principal flaw of the gas turbine was its inefficiency when not working at full load. When other regions of BR gained experience of diesel-electrics, interest in the gas turbine waned and both were withdrawn from regular service by the end of 1960.

Shinkansen 1964 Japan

Shinkansen means "new line", and the significance of the celebrated Shinkansen trains lies more in their method of operation than in technical development. The Japanese had the courage to fund a totally new railway, accepting two prerequisites for the successful attainment of average speeds of 100 mph: a wider gauge than the standard 3 feet 6 inches of Japanese National Railways; and the need for a line dedicated to frequent high-speed trains to guarantee a reliable service.

Their investment was amply rewarded by a 300 percent increase in traffic between 1966 and 1973 over the new 4-foot-$8\frac{1}{2}$-inch gauge line between Tokyo and Osaka. The line had been opened for a year of moderate speed running in 1964, leading to the introduction of services running at up to 130 mph the following year. Each 16-car train has 15,872 hp at its disposal, produced by sixty-four 248-hp motors, one to each axle to ensure high acceleration. New generations of Shinkansens have been produced since the original 480 cars.

Class DD40 AX "Centennial" 1969 US

To take their mammoth freight trains over the Sherman Hills of Wyoming, Union Pacific had to use six or seven diesels on a single train to replace the steam "Big Boy" 4-8-8-4s. The answer to this unsatisfactory arrangement was the "Centennial" diesel-electric, built by General Motors to produce 6,600 hp from two 16-cylinder engines driving two four-axle bogies. It was the most powerful and the largest prime mover unit in the world, with a length of 98 feet 5 inches.

The class name was chosen to commemorate the centenary of the Union Pacific Railroad, the central section of the first transcontinental railroad, which opened in 1869. The use of two engines in a single unit saved a set of electrical control gear, but the modular nature of modern control gear, in which faults can be easily diagnosed and repaired, has diminished the value of this saving.

In common with most railroad companies, Union Pacific has reverted to buying off-the-shelf locomotives since they are more cost effective, but the "Centennials" remain the ultimate development of the most common form of traction on the railways of the world.

ETR 401 Pendolino 1976 Italy

This was the first successful train to have a tilting mechanism that would allow a 9-degree angle. Previously, the first commercial tilting train, the Class 381 on Japanese National Railways, had been limited to 5 degrees. The advantage of a tilting train is that it obviates the need to build a new railway line to achieve significantly higher line speeds, which is the method chosen by SNCF with the TGV.

The tilt mechanism of the Pendolino is made up of accelerometers and gyroscopes, and has been used to good effect on the sharp curves of the line between Rome and Ancona that runs through the Apennines. A new generation of Pendolino trains, the ETR 450, has extended their use, and other countries, such as Sweden, are using comparable technology in the ceaseless quest for higher speeds to capture traffic from road and air transport.

THROUGH THE AIR

Sopwith Camel 1917 Britain

During the early part of World War I, the Royal Flying Corps, forerunner of the RAF, had depended largely on the tiny Sopwith Pup. By 1916, it was apparent that German aircraft technology was outstripping the British, and that a replacement for the Pup was needed.

The Sopwith Camel was therefore introduced in 1917. With its propeller, engine, fuel tank, armament and cockpit all crammed into a comparatively small space at the front of the aircraft, the Camel had extraordinary manoeuvrability, but this feature also had its disadvantages. Although the plane could be turned very tightly, it was difficult to control under those circumstances and was liable to spin rapidly without warning.

Nevertheless, the Camel became the most successful fighter of its age. Between July 1917 and November 1918, Camels destroyed 1,294 enemy aircraft, more than any other in the entire course of the war, and played a particularly significant role in the Battle of Cambrai in March 1918.

Hawker Hurricane 1935 Britain

Developed by Hawker and first flown as a prototype in 1935, the Hurricane was the RAF's first eight-gun monoplane fighter. Like the Spitfire, it had machine-guns mounted on the wings (previous fighter planes had had a smaller number of guns mounted in the fuselage). Although inferior in performance to the Spitfire, it made up in sturdiness and the solidity of its gun platform what it lacked in manoeuvrability. In their first year in combat, Hurricanes shot down some 1,500 Luftwaffe aircraft, almost half the total for all British fighter aircraft over that period.

Douglas DC-3 1936 US

The 21-seater DC-3 flew its first scheduled service for American Airlines in 1936. Its cheapness and reliability made it popular both as a passenger aircraft and for military transport in the US and Great Britain during World War II; by 1945, 10,000 DC-3s had been built. After the war the US Air Force sold many of its aircraft to air forces from Argentina to Yugoslavia; over 2,000 DC-3s are still being used in a military capacity outside the US. Later models could accommodate 36 passengers, but the plane's range never exceeded 1,510 miles and its normal cruising speed was a mere 170 mph—the modern DC-10 has a range and speed more than three times greater. Nevertheless, small airlines throughout the world continue to rely on the DC-3 and it remains the most widely used air transport in history.

De Havilland Comet 1952 Britain

In May 1952, the first commercial jet-propelled aircraft, a BOAC Comet, made its maiden flight from London to Johannesburg. It had five scheduled stops along the way, and the journey took a little under 24 hours, but the effect on long-distance travel was as dynamic as that of Concorde 25 years later. The other end of the world was suddenly accessible.

The de Havilland Comet had been developed in Britain during World War II, with an eye to commercial transport in peacetime. In the United States, military jet aircraft were already in use, but commercial manufacturers had not yet exploited the possibilities. In fact, the Comet was so far ahead of its rivals that none of the other aircraft companies had any clear idea of how to compete.

Jet-propulsion was only a part of the breakthrough in technology that this plane represented—its structure and aerodynamics were also far in advance of anything that had been built so far, and the pressure attained in the cabin was double that of any previous airliner, allowing a cruising height of 40,000 feet.

By 1954, Comet 2 could fly nonstop from London to Khartoum, a distance of 3,064 miles in six and a half hours. And, perhaps most significantly of all, passengers had discovered that the new airliner could cope with bad weather much better than its predecessors.

Vickers Viscount 1953 Britain

The first aircraft designed for turboprop propulsion, the Vickers Viscount almost single-handedly prevented an American monopoly of the world civil aviation market for twenty years after World War II. The chief designer at Vickers in the late 1940s, George Edwards, was not only responsible for the Viscount—he became one of the most prominent figures in the British aircraft industry and was involved in the development of both the VC10 and Concorde.

The Viscount's strength lay in its Rolls-Royce Dart engines. The Dart was a well-established and reliable, if basic, piece of technology. A chief executive of Rolls-Royce in the 1960s described it as "agricultural machinery"; on the other hand, he had to admit, nobody had ever junked a plane with a Dart engine.

The results of the Viscount's first test flight were spectacularly good, but just at that moment British European Airways, potentially the plane's principal customer, announced the purchase of 20 rival aircraft. Edwards's faith in his design was justified within two years, however, when BEA also ordered 20 Viscounts. Air France, Aer Lingus, the Australian airline TAA and TCA (now Air Canada) all bought the aircraft in its early years.

BEA flew the first scheduled Viscount service from Heathrow to Nicosia in 1953 and the aircraft continued in production until 1964. Even today there is a thriving secondhand market for Viscounts, with ex-airline models often being bought by corporate customers.

Boeing 707 1958 US

The development of the Boeing 707 entailed one of the greatest commercial risks in modern aviation history. The British-built de Havilland Comet had shown the world the advantages of jet travel and American companies had to compete. Boeing, known more for their fighters than their commercial aircraft, were aware of the need for in-flight refuelling in air force jets and were already working on the concept of a "jet tanker". It seemed to them that a civil version of the same craft could be their answer to the Comet. It would be powered by a lighter variation of the fuel-efficient Pratt & Whitney engines Boeing had used in their hugely successful B-52 bombers.

Unable to sell this idea up front to commercial airlines or to the US Air Force, or to draw on government funding, Boeing took the decision to develop a prototype using $15 million of their own money. This was in 1952. It was an enormous sum of money. No one could have predicted that the same basic craft would still be in production 30 years later.

By 1954, the $15 million budget had long since been exceeded, but the USAF had ordered enough tankers to subsidize the development of the civil aircraft. The following year, Douglas—a far greater force than Boeing in commercial aircraft manufacture—announced the launch of their DC-8, in direct competition with the proposed 707. Pan Am bought both aircraft, while United opted exclusively for the DC-8. Expensive modifications to both

craft followed as Boeing and Douglas tried to keep one jump ahead of each other.

Pan Am flew the first scheduled 707 flight from New York to Paris in 1958, and the battle between 707 and DC-8 continued throughout the 1960s. Douglas finally abandoned production of the DC-8 in 1972, but the Boeing continued to sell—admittedly in smaller numbers and largely in its military form—well into the 1980s.

Airbus 1972 France, Germany, Netherlands and Spain

The wide-bodied, twin-engined airbus produced by Airbus Industrie is the financial and technical brainchild of French, German, Dutch and Spanish expertise. It was Europe's first significant contribution for many years to what had been very much an American-dominated market—but it was a very significant contribution indeed.

European manufacturers wanted to develop a short-to-medium-haul aircraft that would seat 250 to 300 people, be economical to run and minimize congestion at Europe's overcrowded airports. The aircraft they produced was ordered not only by European airlines but by one major American carrier and, increasingly, by airlines around the world, particularly in the Far East. Within ten years of its launch, Airbus had pushed Boeing into second place in the wide-bodied market, and celebrated a million hours of accident-free flying.

TU-160 1988 USSR

Since the late 1980s, with the end of the Cold War, Westerners have become more aware of the advanced state of Russian aeronautical technology, which reaches its peak in the TU-160, the largest and one of the fastest strategic bombers in the world. It is appreciably faster than its equivalent in the US Air Force, the B-1B Lancer, and can cruise at almost twice the speed of sound. The TU-160 has broken innumerable records in tests of speed and performance, most notably flying a 620-mile course at a speed of 1,068 mph carrying a load of 66,137 lb.

INTO SPACE

Sputnik 1 1957 USSR

The first artificial satellite was launched into space by the Soviet Union on 4 October 1957. Called Sputnik—the Russian for traveller—the satellite was little more than a small sphere fitted with three radio antennae, which it used to broadcast a simple "bleep" to Earth as it made its orbit. The purpose of Sputnik was to advertise Soviet success in building an intercontinental ballistic missile, and at that it was a brilliant success. American opinion was shocked at this evidence of Soviet superiority, and at once began the expansion of its own space programme.

Apollo 13 1970 US

The flight of *Apollo 13*, the third manned mission to the Moon, was an epic journey saved from catastrophe by a series of brilliant extemporizations. Launched on 11 April 1970, *Apollo 13* was well on its way to the Moon with its crew of three (Jim Lovell, John Swigert and Fred Haise) when an oxygen tank exploded. Without oxygen their fuel cells could produce no power, and they were forced to take to the lunar module, the space age's first lifeboat. They coasted around the Moon, correcting their course with the lunar module's engines, and returned to Earth in a cold, powerless vehicle with too little water to drink. Finally they managed a safe splashdown in the Pacific, weak and dehydrated. They had made it, but only just.

Apollo-Soyuz 1975 (US–USSR)

The first and so far only joint project between the Soviet and American space project was the Apollo-Soyuz test project, the "handshake in space". An American Apollo spacecraft, launched on 15 July 1975, made a rendezvous and docked with a Soviet Soyuz spacecraft launched the same day. The two crews moved between the two spacecraft, shook hands, shared meals and toasted each other with soup. The joint project, a result of the period of detente between the superpowers, was meant to signal a new era of cooperation in space—but the Cold War quickly resumed after the Soviet invasion of Afghanistan in 1979 and the experiment was not repeated.

Bibliography

Ackroyd, John. *Just for the record: Thrust 2* CHW Roles & Associates, 1984

Anderson, William R., with Blair Jr., Clay. *Nautilus 90 North* Hodder & Stoughton, 1959

Andrews, Allen. *The Mad Motorists* Harrap, 1964

Barzini, Luigi. *Peking to Paris* Alcove Press, 1972

Bernacchi, L.C. *Saga of the Discovery* Blackie, 1938

Bobrick, Benson. *Labyrinths of Iron* Newsweek Books, 1982

Booth, Henry. *An Account of the Liverpool and Manchester Railway* reprinted Fran Cass & Co., 1969

Botany Bay, the voyage of Governor Phillip printed for John Stockdale, London, 1789

Braddon, Russell. *The Hundred Days of Darien* Collins, 1974

British Trans-Americas Expedition Report (no date)

Brooks, Clive. *Atlantic Queens* Haynes, 1989

Burton, Anthony. *The Rainhill Story* BBC, 1980

Campbell, Gina and Meech, Michael. *Bluebirds* Sidgwick & Jackson, 1988

Carey, John (ed.). *The Faber Book of Reportage* Faber, 1987

Carlson, Robert E. *The Liverpool & Manchester Railway Project, 1821–31* David & Charles, 1969

Carrick, Robert W. *The Pictorial History of the America's Cup Races* W.H. Allen, 1965

Chichester, Francis. *Gipsy Moth Circles the World* Hodder & Stoughton, 1967

Cochrane, Dorothy, Hardesty, Von, and Lee, Russell. *The Aviation Careers of Igor Sikorsky* University of Washington Press for NASA, 1989

Cookridge, E.H. *The Orient Express* Allen Lane, 1979

Dorin, Patrick C. *Canadian Pacific Railway* Superior Publishing Co., 1974

Douglas, Hugh. *The Underground Story* Robert Hale, 1963

Duke, Neville, and Lanchbery, Edward. *Sound Barrier* Cassell, 1954

Freeman Allen, Geoffrey. *Luxury Trains of the World* Bison, 1979

Freeman Allen, Geoffrey. *Railways Past, Present and Future* Orbis, 1982

Gillespie, Charles Coulston. *The Montgolfier Brothers and the invention of aviation* Princeton University Press, 1983

The Great Age of Exploration Reader's Digest, 1971

Grierson, John. *Sir Hubert Wilkins, Pilgrim of Exploration* Robert Hale, 1960

Gunston, Bill. *Flights of Fantasy* Hamlyn, 1990

Heine, William C. *Historic Ships of the World* David & Charles, 1977

Higham, Robin. *Britain's Imperial Air Routes 1918 to 1939* G.T. Foulis, 1960

Hogg, Garry. *The Hovercraft Story* Abelard-Schuman, 1970

Hollingsworth, Brian. *North American Locomotives* Salamander, 1984

Honeywell, Eleanor. *The Challenge of Antarctica* Anthony Nelson, 1984

Howarth, D. *The Dreadnoughts* Time-Life Books, 1980

Hughes, Robert. *The Fatal Shore* Collins Harvill, 1987

Huntley, John. *Railways in the Cinema* Ian Allan, 1969

John, Anthony and Dear, Ian. *The Early Challenges of the America's Cup* Columbus, 1986

Kemp, Peter (ed.). *The Oxford Companion to Ships & The Sea* Oxford University Press, 1976

Kratville, William. *Big Boy* Kratville Publications, Omaha

Lacey, Robert. *The Queens of the North Atlantic* Sidgwick & Jackson, 1973

Landstrom, Bjorn. *Columbus* Allen & Unwin, 1967

Landstrom, Bjorn. *The Ship* Allen & Unwin, 1961

Lawrence, Mike. *The Mille Miglia* Batsford, 1988

Leggett, Robert C. *Railways of Canada* David & Charles, 1973

Lindbergh, Charles. *The Spirit of St Louis* Scribner's, 1953

Lubbock, Basil. *The Log of the Cutty Sark* Brown, Son and Ferguson, 1928

Ludovic (ed.). *A Book of Air Journeys* Collins, 1982

MacGregor, David. *Clipper Ships* Argus, 1979

MacKay, Donald. *The Asian Dream* Douglas & McIntyre, 1986

Masefield, Sir Peter. *To Ride the Storm* William Kimber, 1982

Mauretania, facsimile reprint of articles from *Engineering*, Patrick Stephens, 1987

Miller, Jay. *The X-Planes* Orion, 1988

Mondey, David (ed.). *The International Encyclopedia of Aviation* Octopus, 1977

Mosley, Leonard. *Lindbergh* Hodder & Stoughton, 1976

Newkirk, Dennis. *Almanac of Soviet Manned Space Flight* Gulf Publishing, 1990

Nicholson, John. *Great Years in Yachting* Nautical Publishing Co., 1970

Orlebar, Christopher. *The Concorde Story* Temple Press, 1986

Osman, Tony. *Space History* Michael Joseph, 1983

Page, Martin. *The Lost Pleasures of the Great Trains* Weidenfeld & Nicolson, 1975

Pittenger, William. *Capturing a Locomotive* J.B. Lippincott, 1882

Politovsky, Eugene. *From Libau to Tsushima* John Murray, 1906

Rails Across Canada VIA Rail, 1986

Rutherford, Michael. *Mallard, the record breaker* Newburn House, 1988

Sawyer, L.A. and Mitchell, W.H. *The Liberty Ships* David & Charles, 1970

Simpson, C.R.H. *The Rainhill Locomotive Trials* Rainhill Trials Celebration Committee, 1979

Slocum, Captain Joshua. *Sailing Alone around the World* Rupert Hart-Davis, 1948

Specifications for the "Discovery" Royal Geographical Society, 1899

Stevens, Thomas. *Around the World on a Bicycle* Sampson Low, Marston, Searle, and Rivington, 1887; Century, 1988

Talbot, Frederick A. *The Railway Conquest of the World* William Heinemann, 1911

Tremayne, David. *The Fastest Man on Earth* 633 Club, 1986

Turnill, Reginald. *Spaceflight Directory* Frederick Warne, 1978

Villa, Leo and Desmond, Kevin. *The World Water Speed Record* Batsford, 1976

Walder, David. *The Short Victorious War* Hutchinson, 1973

White, William J. *Airships for the Future* Sterling, 1978

Wilson, Andrew. *Space Shuttle Story* Hamlyn, 1986

Wolfe, Tom. *The Right Stuff* Jonathan Cape, 1980

Yenne, Bill. *All Aboard! The Golden Age of American Rail Travel* Dorset Press, 1984

Index

Acknowledgments

The author and publisher would like to express their gratitude to the following for their kind assistance in the production of this book:

Airship and Balloon Company, Telford; Col. J. Blashford-Snell; British Airways Archives, Heathrow; HoverSpeed, London; London Library; Peter Mills, SNCF, London; Rear-Admiral R.O. Morris; Mystic Seaport Museum, Connecticut; National Maritime Museum, London: Graham Slatter, R.G. Todd and David Topliss; National Motor Museum Library, Beaulieu; Nautilus Memorial, Groton, Connecticut; Charles Noble; Science Museum, London; Short Brothers PLC, Belfast; David Smithers; Smithsonian Institution, Washington; SNCF, Paris; Thunder & Colt, Oswestry; Virgin Atlantic Airways, Crawley; Westland Helicopters, Yeovil.

The publishers gratefully acknowledge the permission granted by Harper Collins for the use of material from *Columbus* by Bjorn Landstrom. They are also grateful to *Motor Sport* for permission to quote from an account of the Mille Miglia by Denis Jenkinson.

CONVERSION TABLES

1 inch = 2.54 cm
1 foot = 0.3048 metre
1 yard = 0.9144 metre
1 mile = 1.6093 km

1 square foot = 0.092 square metre
1 square yard = 0.8361 metre

1 pint = 0.568 litre
1 gallon = 4.546 litres

1 lb = 0.4536 kg
1 cwt = 50.8 kg
20 cwt = 1 ton
1 ton = 1.016 tonnes

$C = \frac{5}{9} \times (F - 32)$
$F = \frac{9}{5} \times C + 32$

1 hp = 746 watts = 0.746 kilowatt

1 knot = 1.15 mph = 1.852 km/h
Mach 1 (at sea level) = 760 mph = 1,222 km/h

Picture Credits

l = left; *r* = right; *c* = centre; *t* = top; *b* = bottom

11 Museo Civico Como/Scala; 12 National Maritime Museum/Angelo Hornak; 13 Adam Woolfitt/Susan Griggs Agency; 14 National Maritime Museum, 14–15 E.P. Goldschmidt & Co/Ann Ronan Picture Library; 17 Uffizi/Scala; 19 National Maritime Museum; 20 Collection, Duke of Alba/Michael Holford; 21 National Maritime Museum; 22–23 Commonwealth Club/Bridgeman Art Library, 23 Mary Evans Picture Library; 24–25 National Maritime Museum, 25*t* Mary Evans Picture Library, 25*b* Beken of Cowes; 27 Mary Evans Picture Library; 30–31 Hulton-Deutsch Collection, 31–33 Royal Geographical Society; 34 Popperfoto; 35 Royal Geographical Society; 36 Popperfoto; 37–38 Town Docks Museum, Hull; 40–41 Rear-Admiral R.O. Morris; 42–43 David Cobb/Pitkin Pictorials, 43 Mary Evans Picture Library; 46 Beken of Cowes; 47 The Mansell Collection; 49 Kos; 50*t&c* Topham Picture Source, 50*b* Rosenfeld Collection, Mystic Seaport Museum, Inc; 51 Beken of Cowes; 52 Rosenfeld Collection, Mystic Seaport Museum, Inc; 53 Kos; 54–55 Trafalgar House/Cunard, 55 Peter Radmore; 56–58 Hulton-Deutsch Collection; 59 P&O; 60 Anthony J. Lambert; 61 UPI/Bettmann; 62 The Bettmann Archive; 63*t&l* US National Archives/MARS, 63*r* Maritime Commission; 64 Popperfoto; 65*t* Associated Press, 65*b*–72 Popperfoto; 73–74 The Nautilus Memorial; 75*t* Popperfoto, 75*b* Submarine Museum, Gosport; 76–79 Sea Containers; 82 Retrograph Archive; 86 National Motor Museum; 87 Mary Evans Picture Library; 88 Fiat; 89 Quadrant Picture Library; 90 The Bettmann Archive; 90–91 Mary Evans Picture Library; 92–93 Terence Cuneo/Peter Roberts Collection/Neill Bruce, 93 (*inset*) SNCF/La vie du rail; 94–95 Neill Bruce; 95 Quadrant Picture Library; 97–98 Operation Raleigh; 100 All Sport; 101 Classic and Sports Car; 103–5 Daimler-Benz Archiv; 106–7 Pascal Rondeau/All Sport; 107 Agence Vandystadt/All Sport; 108*t* Pascal Rondeau/All Sport, 108*b* Darrell Ingham/All Sport, 108–9 Agence Vandystadt/All Sport, 109 Pascal Rondeau/All Sport; 110–13 Charles Noble; 114–17 David Smithers; 120–21 The Mansell Collection; 122–23 Science Museum, 123*tl* Roland Lewis, 123*tr* National Railway Museum/Bridgeman Art Library; 125 US National Archives/Robert Hunt Library; 126–27 Peter Newark's Western Americana; 129*t* Guildhall Library/Bridgeman Art Library, 129*b*–131*t* Hulton-Deutsch Collection, 131*b* London Transport Museum; 132 Coll. Commault/La vie du rail; 133 SNCF/La vie du rail; 134–35 Coll. Illustration/La vie du rail; 136*t* Hulton-Deutsch Collection, 136*b* The Kobal Collection; 137 Venice Simplon Orient Express; 138–39 Canadian National Railways, 139 (*inset*) Canadian Pacific Archives; 140 Canadian National Railways; 141 Canadian Pacific Archives/Millbrook House; 143 Cecil J. Allen Collection/G. Freeman Allen; 145 Cecil J. Allen Collection/G. Freeman Allen; 146 National Railway Museum; 147 Quadrant Picture Library; 148–49 Colour-Rail; 150*t* Eric Treacy/Millbrook House, 150*b* Colin Garratt; 151*t* Colour-Rail, 151*b* Colin Garratt; 152–55 SNCF; 159 H. Roger-Viollet; 160 Mary Evans Picture Library; 161*tl* Derek Bayes/Aspect Picture Library, 161*tr&br* H. Roger-Viollet; 162 Hulton Deutsch Collection, 162–67 Popperfoto; 168*t&b* Hulton-Deutsch Collection, 168*bl* Popperfoto; 169*t* National Motor Museum, 169*b* Chris Allen Aviation Library; 170–72*t* Quadrant Picture Library, 172*b* Topham Picture Library; 173 Popperfoto; 174–75*t* Luftschifbau Zeppelin/MARS, 175*b* Popperfoto; 177 Shorts Brothers/MARS, 177 (*inset*)–179 British Airways Archive; 180–81 Westland Helicopters Ltd, 181 Press Association; 182*t* United Technologies Corporation Archive, 182*c&b* Westland Helicopters Ltd; 184–87 Canadair; 188 Aviation Picture Library; 189 Quadrant Picture Library; 190*t* SIPA/Rex Features, 190*b* M. Roberts/The Research House; 191 Aviation Picture Library; 192*t* USAF/The Research House, 192*b* Quadrant Picture Library, 192–93 USAF/The Research House, 193 Quadrant Picture Library; 194 Smithsonian Institution; 195 Smithsonian Institution/Aviation Picture Library; 196 Bristol Museum/Aviation Picture Library, 196–97 Steve Krongand/The Image Bank; 198 British Aerospace/MARS; 199 Aviation Picture Library; 200 British Aircraft Corporation; 201 Quadrant Picture Library; 202–3 Boccon-Gibod/SIPA/Rex Features; 204–5 Thunder & Colt; 208–9 Novosti/Science Photo Library; 210–11*l* TASS; 211*tr* Novosti/Science Photo Library, 211*br* V. Haende-Rothe/TASS; 212–15 NASA/Science Photo Library; 216 NASA/The Research House, 216–17 Salaber/Liaison/Frank Spooner Pictures; 218 NASA/Science Photo Library; 220 Luis Castañeda/The Image Bank; 221 Roger Ressmeyer, Starlight/Science Photo Library; 222–26 NASA/Science Photo Library, 226*l* Novosti/Science Photo Library; 227 NASA/Science Photo Library.

Artwork Credits

Trevor Hill: 18–19, 48, 70–71, 84–85, 88–89, 110, 128, 134, 173, 178–79, 182–83.
Ian Howatson: 143, 192, 164–65.
Mick Saunders: 39, 78–79, 102, 107, 186, 219.
Paul Selvey: 32–33, 66, 75, 77, 126, 130, 158, 166, 195.
Simon Roulstone: 12, 25, 28–29, 44–45, 94, 98, 116, 121, 141, 148–49, 154–55, 205, 215.